Queer International Relations

Oxford Studies in Gender and International Relations

Series editors: J. Ann Tickner, University of Southern California, and Laura Sjoberg, University of Florida

Queer International Relations

*Sovereignty, Sexuality
and the Will to Knowledge*

CYNTHIA WEBER

OXFORD
UNIVERSITY PRESS

OXFORD

UNIVERSITY PRESS

Oxford University Press is a department of the University of
Oxford. It furthers the University's objective of excellence in research,
scholarship, and education by publishing worldwide.

Oxford   New York
Auckland   Cape Town   Dar es Salaam   Hong Kong   Karachi
Kuala Lumpur   Madrid   Melbourne   Mexico City   Nairobi
New Delhi   Shanghai   Taipei   Toronto

With offices in
Argentina   Austria   Brazil   Chile   Czech Republic   France   Greece
Guatemala   Hungary   Italy   Japan   Poland   Portugal   Singapore
South Korea   Switzerland   Thailand   Turkey   Ukraine   Vietnam

Oxford is a registered trademark of Oxford University Press
in the UK and certain other countries.

Published in the United States of America by
Oxford University Press
198 Madison Avenue, New York, NY 10016

© Oxford University Press 2016

Cataloging-in-Publication data is on file at the Library of Congress

ISBN 978-0-19-979585-7 (hbk.); 978-0-19-979586-4 (pbk.)

For Rick, Rob, and Thäis

CONTENTS

ACKNOWLEDGMENTS

When I pitched this book to Laura Sjoberg and Ann Tickner at the International Studies Association conference in New York in 2009, I expected to write it quickly. I'm glad I failed to do so. For in the intervening years, not only has the proliferating scholarship in transnational/ global queer studies and queer IR enriched my thinking, but so, too, have my students and colleagues. First and foremost, I had the opportunity to test and refine this material in discussions with my master's students in my Queer IR and later Global Queer classes over a three-year period. This was thanks in part to the efforts of Andrea Cornwall, Rachel O'Connell, and Richard Black to broaden Sussex University's MA in Sexual Dissidence to include global queer issues by offering the MA as a joint English-Global Studies project and thanks in part to my then-Head of Department, Justin Rosenberg, who released me from some administration so I could do (more) research-led teaching. Without the opportunity to consistently teach Global Queer as a core option on the Sexual Dissidence MA, without my on-going conversations about global queer issues with my Sexual Dissidence colleagues (especially Rachel, Andrea, and Paul Boyce), and without each and every one of the students in those classes, this would have been an intellectually poorer project.

Like my students, my colleagues at the University of Sussex helped me to improve this work. Zdenek Kavan, who has been teaching me about foreign policy since I was an MA student at Sussex three decades ago, offered invaluable guidance on chapter 6, as did Stefanie Ortman and my colleagues at the Sussex IR Research-in-Progress seminar, especially Synne Laastad-Dyvik and Paul Kirby. Melanie Richter-Montpetit and I had innumerable conversations about IR and queer studies over the course of this past year, which greatly influenced my thinking. Melanie also generously read and commented on the entire manuscript, making many improvements along the way. And Louiza Odysseos has been in discussions with me about this project since long before I was able to write it. Indeed, it is in part because I wasn't satisfied with my submission to the *Millennium* special issue 'Gender and International Relations' that the then-PhD student Louiza was coediting with Hakan Seckinelgin in the late 1990s (Odysseos and Seckinelgin 1998)[1] that I have long felt the need to return to this project. Louiza's influence is found throughout these pages, especially in chapters 2 and 5, which she read and commented upon and which owe debts to her own work on human rights.

Some of the ideas I struggled to articulate for Louiza and Hakan back in the 1990s first appeared in print in my 2015 *European Journal of International Relations* article 'Why Is There No Queer International Theory?'[2] While none of that article appears in this book, it was never far from my mind as I wrote this text. For in many respects, this book begins where that article left off—by offering some (but by no means the only) concrete answers to questions like these: What are 'queer' and 'queer IR'? How can and do IR scholars conduct research in the field of queer IR? What research questions does queer IR address? And how and why does queer IR research matter for the field of international relations more generally? The Sussex-based editorial team of Beate Jahn, Patricia Owens, and Pete Newell, the anonymous non-Sussex board member who oversaw this submission, and the anonymous reviewers of that piece all pushed me to improve that article and complete this book. Thanks also to Rebecca Adler-Nissen, Angela Chnapko, Lisa Duggan, Anne-Marie Fortier, Lene Hansen, Rachel O'Connell, Louiza Odysseos, and Laura Sjoberg, who read and/or commented on that piece. I also received valuable research support from Aristea Fotopoulou and editing assistance from Joanna Wood in the early stages of this work.

Beyond Sussex, Lene Hansen and Rebecca Adler-Nissen of the University of Copenhagen workshopped this book with me over a number of years and provided detailed comments on parts of the manuscript, especially chapters 1, 2, and 6. Indeed, it was Rebecca's suggestion and Rebecca and Lene's encouragement that led me to pursue the case of Tom Neuwirth and/as Conchita Wurst as an illustration of the 'normal *and/or* perverse homosexual'. At critical moments, their intellectual and personal support revitalized me and my work, on this project certainly, but also more widely as part of the 'Outfoxing IR Collective'. Catherine Baker—both as a reader of chapter 6 and as an academic commentator on the Eurovision Song Contest—also helped shape the Neuwirth/Wurst case study. Discussions with Kate Nash, Neil Washbourne, and Anthony Langlois significantly influenced my work in chapter 5, as did Kate and Anthony's respective work on human rights. A version of chapter 2 was first published in *International Studies Quarterly* by Wiley (before the journal went on to be published by Oxford) as "Queer Intellectual Curiosity as International Relations Method: Developing Queer International Relations Theoretical and Methodological Frameworks" (Weber, 2015, doi: 10.1111/isqu.12212). That manuscript benefited from extremely detailed comments from three anonymous reviewers and clear guidance from the *ISQ* editorial team, especially Dan Nexon, much of which made its way into this manuscript. Halit Mustafa Tagma also read and commented on chapter 2, helping me to improve my discussion of statecraft as mancraft. Parts of chapter 1 appeared in my coedited (with Laura Sjoberg) introduction to the *International Studies Review* 'Queer International Relations' (2014) symposium entitled 'From Queer to Queer IR'. Thanks to *ISR* editor Janice Bially Mattern and the anonymous reviewers of that article for their helpful comments. Audiences at the *International Feminist Journal of Politics* conferences at the University of the Free State and the University of Sussex, the International Studies Association conference in New Orleans, the University of Manchester (especially Cristina Masters, Laura McLeod, Veronique Pin-Fat, Andreja Zevnik), the London School of Economic and Political Science (especially Mark Hoffmann), the University of Edinburgh (especially Darcy Leigh, Andrew Neal, and Xavier Guillaume), and the Copenhagen-Sussex Research Network all helped me to refine my arguments. Darcy also read and commented on the entire manuscript, as did longtime friends and colleagues Spike Peterson, Miranda Joseph, and Mark Lacy. In addition to those mentioned above, I have also benefited from ongoing conversations about queer studies, queer IR, and IR methods with Rahul Rao, Amy Lind, Meghana Nayak, Lauren Wilcox, Kai Wilkinson, Anna Agathangelou, Lily Ling, Maureen McNeil, Jackie Stacey, Eithne Luibhéid, Mary Hawkesworth, Ilan Kapoor, Momin Rahman, akshay khanna, François Debrix, Patrick Thaddeus Jackson, and many more scholars and activists working at the intersections of IR and queer studies. All of them made this a better book.

I could not have asked for more supportive or engaged editors than Ann Tickner, Laura Sjoberg, and Angela Chnapko. Not only did they wait five years for me to produce this book, but once I started writing it, they endured me sending it to them chapter by chapter, as my way of keeping myself on track. Their ongoing commentaries on these chapters and on the final manuscript as a whole—as well as the detailed and astute comments of an anonymous reviewer of the manuscript—indelibly mark this work, all to its benefit. Thanks also to Princess Ikatekit, production editors Eswari Marudhu and Alphonsa James, and copy editor Richard Isomaki from Oxford University Press for getting the final manuscript into shape.

More than anyone else, though, it is my partner Anne-Marie Fortier who made sure this project made its way into print. Anne-Marie suffered endless conversations in which I expressed my desire to write this book, my distress that—particularly as a statement addressed to the discipline of IR—it (still) needed to be written, and my aversion to writing it. Had it not been for her repeated insistences, I may very well have abandoned this project. She not only made sure I wrote it, but through her own research and through her commentaries on various drafts of the entire manuscript she brought clarity and intellectual depth to specific arguments (especially in chapter 4) and to the book as a whole.

This book is dedicated to Rick Ashley and Rob Walker, who introduced me to poststructuralist IR readings of sovereignty, and to the late Thäis Morgan, who introduced me to queer studies. I met all of them when I was a graduate student at Arizona State University, when poststructuralism was first making an impression in IR and when queer studies were first making an impression just about everywhere but in IR. It was Rick, Rob, and Thäis (as well as my colleague at Purdue University Diane Rubenstein) who made my first queer IR book, *Faking It*, possible. That was a book few in IR read much less embraced when it was published in 1999, although Rick has long championed that work. Unlike *Faking It*, this book does some of the work that Rick, Rob, and Thäis did in their respective fields of IR and English. It painstakingly maps some of the terrain at the intersections of transnational/global queer studies and queer IR in terms that I hope are accessible and legitimizing of (emerging) research programs in and across both fields. While I undoubtedly fall short of the standards Rick, Rob, and Thäis set in their pathbreaking writing and teaching, I remain most inspired and sustained by their scholarship, their mentorship, and their friendship.

Queer International Relations

Sovereignty, Sexuality, and the Will to Knowledge

In his fable *Les Bijoux Indiscrets* (*The Indiscreet Jewels*), the eighteenth-century French writer Denis Diderot tells the story of a Congolese sultan named Mangogul whose frustration with the impossibility of knowing for sure 'the adventures of the women in my court' is addressed by his genie, Cucufa.

> 'You see this ring?' he said to the sultan. 'Put it on your finger, my son. Every woman toward whom you turn the stone will recount her intrigue in a loud, clear, and intelligible voice. But do not imagine that they shall speak through their mouths'.
>
> 'From whence', cried Mangogul, 'shall they then speak?'
>
> 'From the most honest part of them, and the best instructed in the things you desire to know', said Cucufa. 'From their jewels'. (Diderot 1993, 11)[1]

It is to this orientalist, sexist tale that Michel Foucault refers as he articulates the aim of his project on the history of sexuality. That aim is 'to transcribe into history the fable of *Les Bijoux Indiscrets*' (1980, 77) because it expresses contemporary Western society's demand that the sexed and sexualized organ/body speak, and it elucidates how the will to knowledge and the games of power are always part of the process of speaking sex and sexuality. As Foucault puts it, 'Our problem is to know what marvelous ring confers a similar power on us, and on which master's finger it has been placed; what game of power it makes possible or presupposes. . . . We must write the history of this will to truth' (1980, 79).

Feminist, queer studies, and international relations (IR) scholars have long been writing this history of the will to knowledge, as well as challenging its orientalist, racist, and sexist terms (see, e.g., JanMohamed 1992; Stoler 1995, 203).[2] Yet even those scholars who (critically) root themselves in a Foucauldian tradition can have as much regard as disregard for one another's work. This is in part because they each (critically) foreground different questions—the woman (and later man) question for feminists, the homosexual (and later queer) question for queer studies scholars, and the game-of-power question for IR scholars.[3] It is also because—as interdisciplinary as they may believe themselves to be—they often overlook one another's scholarship as they address themselves to different audiences.

This state of affairs is particularly acute among IR scholars and queer studies scholars—even among IR scholars working on sexualities and queer studies scholars working on global issues. It has significant consequences. By failing to fully take on board the insights of their queer studies colleagues about the possibility and impossibility of producing and deploying sexualized subjectivities, most IR scholars regularly undertheorize how the will to knowledge about *sexualities* is part of what makes international games of power possible and impossible.[4] Similarly, by ignoring the insights of their IR colleagues about how sovereignties[5] are deployed to produce identities that are claimed to authorize national and international orders, most queer studies scholars undertheorize how the will to knowledge about sexualities is a specifically *sovereign* will that makes possible and presupposes specifically sexualized *sovereign* subjectivities.[6] The unfortunate result of this mutual neglect is that it can appear as if there is no (need for) queer theory in IR and no (need for) IR theory in queer studies.

The aim of this book is to contest this proposition. It does so by putting queer studies scholarship and IR scholarship in conversation around sexuality and sovereignty.[7] More specifically, it argues that what queer studies scholars say about queer is akin to what poststructuralist IR and queer IR scholars have long argued is the case about sovereignty.

What queer studies scholars say about queer is that—in Eve Kosofsky Sedgwick's terms—queer designates a refusal or an inability to signify monolithically in relation to sex, to gender, and to sexuality.[8] Queer subjectivities are those subjectivities that do not signify as *either* one sex, gender, and/or sexuality *or* another; they are subjectivities that signify as (also) *more than one* sex, gender, and/or sexuality, often at the same time. In this respect, queer subjectivities more than exceed binary logics of the *either/or*. They often make more sense when read through what Roland Barthes calls the (plural) logic of the *and/or*, in which subjectivities signify as *either* one thing *or* another (*or* yet another) while simultaneously signifying as one thing *and* another (*and* yet another).[9] These 'impossibly queer' subjectivities (Gopinath 2005) can ignite in modern surveyors of sexuality—from physicians to TV chat show hosts—a frustration with the impossibility of knowing for sure what or who these queer subjectivities are, sending them in search of some genie's ring that will satisfy their will to knowledge.[10] Much of what queer studies scholarship does is trace how this will to knowledge produces sexualized subjectivities like the 'homosexual', the 'gender variant', and the 'trans*'[11] through the anxious labor of enforcing powerful regimes of normalization and perversion. It also traces and/or proposes how to resist these regimes.

What poststructuralist IR scholars say about sovereignty is that it refers to those practices that attempt to craft an agent in whose name a political community governs by investing that agent with legitimate political authority.[12] Richard K. Ashley refers to this practice as 'statecraft as mancraft' (1989), which takes classical and modern forms. Argues Ashley, 'If medieval statecraft was in part an art of fixing an interpretation of God that the king could mirror and serve . . . then modern statecraft is in significant measure an art of fixing a paradigmatic interpretation of sovereign man that the state can mirror and serve' (1989, 303). Through modern statecraft as modern mancraft, a modern state (or other political community) attempts to present its sovereign foundation—its phantastical yet presumed-to-be-factual 'sovereign man'—as if it were the singular, preexisting, ahistorical ground that authorizes all sovereign decisions in its political community.[13] Yet 'modern man' as 'sovereign man' is neither singular nor ahistorical; he is as impossibly plural and as much a product of specific histories as the queer subjectivities queer studies scholars investigate.[14]

These impossibly plural sovereign subjectivities can ignite in modern surveyors of sovereignty—from scholars to statespeople—a frustration with the impossibility of knowing for sure who 'sovereign man' really is, thwarting their attempts to craft plurally 'modern man' as singularly 'sovereign man' and sending them in search of some genie's ring to satisfy their will to knowledge about 'sovereign man' to solidify their denials that statecraft as mancraft is fundamental to their disciplinary and diplomatic games of power.[15] Much of poststructuralist IR scholarship on sovereignty traces how this will to knowledge about sovereignty and the regimes of truth about 'sovereign man' it establishes produce seemingly binary sovereign subjectivities (citizen vs. foreigner; patriot vs. traitor) and sovereign orders (domestic vs. international; the West vs. the rest) through the anxious labor of constructing and enforcing powerful formulations of sovereign order versus dangerous anarchy. It also traces and/or proposes how to resist these regimes.

What queer IR and transnational/global queer studies scholars[16] say about sexuality and sovereignty is that the anxious labor required to produce sexualized subjectivities like the 'homosexual', the 'gender variant', and the 'trans*' and that is required to produce order as opposed to anarchy nationally and internationally are intimately intertwined.[17] In queer IR terms, this is because the 'sovereign man' of sovereign statecraft is always produced as knowable as/in relation to various 'normal' and 'perverse' sexed, gendered, and/or sexualized figures.[18]

The story this book tells is about how the crafting of sovereign *and* sexualized figures is a tool in domestic and international games of power that confirms as well as contests traditional logics of modern sovereign statecraft as modern sovereign mancraft. Traditional logics of statecraft as mancraft are confirmed when sexualized 'sovereign man' is crafted as Ashley claims the ideal type of 'sovereign man' must be—as a necessarily singular, *either* normal *or* perverse figure who authorizes (or opposes) a specific binary arrangement of order versus anarchy. These same logics are contested when sexualized 'sovereign man' is crafted as a queerly plural figure—as a 'sovereign man' who is *either* normal *or* perverse while at the same time being normal *and* perverse. It is this move that takes us from a traditional logic of statecraft as mancraft that abide by the logic of the *either/or* into what I call a queer logics of statecraft that abides by a pluralized Barthesian *and/or*. My argument is that by putting (transnational/global) queer studies scholarship and (queer) IR scholarship in conversation around sexuality and sovereignty, not only do a plethora of sexualized *and* sovereign national, regional, and international figurations and their stakes for IR and for queer studies come into focus. So, too, do queer logics of statecraft that confirm, contest, and extend understandings of how the will to knowledge about sexualized sovereign subjectivities functions in domestic and international games of power.

PLAN OF THE BOOK

This story is framed through four questions:

- What is 'homosexuality'?
- Who is the 'homosexual'?
- How is the 'homosexual' figured as/in relation to 'sovereign man'?
- Why are these questions relevant for IR and for transnational/ global queer studies?

This book seeks to answer the last two of these questions by tracing how the will to knowledge about male 'homosexuality' and the male 'homosexual' drives some always imagined and unstable 'Western' hegemonic discourses of sovereign statecraft as sovereign mancraft.[19] Certainly, not all figurations of the 'homosexual' are male. Yet throughout this book I trace various figurations of the 'homosexual' that are described as male and (often) as masculine because—as Foucault argues—the 'homosexual' was 'birthed' and therefore 'known' in Western hegemonic discourses as male in relation to the practice of sodomy among men. It is this male (if not always masculine) figure of the 'homosexual' who—I go on to argue—appears in discourses of statecraft as mancraft, as a figure who is or is opposed to 'sovereign man' (Ashley 1989). My aim is not to reify 'homosexuality' or the 'homosexual' as male and/or masculine but to trace how practices of 'statecraft as mancraft' are destabilized because of their insistence upon a knowable figure of the 'homosexual' as or against 'sovereign man'.

The heart of the book is its four empirical chapters that set out this story, which begins in chapter 3. These chapters tell the story of how specific figurations of the 'homosexual' function first through traditional *either/or* logics of statecraft as mancraft (chapters 3, 4, and 5) and then also through queer logics of statecraft (chapter 6). In a traditional logic of statecraft as mancraft, the 'homosexual' is figured as *either* normal *or* perverse so he may function as or against 'sovereign man'. In queer logics of statecraft, the 'homosexual' is figured as normal *and/or* perverse so that he may function as *and/or* against 'sovereign man' at the same time in the same place, in ways that contest traditional *either/or* logics of statecraft as mancraft that demand 'sovereign man' is, always was, and always will be knowable as singular and ahistorical. Readers seeking a clear statement of the theoretical and methodological framework employed to investigate figurations of the 'homosexual' as/in relation to 'sovereign man' may wish to begin the story with chapter 2, which is entitled 'Queer Intellectual Curiosity as International Relations Method'. However, the book works as a complete text with or without chapter 2.

Chapter 2 offers two theoretical and methodological approaches for analyzing figurations of the 'homosexual' and what I call sexualized orders of international relation. The first combines Michel Foucault's concepts of 'putting sex into discourse', 'productive power', and 'networks of power/knowledge/pleasure' with feminist technoscience studies scholar Donna Haraway's conceptualization of 'figuration', feminist and queer theory scholar Judith Butler's theory of performativity, and poststructuralist IR scholar Richard Ashley's arguments about 'statecraft as mancraft' to develop a method for analyzing figurations of the 'homosexual' and sexualized orders of international relation that are inscribed in IR as *either* normal *or* perverse. The second recombines these elements—especially Ashley's 'statecraft as mancraft'—with a pluralized rendering of Roland Barthes's rule of the *and/or*, which offers instructions on how to read plural figures and plural logics that signify as normal *and/or* perverse, figures that might be described as queer.[20] In so doing, it proposes an additional lens through which to investigate singularized and pluralized figurations of the 'homosexual' and sexualized orders of international relation—queer logics of statecraft.

Chapters 3 through 6 apply these queer IR theoretical and methodological frameworks to their investigations of the 'perverse homosexual', the 'normal homosexual', and the 'normal *and/or* perverse homosexual' respectively.

Chapters 3 and 4 trace how 'the institutions, structures of understanding, and practical orientations that make heterosexuality seem not only coherent ... but also privileged'—what queer studies scholars Lauren Berlant and Michael Warner call 'heteronormativity' (1995, 548 n. 2)—are productive of and are produced by figurations of the 'homosexual' in domestic and international politics. Specifically, these chapters examine how four figures that consistently appear in IR and transnational/global queer studies theory and practice as perverse—the 'underdeveloped', the 'undevelopable', the 'unwanted im/migrant', and the 'terrorist'—are among the specific (if surprising) articulations of the 'perverse homosexual' in Western discourses of sovereign statecraft as sovereign mancraft. Over these two chapters, I read these figures first separately and then together.

My discussion begins in chapter 3 with an analysis of how the figures of the 'underdeveloped' and the 'undevelopable' owe debts to the figuration of the 'temporally perverse homosexual'. After situating this discussion in relation to IR theory and policy, I summarize queer studies theorist Neville Hoad's account of how the 'male homosexual' is figured as the 'underdeveloped' through (neo)imperial evolutionary narratives. I focus exclusively on Hoad's discussion of how Sigmund Freud's use of the temporal trope of degeneracy explicitly figures the 'homosexual' as 'arrested' both sexually and civilizationally. If Freud's 'degenerate homosexual' provides a general Western cultural figuration of the 'underdeveloped' that has been imported into IR, Gabriel Almond's figuration of the 'decadent homosexual' (a trope also discussed by Hoad) as the 'undevelopable' in his modernization and development theory is a specifically IR/comparative politics supplement to Freud's figuration. I trace how Almond implicitly figures the 'undevelopable' as the 'decadent homosexual' through his acceptance of Talcott Parsons's nuclear family as the engine of biological, social, and—thanks to Almond—political reproduction and development. I conclude this chapter by exploring how—in combination and in competition—these figurations ground various sexualized orders of international relation.

Figurations of the 'underdeveloped' and the 'undevelopable' also underwrite contemporary understandings of the 'unwanted im/migrant' and the 'terrorist' These latter figures are often conceived of in Western discourses as dangerous because they have moved out of the places modernization and development theory crafted to contain them, either spatially, temporally, or in terms of their desires.

It is how the sexually perverse 'underdeveloped' and 'undevelopable' *move* within and beyond their assigned spaces in Western developmental discourses that incites their refigurations by Westerners as the sexually perverse 'unwanted im/migrant' and 'terrorist'. Chapter 4 analyzes these figurations through IR literatures on the securitization of the 'unwanted im/migrant' and the 'terrorist' (specifically the 'al-Qaeda terrorist')[21] with queer migrations literatures on how the 'queer', the 'migrant', and the 'queer migrant' put sexuality on the move in relation to the home and the homeland.

Chapter 5 shifts the focus from the 'perverse homosexual' to the 'normal homosexual' by tracing how Western discourses of statecraft as mancraft address the question, Who is the 'normal homosexual' in IR? In the dominant transnational/global queer studies readings of this figure, the 'normal homosexual is understood to be embedded not only in heteronormativities but also in the 'new homonormativities'. Queer theorist Lisa Duggan describes homonormativity as 'a politics that does not contest dominant heteronormative assumptions and institutions, but upholds and

sustains them, while promising the possibility of a demobilized gay constituency and a privatized, depoliticized gay culture anchored in domesticity and consumption' (2003, 50; also see Duggan 2002). Specifically, this
chapter analyzes how the United States under the Obama administration
figures the 'LGBT' as the 'gay rights holder' and the 'gay patriot', particularly through Secretary of State Hilary Clinton's 'Gay rights are human
rights' speech. Following the work of transnational/global queer studies theorist Jasbir Puar (2007; 2010) and Amit Rai (Puar and Rai 2002)
and queer IR theorists Rahul Rao (2014) and Anna Agathangelou (2014),
it traces how Clinton's speech maps the world into normal states versus
pathological states according to how they are judged by the United States
to be responding to a specific 'homosexual question': How well do you
treat your homosexuals? Normal states are those states that champion gay
rights as human rights and fold the 'LGBT' into state and social institutions as a moral and legal equal. Pathological states are those that deny
human rights and state protection to the 'LGBT'.

What makes this 'normal homosexual' and the 'normal' and 'pathological' states that are figured through discourses of statecraft as mancraft possible is the way a specific form of homonormativity has become
nationalized and internationalized as what Puar calls 'homonationalism'
(i.e., homonormativity plus nationalism that normalizes the 'homosexual'
as the 'national patriot', for example; see Puar 2007).[22] Yet this does not
mean that there are no longer 'homosexuals' figured as perverse in international discourses of statecraft as mancraft. Rather, it means that the figure of the 'perverse homosexual' in these contemporary discourses is a
figure whose unruliness and irrationality threatens national (gay) patriotisms and national and international neoliberalisms. Thus, the 'underdeveloped', the 'undevelopable', the 'unwanted im/migrant', and the 'terrorist'
continue to be feared, excluded, and sometimes killed, while the 'gay rights
holder' and the 'gay patriot' are celebrated, included, and protected (see,
for example, Kuntsman 2008; 2009).

Read together, chapters 3, 4, and 5 demonstrate how the 'perverse
homosexual' can be refigured as the 'normal homosexual'. Yet what they
also demonstrate is how the 'homosexual' is always necessarily figured as

either normal *or* perverse in traditional logics of statecraft as mancraft. Chapter 6 argues that a range of diverse figurations of 'homosexuality' and the 'homosexual' in international politics exceed categorization as exclusively normal or perverse in relation to sex, gender, and/or sexuality *and* in relation to sovereign forms of authority. For these figures are both *either* normal *or* perverse while simultaneously being normal *and* perverse. Through a close reading of the 2014 Eurovision Song Contest winner and self-identified 'homosexual' Tom Neuwirth and/as the bearded drag queen Conchita Wurst (a figure I call Neuwirth/Wurst), this chapter analyzes how the 'normal *and/or* perverse homosexual' functions as both a deliberate static (Barthes 1976, 9) in traditional logics of statecraft as mancraft and as a potentially plural 'sovereign man' in a queer logic of statecraft. It does this by considering how Neuwirth/Wurst's queer forms of 'unstoppable unity'[23] in the registers of sex, gender, sexuality, race, nationality, and religious and secular authority challenge traditional discourses of European integration. Read through the lens of a queer logics of statecraft, Neuwirth/Wurst arguably makes possible a thorough rethinking of what the process of 'European integration' might mean and what a sovereign 'integrated Europe' might become, without reducing the 'plural' or the 'queer' to *necessarily* liberating or transgressive forms of sovereign subjectivity.[24]

Chapter 7 concludes by considering the limits of the will to knowledge about 'homosexuality' and the 'homosexual' in the dual registers of sexuality *and* sovereignty through Foucault's provocations about the 'end of man'.

This story about how *sovereignty* is entangled with sexuality is not meant to reduce the field of IR scholarship to (state) sovereignty studies. Nor is it meant to erase the 'phantasmical qualities' of sovereignty (Berlant 2007, 756) that prevent its practical deployment from ever matching some ideal form, either as 'sovereign man' or the 'sovereign state'. Rather, it is meant to acknowledge that this 'essentially contested concept' (Gallie 1955–1956) remains the primary signifier of the state. For when IR theorists and practitioners speak of the 'state', they mean (and often evoke) the 'sovereign state' or the 'sovereign nation-state'. In so doing, they affirm that it is some presumed yet always disputed, always fictive ('post') sovereignty[25] that functions in IR discourses to secure the political authority of the state domestically and internationally. It is because sovereignty continues to fuel innumerable 'political delusions' (Cocks 2014) about states, about capital, about security, and about their combination that makes sovereignty among the most relevant ongoing concerns for IR scholars and practitioners.

By putting queer studies and IR in conversation around *sexuality* and sovereignty, it is not my aim to answer Berlant and Warner's rhetorical question, 'What does queer theory teach us about *X*?' (1995). It is not my aim, in other words, to answer either the question 'What does queer theory teach us about international relation?' or 'What does international relations teach us about queer theory?' Rather, it is to reject the terms in which Berlant and Warner cast 'queer' and 'disciplines that have long histories of affiliation with the state' like IR (1995, 348) that effectively separate and oppose 'queer' and 'IR'. For Berlant and Warner, queer seeks to unsettle rather than systematize the world by refusing to 'undertake the kind of general description of the world that would allow it to provide practical solutions' (1995, 348). In contrast, state-facing disciplines like IR seem to be apparatuses 'for falsely translating systematic and random violences into normal states, administrative problems, or minor constituencies' (1995, 348). While this dichotomizing description might have been and might still be valid for *some* queer and *some* IR theory and practice, it never defined the wide range of research and practice that took place in the name of either field. Indeed, Berlant's own critical reflections on sovereignty (2007) arguably have more in common with Ashley's interruption of IR theorizations of sovereignty than they do with many other (transnational/global) queer studies engagements with sovereignty.[26]

Certainly, Berlant and Warner's move was politically and intellectually important for its time for a variety of reasons.[27] Yet to cling to it today would have three effects. It would erase how queer can be, and is, captured in the name of state power, something IR scholars commented on before Berlant and Warner's influential article (Weber 1994a; 1994b; also see Weber 1999). It would erase rich traditions of critical IR scholarship that systematically *challenge* state violences and the IR theories that make them possible, be they (neo)realist, (neo)liberal, or some constructivist combination of the two (for IR critiques that precede Berlant and Warner's article, see, e.g., Cox 1981; Ashley 1984; Walker 1993). And it would continue to enforce the mutual neglect of IR scholarship by queer studies scholars and queer studies scholarship by IR scholars that I argue impoverishes theoretical and practical endeavors by scholars and practitioners affiliated with these rich, productively overlapping traditions.

This mutual neglect is palpable in some of the preeminent work in transnational/global queer studies and in IR. On the one hand, the insights generated by transnational/global queer scholars like Jasbir Puar, Amit Rai, and Adi Kuntsman (Puar and Rai 2002; Puar 2007; Kuntsman 2008; 2009) that trace figurations of the 'homosexual' as the 'terrorist', the 'soldier', and the 'gay patriot' in the US War on Terror and in Israeli-Palestinian relations, for example, speak directly to interests IR scholars have with state and nation formation, war and peace, and international political economy—themes that are all developed in this transnational/ global queer scholarship. Yet these figurations—which are necessarily analyzed in their specific historical and geographical settings—are also situated within larger discourses of sovereignty and security. It is these broader issues about sovereignty and security that are undertheorized in these powerful works of transnational/global queer scholarship, and it is precisely these issues that IR theorists are adept at drawing out.

On the other hand, IR scholars of sovereignty and security have a propensity to ignore figurations of the 'homosexual', even when they draw upon methods developed by queer theorists to perform their analyses. For example, Richard Ashley's formulation of 'statecraft as mancraft' (1989) is grounded in Roland Barthes's discussion of connotation and denotation as it is presented in Barthes's classic text *S/Z* (1974). Yet at no point does Ashley ponder what it means that Barthes's arguments about reading and writing emerged from Barthes's engagement with Honoré de Balzac's story 'Sarrasine', which is about the figure of the castrato. Similarly, David Campbell's analysis of IR through Judith Butler's notion of performativity was and remains a significant intervention in the field of IR. Yet when reading Campbell's *Writing Security* (1992), one has no idea that among Butler's fundamental claims in *Gender Trouble* (1999) is that homosexuality makes heterosexuality possible. By neglecting Butler's insight, Campbell—like Ashley—erases sexuality from his consideration of sovereignty and security, thereby missing opportunities to theorize how sexuality participates in the figuration of sovereignty and security in domestic and international politics.[28]

These examples do not arise out of any intentional slight on the part of any of these authors but out of an academic context in which 'queer' and 'IR' have for too long been treated as separate (disciplinary) domains of inquiry, especially around issues of sovereignty and sexuality. Abandoning some artificial queer studies versus IR binary, I want to suggest, can go some way toward rectifying this situation, by creating opportunities to think 'queer questions' (Rao 2014) together with 'IR questions' in ways that can enhance scholarship in both fields.

In staging this conversation among transnational/global queer studies and IR scholars, I am not aiming to define what some emerging field that might be called 'queer IR' is or must become. Rather, my aim is to stage but one idiosyncratic engagement among the always plural, always contested, 'undomesticated, unsymbolized' set of forces (de Lauretis 2011, 245) some call queer and some call IR that never quite stabilize into disciplines or distinctive fields of practice, much less into some newly defined field called 'queer IR.'

Having said that, I want to be clear that my idiosyncratic enactment of queer IR is very specific—in terms of both its content and its politics. For example, even though the term 'queer' and more specifically some notion of queer IR is always plural and contested, to me this does not mean that queer designates anything and everything, nor should it, as I do not find an 'Everything is always already queer' usage of the term 'queer' very useful either analytically or politically (also see Butler 1993; Warner 1999a and 1999b). Not only does such a usage of the term lack analytical specificity; it just as importantly lacks an analysis of power. In our current age—some twenty years since the term 'queer' first entered the academic lexicon (de Lauretis 1991; also see Warner 2012)—scholars and activists are abundantly aware of how the term queer and things generally associated with queer (e.g., various figurations of 'homosexuality' and the 'homosexual', for example) can be and have been appropriated by those in power for nonprogressive purposes (see, e.g., Weber 1994a; 1994b; 1998; 1999; 2002; Duggan 2003; Puar and Rai 2002; Puar 2007; 2010). What that suggests to me is that the time (if there ever was such a time) for an 'anything goes' celebration of 'queer' has passed.

This means that, analytically, my own usage of queer has a specific content, even if that content's function is to keep open spaces for critical queer thinking and practice. For me, that analytical content does not extend to all things nonnormative (as it does for some queer theorists). Rather, it extends specifically to how queer is deployed in relation to normative *and/ or* perverse understandings of sex, of gender, and of sexuality in ways that make two refusals. The first refusal is to reduce 'queer' to only that which is antinormative (Wiegman and Wilson 2015; also see Weber 1999). As I use it, queer is, for example, a never-quite-achieved or coherent concept, subjectivity, field of political practice, or sexualized ordering of the intimate, the national, and/or the international that combines normativities and perversions in ways that confuse and confound what is said to be normative *and/or* antinormative by eschewing *or* embracing while at the same time and place eschewing *and* embracing normativities and perversions (as the case of the 'Eurovisioned drag queen' Neuwirth/Wurst illustrates in detail in chapter 6). The second refusal is to disconnect queer from any consideration of sexes, genders, and sexualities and from those bodies that refuse/fail to signify monolithically in these terms, because this move enables a foreclosure on these types of analyses. This is why I am most comfortable with Eve Sedgwick's understanding of queer as 'the open mesh of possibilities, gaps, overlaps, dissonances and resonances, lapses and excesses of meaning when the constituent elements of anyone's gender, of anyone's sexuality aren't made (or *can't be* made) to signify monolithically' (1993, 8). For in this definition of queer, sexes, genders, and sexualities and their complex attachments matter.

Insisting upon linking queer to sexes, genders, and sexualities rather than to a broader understanding of queer as encompassing all things nonnormative allows me to do two further things. The first is to distinguish queer from a more generalized (especially Foucauldian) type of poststructuralism. The second is to insist that how queer and things associated with queer are mobilized must themselves be the subject of political (and feminist) analysis.

Both of these points are illustrated in a story about an IR theorist's evocation of the term queer. That story begins with this declaration: 'My work is queer'.

This is what a white, heterosexual, cismale, poststructuralist IR professor declared at a public lecture about his Foucauldian-informed project. His lecture included no analysis of the function of nonmonolithic expressions of sexes, genders, or sexualities. Quite the contrary, not once did he even mention any of these terms. Instead, as he laid out his project, it had nothing to do with sexes, genders, or sexualities, even though there were multiple opportunities to analyze their normative *and/or* perverse functions in the context of his project.

Sitting in the audience that day next to another self-identified queer person and queer studies scholar, I remember how we both squirmed with discomfort. I remember our conversation afterward, in which we both discussed how profoundly disturbed we were by this professor's declaration. For what we both felt was that this specific enactment of queer was not queer in any sense we understood it. It felt to us like an appropriation of the term queer and of the thinking space that comes with it by this 'mythically normative' professor (Lorde 1984, 116)[29] in order to augment his own individual power and to further his appeal to his audience of admirers. It made me admire him less. For his mobilization of queer—which, had it been mobilized differently, could have created a range of possibilities for scholarship and practice with respect to nonmonolithic sexes, genders, and sexualities—closed down any consideration of sexes, genders, and sexualities in the very name of queer.

This story illustrates why I disagree with Sedgwick's suggestion that 'what it takes—all it takes—to make the description "queer" a true one is the impulsion to use it in the first person' (Sedgwick 1993, 9). To me, this particular claim by Sedgwick expresses a naiveté about power relations.

For not everyone uses queer in the first person in the same way, to empower the same 'truth'. This is why the mobilization of the term queer matters. And this is why I insist on linking queer to analyses of nonmonolithic expressions of sexes, genders, and sexualities.

My move with respect to queer is akin Cynthia Enloe's move with respect to feminism. As Enloe puts it,

> I think you can't claim to describe your analysis as feminist if you have no interest in women's ideas and experiences and lives, and if you have no interest in the workings of both masculinities and femininities. You have to have curiosity about the workings of both to be feminist. You also have to be interested in the way that power works in gender and in women's lives. You have to add an explicit exploration of *power* if you're not just going to do *gender* analysis, but (a more useful) *feminist* analysis. (Enloe 2013)[30]

Let me borrow Enloe's terms to explain how I use the term queer. I cannot claim to be doing queer work if I have no genuine interest in those who refuse/fail to signify monolithically in terms of sexes, genders, and sexualities. I cannot claim to be doing queer work if I neglect to analyze how power circulates in and through sexes, genders, and sexualities to attempt to normalize *and/or* pervert them. I cannot claim to be doing queer work if my evocation of the term queer closes down possibilities for critical thinking and practice in relation to nonmonolithic sexes, genders, and sexualities. I cannot claim to be doing queer work if I do not analyze how any evocation of the term queer is itself always made through a particular expression of power on behalf of some kind of intimate, national, and/or international politics.

If I or other IR scholars were to call our work queer without doing these things, this could be just as harmful to some presumed field called 'queer IR' as would declarations that dismiss queer IR research altogether. For this kind of enthusiastic embrace of queer and queer IR squeezes the content of nonmonolithic sexes, genders, and sexualities right out of considerations of queer and queer IR. And that has the effect of closing down innumerable spaces of critical thinking and practice, whether that is our intention or not.

Queer and queer IR, then, are not equivalent to poststructuralism or poststructuralist IR. While they have similar origins and overlapping political concerns, there can be and often are important differences between them, both in terms of their content and in terms of their political deployments and effects. This is not to say that a white, heterosexual, cismale (or cisfemale), poststructuralist (or other) IR scholar cannot be a queer IR scholar or cannot be an advocate on behalf of queer IR scholars and scholarship. Many are (see Nayak 2014). Rather, it means that those deploying the term queer ought to ask themselves: On whose behalf am I deploying this term, and what are the practical political effects of my deployment? Also, how, in particular, does my deployment of queer affect those who refuse/fail to signify monolithically in relation to sexes, genders, and sexualities?

One final point. There is nothing inherently feminist about queer or queer IR. Queer and queer IR's relevance for the discipline of IR and even its existence in the discipline of IR have been challenged by some feminist scholars and some feminist IR scholars.[31] Additionally, queer and queer IR can be and have been mobilized for nonfeminist purposes. Like many queer theorists and IR theorists, my political commitment is to a queer IR that is also a feminist IR, or is at least compatible with a feminist IR. What follows here is offered in that spirit.

Queer Intellectual Curiosity as International Relations Method

Developing Queer IR Theoretical and Methodological Frameworks

The new persecution of the peripheral sexualities entailed an *incorporation of perversions* and a new *specification of individuals....* Homosexuality appeared as one of the forms of sexuality when it was transposed from the practice of sodomy onto a kind of interior androgyny, a hermaphrodism of the soul. The sodomite had been a temporary aberration; the homosexual was now a species.

—MICHEL FOUCAULT (1980, 42–43)

Like being a woman, like being a racial, religious, tribal, or ethnic minority, being LGBT does not make you less human. And that is why gay rights are human rights, and human rights are gay rights ... The Obama Administration defends the human rights of LGBT people as part of our comprehensive human rights policy and as a priority of our foreign policy.

—US SECRETARY OF STATE HILARY CLINTON (2011)

We are unity, and we are unstoppable.

—EUROVISION SONG CONTEST WINNER TOM NEUWIRTH
AND/AS CONCHITA WURST (2014)[1]

What is 'homosexuality'? Who is the 'homosexual'? How might theoretical and methodological frameworks draw out the relevance of these questions for International Relations?

This chapter outlines theoretical and methodological approaches that take a queer intellectual curiosity about figurations of 'homosexuality' and the 'homosexual' as its methodological core to offer ways to conduct IR research. A queer intellectual curiosity—akin to Cynthia Enloe's feminist curiosity (Enloe 2004)—is a method that refuses to take for granted the personal-to-international institutional arrangements, structures of understanding, and practical orientations that figure 'homosexuality' and the 'homosexual'. It investigates how these figurations—these distillations of shared meanings in forms or images[2]—powerfully attach to and detach from material bodies and are powerfully mobilized in international politics, challenging the common assumption that (homo)sexuality is trivial in international politics.

The quotations that open this chapter demonstrate that understandings of 'homosexuality' and the 'homosexual' have changed throughout history. To the nineteenth-century Victorians whom Foucault discusses, homosexuality referred to sexual practices of sodomy between men. Not only did Victorians consider homosexuality an aberrant sexual practice, but they specified the 'sodomite' as a new 'alien strain' (Foucault 1980, 53–73), a new 'species' called the 'homosexual' (also see Somerville 2000; Hoad 2000). It was by discursively implanting the 'perversion' (Foucault 1980, chap. 2) of 'homosexuality' into the bodies of individual members of this new population that the perverse 'homosexual' as an 'abomination' of normal sexuality was invented (Foucault 1980, 36). Subjected to scientific study and biopolitical management, this white Western European 'homosexual' with his naturalized 'homosexual' desire for same-sex sodomy was pathologized and subjected to moral, medical, and psychological correction.

These dominant understandings of 'homosexuality' and the 'homosexual' as perverse persist, even as they are increasingly accompanied by understandings of 'homosexuality' and the 'homosexual' as normal. As they are articulated in and legitimated by US secretary of state Hilary

Clinton's 2011 Human Rights Day speech (Clinton 2011), 'homosexual-ity' refers less to perverse sexual conduct than to love within a same-sex couple. The 'cringeworthy' term 'homosexual' that connotes perver-sion (Peters 2014) disappears altogether, to be replaced by 'lesbian, gay, bisexual, transgender' or 'LGBT' for short. Imagined in the image of the white, modern, Western, neoliberal citizen, the 'LGBT' is not a perverse, alien strain. Rather, the 'LGBT' is cast as a normal minority human being within a universal population of normal human beings. What distin-guishes the 'LGBT' is unjust discrimination associated with the object of its love/affection. The 'LGBT' with its naturalized 'homosexual' desires for same-sex love is normalized and subjected to domestication through gay marriage, gay consumerism, and gay patriotism (Duggan 2003).[3]

It is not uncommon for people to understand 'homosexuality' and the 'homosexual' as *either* normal *or* perverse. This is especially the case when statespeople and religious leaders mobilize these understandings for political gain. We see this in how 2014 Eurovision Song Contest winner Tom Neuwirth and/as Conchita Wurst (hereafter Neuwirth/Wurst) was taken up by some European leaders as a figure who embodied either a normal or a perverse image of an integrated Europe. Russian national-ist politician Vladimir Zhirinovsky, for example, claimed Wurst signified 'the end of Europe' because 'they don't have men and women any more. They have "it"' (Davies 2014). In contrast, Austrian Green member of the European Parliament Ulrike Lunacek commented, 'Conchita Wurst has a very important message that . . . has to do with what the EU stands for: Equal rights, fundamental rights, the right to live your life with-out fear, for LGBT and other minorities' (EurActiv 2014). The figure of Neuwirth/Wurst inspired such strong views not because Neuwirth/Wurst could be read as exclusively normal *or* perverse but because Neuwirth/Wurst could also be read as normal *and* perverse at the same time in a number of registers. Certainly, Neuwirth/Wurst appeared as normal *and/or* perverse in the registers of sex (male *and/or* female), gender (masculine *and/or* feminine) and sexuality (heterosexual *and/or* homosexual), as the name Conchita Wurst in part implies (which combines the Spanish slang for vagina [*conchita*] with the German word sausage [*wurst*] and—read

together—is Austrian slang for 'It's all the same to me'). But Neuwirth/
Wurst can also be read as normal *and/or* perverse in registers that matter intensely in international relations. These include nationality (where
Neuwirth/Wurst is Austrian *and/or* German *and/or* Colombian) and 'civilization' (where Neuwirth/Wurst is Indigenous *and/or* Hispanic *and/or*
European). What is striking about these figurations of Neuwirth/Wurst
(as I elaborate later) is that Neuwirth/Wurst's IR registers of normality
and/or perversion always function through, and never independently of,
Neuwirth/Wurst's *and/or* sexes, genders, and sexualities.

These three very different figurations of 'homosexuality' and the
'homosexual' are important not only because they mark major historical
shifts in dominant Western perspective on the 'homosexual' and 'homosexuality'. They also illustrate how specific figurations of 'homosexuality'
and the 'homosexual' make it (im)possible for Western 'experts' to cat-
egorize people and geopolitical spaces as normal or pathological and to
react to them accordingly. This matters for IR because specific figurations
of 'homosexuality' and of the 'homosexual' enable and contest specific
modes of organization and regulation of national, regional, *and* international politics.

For example, figurations of 'the savage, the primitive, the colonized'
(Stoler 1995, 7) and the 'underdeveloped' and 'undevelopable' (Hoad
2000) all appear in Victorian colonial discourse as sexualized and racially
darkened degenerate and/or deviant 'perverse homosexuals'.[4] These
figurations played a role in licensing Victorian sovereign states to subject entire colonized populations to imperial rule, as Stoler's analysis of
colonial educational practices evidences (1995; also see chapter 3 in this
volume). Traces of these figurations linger in contemporary Western figurations of the 'unwanted im/migrant' and the 'terrorist', which inform
policies on immigration and security (Luibhéid 2002; 2005; 2008; 2013;
Luibhéid, Buffington, and Guy 2014; Puar and Rai 2002; Puar 2007; also
see chapter 4 in this volume). Figurations of the 'homosexual' as the normal 'LGBT' justified the Obama administration's global support for gay
rights as human rights. This support both promised to extend human
rights to all 'LGBT populations' (Langlois 2015) and justified the Obama

administration's monitoring of how some states performed against US standards of tolerance toward the 'LGBT' (Rao 2012). Finally, figurations of the 'homosexual' as normal *and/or* perverse sparked debate in contemporary Europe about how the (dis)ordering of sexes, genders, and sexualities in traditional binary terms might progress or imperil Europe 'itself'. In these debates, Neuwirth/Wurst was 'weaponized' (Black 2014) by European leaders who selected *some* elements of Neuwirth/Wurst's 'unstoppable unity' to enable or disable specific renderings of European integration and of Europe 'itself'. Yet because there were at least three legitimate readings of Neuwirth/Wurst circulating in debates about Europe—Neuwirth/Wurst as normal, Neuwirth/Wurst as perverse, and Neuwirth/Wurst as normal *and/or* perverse—attempts to use Neuwirth/Wurst to anchor any singular vision of an integrated Europe did as much to disorder (knowledge about) European integration as they did to order it/them (see chapter 6 in this volume).

Because policymakers occasionally employ these figurations to construct and legitimate how they order international politics and tame anarchy, figurations of 'homosexuality' and the 'homosexual' participate in constructing 'sexualized orders of international relations' (i.e., international orders that are *necessarily* produced through various codings of sexes, genders, and sexualities) that have practical empirical consequences for individuals, populations, nation-states, and the conduct of foreign policy. Viewed through queer intellectual curiosity, a plethora of sexualized and queer IR figurations and their stakes for IR come into focus. Discussing each sexualized and queer IR figuration and its importance in IR is beyond the scope of this book. I limit my analysis to the three sets of figurations that correspond to the illustrations that open this chapter—Victorian colonial practices that gave us the 'underdeveloped' and the 'undevelopable' and in contemporary form the 'unwanted im/migrant' and the 'terrorist', Obama administration foreign policy leveraging of gay rights as human rights that gave us the 'gay rights holder' and the 'gay patriot', and EU Eurovision debates about Neuwirth/Wurst as the 'Eurovisioned bearded drag queen'— for two reasons. First, each illustrates a different alignment of 'homosexuality' with (ab)normality, producing three distinct sexualized figurations of the 'homosexual' for analysis—the perverse Victorian 'homosexual', the normal Obama administration 'homosexual', and the normal *and/or* perverse Eurovisioned 'homosexual'. Second, separately and together these examples demonstrate that by placing a queer intellectual curiosity about figurations of 'homosexuality' and the 'homosexual' at its methodological core, this particular queer IR method does more than just 'add (homo) sexuality' to IR. It offers ways to map phenomena as diverse as colonialism, human rights, and the formation of states and international communities that provide vastly different renderings of international politics than those that emerge when we include a 'sexuality variable' in our survey research instruments, for example.

In this chapter, I develop two theoretical and methodological approaches that put a queer intellectual curiosity about 'homosexuality' and the 'homosexual' at the core of their investigations of international relations. I develop one such approach first by mining classic texts in queer theory, feminist technoscience studies, poststructuralist international relations, and queer international relations for theoretical concepts and methodological procedures that—in combination—provide one such approach. Specifically, I read Michel Foucault's *History of Sexuality*, volume 1 (1979) to recover three specific elements from his analysis: putting sex into discourse, productive power, and networks of power/knowledge/ pleasure. I suggest that these elements, together with feminist technoscience studies scholar Donna Haraway's conceptualization of 'figuration' as the distillation of shared meanings in forms or images (1997), feminist and queer theory scholar Judith Butler's theory of performativity (1999), and poststructuralist IR scholar Richard Ashley's arguments about 'statecraft as mancraft' (1989), provide the necessary concepts and devices to analyze figurations of the 'homosexual' and sexualized orders of international relations that are inscribed in international discourse and practice as either normal or perverse.

While these theories in combination generate important research questions, they neglect to analyze plural figures like Neuwirth/Wurst that defy categorization as either normal or perverse and the sexualized (dis)orders of international relations to which they may give rise. In a second reading of these theories—especially Ashley's statecraft as mancraft—I attempt to correct this oversight by turning to Roland Barthes's logic of a pluralized *and/or* (1974 and 1976). Barthes offers instructions for reading plural figures and logics that signify as normal *and/or* perverse through what can be vast matrices of sexes, genders, and sexualities. I view plural figures and logics that are constructed in relation to (but not necessarily exclusively through) sexes, genders, and sexualities as queer, in accordance with Eve Sedgwick's description of queer as 'the open mesh of possibilities, gaps, overlaps, dissonances and resonances, lapses and excesses of meaning when the constituent elements of anyone's gender, of anyone's sexuality aren't made (or *can't be* made) to signify monolithically' (1993, 8). Reading Ashley's statecraft as mancraft with Barthes's queer logic of a pluralized *and/or*, I propose an additional lens through which to investigate figurations of 'the homosexual', sovereign man, sovereign states, and sexualized orders of international relations—what I call 'queer logics of statecraft'.

DEVELOPING A QUEER IR METHOD

Discourse, Productive Power, and Networks of Power/Knowledge/Pleasure

Michel Foucault's *The History of Sexuality*, volume 1 instructs its readers how to analyze modern sexuality by offering four primary recommendations:

1. Analyze how sex is put into discourse.
2. Analyze the functions and effects of productive power.
3. Understand productive power as working through networks of power/knowledge/pleasure.
4. Analyze how understandings of the 'normal' and the 'perverse' are frozen, without assuming they are either true or forever fixed.

In this section, I offer a reading of *The History of Sexuality* that draws out these instructions.

All of these instructions follow from Foucault's central claim in *The History of Sexuality* that the organizing principle of sexuality from nineteenth-century Europe to 'the contemporary West' is how 'sex is "put into discourse"' (Foucault 1980, 11), for example, how specific meanings of sexualities and sexual subjectivities are produced through specific—even repressive—discursive formulations that bring sexualities like 'homosexuality' and sexual subjectivities like the 'homosexual' into being. For while Victorian institutions from law to medicine certainly repressed 'deviant' sexual practices and sexuality, in so doing they also discursively invented both sexual norms and the 'sexual deviants' who defied them. Foucault's instruction 1, analyze how sex is put into discourse, follows from this observation.

How specifically was sex put into discourse by Victorians? Foucault's answer is through scientific discourses about sexuality—a 'scientia sexualis' including biology, physiology, and psychology—that sought to make the 'homosexual body' confess its scientific truth. 'Scientia sexualis', Foucault claims, functioned as a kind of productive power to invent the 'homosexual' and other sexual figurations like the 'hysterical woman' and the 'masturbating child; during the Victorian era.[5] This is why Foucault offers us instruction 2: Analyze the functions and effects of productive power.

How specifically did productive power work to figure the 'homosexual'? Working on every surface of the 'homosexual body' and penetrating deep into the 'homosexual soul', theologians, doctors, and psychiatrists medicalized, surveilled, and managed the 'homosexual'. Their biopolitical apparatuses produced the 'alien strain' of the 'homosexual' as scientific fact (Foucault 1980, 42–44, 53–73). The 'homosexual', then, was not a discovery whose empirical reality Victorian scientists examined. Rather, it was through the scientific examination of his 'sexual deviance' and the therapeutic correction he was subjected to that Victorian society brought the 'homosexual' into being.

This scientifically produced 'homosexual' was prescribed a regimen of normalization, presumably to make possible his sexual reconstitution from one who desired perverse sex[6] to one who desired normal sex, where normal sex was represented by the white, Christian, bourgeois, able-bodied, cisgendered, procreative, heterosexual 'Malthusian couple'. But what this regime of normalization also did was subject the 'homosexual' to constant surveillance, management, and correction. This is how the 'homosexual' was located in a complex nexus of what Foucault calls the system of power/knowledge/pleasure. This brings us to Foucault's instruction 3: Understand productive power as working through networks of power/knowledge/pleasure.

Why did Victorian society invent 'the 'homosexual', diagnose individuals as afflicted with 'homosexuality', and subject them to processes of normalization? Foucault offers several reasons. One reason is that the 'homosexual' (like other perverse Victorian figures) made it possible to identify normal sexual behavior, discursively implant normality in the Malthusian couple, and circulate social understandings of this couple as exemplary of normal, healthy, moral Victorian sexuality. Thus, a perverse/normal dichotomy produced all manner of Victorian sexual subjectivities (Stoler 1995; Somerville 2000) and organized them socially, scientifically, and morally in ways that made the 'normal', privileged, heterosexual, procreative couple appear to be coherent and whole.

It is only by abandoning what Foucault calls the 'repressive hypothesis'—'the hypothesis that modern industrial societies ushered in an age of increased sexual repression' (Foucault 1980, 49)—that we can appreciate how systems of power/knowledge/pleasure actually function. 'Pleasure and power do not cancel or turn back against one another; they seek out, overlap, and reinforce one another. They are linked together by complex mechanisms and devices of excitation and incitement' (Foucault 1980, 48). What they make possible are figurations of sexualized subjects like the 'homosexual' as well as 'institutions, structures of understanding, and practical orientations that make [normative sexualities like] heterosexuality seem not only coherent—that is, organized as a sexuality—but also privileged' (Berlant and Warner 1995, 548 n. 2; also see Butler 2004, 124).[7]

Foucault takes seriously the question 'Who is the "homosexual"?', then, not so he can get to 'the truth' about the 'homosexual' but to understand how systems of power/knowledge/pleasure function to produce the 'perverse homosexual' and his presumed 'opposite', the 'normal' Malthusian couple. This makes possible exploration of the circulation of these apparent representations in intimate as well as national, regional, and international contexts. For example, we can explore how our knowledge of the 'underdeveloped' as perverse (chapter 3) and the 'LGBT' as normal (chapter 6) is in part produced by/through some of the same scientific systems of power/knowledge/pleasure that produce the 'perverse homosexual' and the 'normal homosexual' respectively. In IR, we see this in how modernization and development theory draws upon Talcott Parsons's structural-functionalist evolutionary sociology to mark the 'underdeveloped' as the 'perverse homosexual' who is the deviant, dysfunctional remainder of social, biological, and political development. This is in contrast to how Hilary Clinton extends the 'normal' to include the 'LGBT couple' which is reproductive for their nation-state, to refigure the 'perverse homosexual' as the 'normal homosexual' (Clinton 2011; also see Peterson 2014). What disconcerts many scholars and statespeople is how Neuwirth/ Wurst combines aspects of the 'perverse, underdeveloped homosexual' (e.g., as the rural Colombian Conchita Wurst) and the 'normal, developed homosexual' (e.g., as the European 'LGBT') at the same time (chapter 6).

Foucault's instruction 4—analyze how understandings of the 'normal' and the 'perverse' are frozen, without assuming they are either true or forever fixed—exposes figurations of the 'homosexual' as the 'underdeveloped', the 'LGBT' and the 'Eurovisioned bearded drag queen' not as true or false but as powerful apparent representations whose meanings and functions vary radically throughout history and across the globe.

Foucault's genealogical method highlights the changeable nature of figurations of the 'homosexual', by focusing on different historical representations of the 'homosexual' and asking, 'How did these very different understandings of the "homosexual" as, for example, the Victorian sexual and developmental "primitive" or "underdeveloped" and the Obama administration's normal "LGBT" come about?' Yet because Foucault's instructions about analyzing modern sexuality and sexual subjectivities are very sweeping (and problematically limited to a self-referential

'Europe' as his analytical terrain; Stoler 1995), it is useful to look to additional theorists to provide more precise concepts and devices. In this vein, I turn to Donna Haraway's Butlerian theorization of figuration.

Figuration

What exactly might we look for when we examine figurations of the 'homosexual'? Writing in a context very different from Foucault's,[8] Donna Haraway discusses some specific techniques of 'figuration' that allow us to employ figuration as a critical conceptual device (Kuntsman 2009, 29; also see Castañeda 2002). Haraway's conceptualization of figuration—which is compatible with Foucault's analysis and builds upon Butler's notion of performativity—can help us explore in more detail the figure of the 'homosexual'.

Figurations are distillations of shared meanings in forms or images. They do not (mis)represent the world, for to do so implies the world as a signified preexists them. Rather, figurations emerge out of discursive and material semiotic assemblages that condense diffuse imaginaries about the world into specific forms or images that bring specific worlds into being. This makes figurations powerful signifiers that approximate but never properly represent seemingly signified worlds, even though figurations are evoked as if they did represent preexisting worlds. It is this latter move that reifies figurations and the worlds they create, making both potentially 'flat, unproductive, stifling and destructive' (Grau 2004, 12; McNeil 2007). This is why we need techniques like Haraway's to analyze precisely how figurations are crafted and employed.

Haraway describes figuration as the act of employing semiotic tropes that combine knowledges, practices, and power to shape how we map our worlds and understand actual things in those worlds (1997). Unpacking Haraway's description, we are left with four key elements through which figurations take specific forms: tropes, temporalities, performativities, and worldings (1997, 11).

Tropes are material and semiotic references to actual things that express how we understand them. Tropes are figures of speech that are not 'literal or self-identical' to what they describe (Haraway 1997, 11). Figures of speech enable us to express what something or someone is *like* while (potentially) at the same time grasping that the figuration is not identical to the figure of speech we have employed. This is what makes figuration something that both makes representation appear to be possible and interrupts representation in any literal sense.

Haraway argues that language necessitates deployment of figuration and its inability to achieve literal representations. This is because all language—textual, visual, artistic—involves 'at least some kind of displacement that can trouble identifications and certainties' (Haraway 1997, 11) between a figure and an actual thing. Investigating figurations of the 'homosexual' as 'an alien species' to the Victorians as opposed to the 'homosexual' as the 'LGBT rights holder' to the Obama administration and as *both* 'an alien species' *and* the 'normal LGBT rights holder' in the figure of Neuwirth/Wurst allows analysis of what makes these figurations possible but also what keeps them from referring to specific material bodies engaged in specific forms of sexual practices, specific forms of loving or specific forms of (singular) being.

Haraway's second element of figuration is temporalities. Temporality expresses a relationship to time. Haraway notes that figurations are historically rooted in 'the semiotics of Western Christian realism', which is embedded with a progressive, eschatological temporality. Western Christian figures embody this progressive temporality because they hold the promise of salvation in the afterlife (Haraway 1997, 9). This medieval notion of developmental temporality remains a vital aspect of (some) contemporary figurations, even when figures take secular forms (e.g., when science promises to deliver us from evil with a new technological innovation; Haraway 1997, 10).

But this developmental time may not be applied to every figuration in the same way. For example, because the Victorian 'homosexual' was figured not only through European scientific discourses but also through discourses of race and colonialism (Stoler 1995), how the 'homosexual' was related to developmental temporalities depended very much on who it was (colonizer vs. savage) and where it was (Europe vs. the colonies). It was in part thanks to how developmental temporalities were racialized (Stoler 1995) and spatialized (Hoad 2000) that it was possible for the racially whitened, Western European 'homosexual' to be put on a course of progressive correction so he could live *within* Victorian society, while figurations of whole populations of (queerly) racially darkened colonial subjects endlessly oscillated between the irredeemable 'nonprogressive homosexual' and the redeemable 'morally perfectible homosexual' (Bhabha 1994, 118), both of whom must live *under* Victorian imperial rule.

Centuries later, these racialized and colonial legacies of the 'homosexual' live on, but in ways that appear to be completely different from those of their Victorian predecessors. For example, Clinton's 'LGBT rights holder' is not cast as progressing; rather, the 'LGBT' is a temporally static figure articulated in universal moral terms. By definition, this figure always was and always will be a human being like every other human being. This is what empowers the 'LGBT' to claim gay rights as human rights, as every human being has a claim to human rights.

This does not mean that a developmental temporality is absent from Obama administration discourse on the 'LGBT'. Rather, developmental temporality is central to Obama administration discourse, albeit differently than it was to the Victorians. This is because developmental temporality is not implanted in the figure of the 'LGBT' per se. Instead, it is located in relations between sovereign nation-states, where the Obama administration uses a state's progress toward the appreciation of gay rights as human rights as the measure of development. This is evident in US policies toward Uganda and Russia, for example (Rao 2014b; Wilkinson and Langlois 2014). Striving toward this specific kind of development is what it means to the Obama administration 'to be on the right side of history' (Clinton 2011; also see Rao 2012).

As we will see in chapter 6, it is, somewhat surprisingly, Tom Neuwirth's Euro-pop bearded drag queen Conchita Wurst that most closely engages with Western Christian realism and its progressive, eschatological temporality as described by Haraway. While Neuwirth/Wurst's declaration,

'We're unstoppable', aligns Neuwirth/Wurst with a modern progressive developmental temporality, as a cisman styled with long flowing hair and a beard while wearing a gown and singing 'Rise like a Phoenix, Neuwirth/ Wurst has been read as a resurrected Christlike figure (Ring 2014). This has led some European political and religious leaders to debate whether Neuwirth/Wurst is a developmental vision of salvation or sacrilege for contemporary Europe.

These differences in how figurations of the 'homosexual' relate to temporalities underscore the importance of Haraway's third element—performativities. Coined by Judith Butler to explain how sexes, genders, and sexualities appear to be normal, natural, and true, the term 'performativity' expresses how repeated iterations of acts constitute the subjects who are said to be performing them (Butler 1999, xv). Applying Nietzsche's idea that there is no doer behind the deed and that the deed is everything (1999, 33) to an analysis of sexes, genders, and sexualities, Butler argues that enactments of gender make it appear as if sex—which Butler understands as a social construct—is natural and normal, and as if particular sexed bodies map 'naturally' onto particular genders. It is through the everyday inhabiting of these various sexes, genders, and sexualities by everyday people who enact them that the subjectivities of these doers of sexes, genders, and sexualities appear to come into being. This does not mean that—once enacted—performativities freeze sexed, gendered, and sexualized subjectivities and the networks of power and pleasure that are productive of them. Rather, because each enactment is itself particular, it holds the possibility of reworking, rewiring, and resisting both 'frozen' notions of sexes, genders, and sexualities and their institutionalized organizations of power, including those that participate in 'build[ing] the fantasy of state and nation' (Butler 2004, 124; in IR, see Campbell 1992).

Following Butler, Haraway argues that 'figurations are performative images that can be inhabited' (Haraway 1997, 11). In the case of the Victorian 'homosexual', the 'LGBT rights holder', and the 'Euro-pop bearded drag queen', this means these figurations—these figures of speech—through their repetition under specific conditions come to be understood as inhabitable images of oneself (or, e.g., one's vision of Europe) or of others. The 'homosexual' may choose to performatively inhabit these figurations, or this inhabiting might be imposed upon the 'homosexual'. For example, it is hard to imagine the Victorian 'homosexual' willingly embracing himself as 'perverse'. It is even harder to imagine colonial subjects embracing their figuration by Victorians as akin to the 'homosexual' in their perversion while distinct from the 'homosexual' because their racialization and 'primitiveness' designate them as incapable of progression or as slow to progress.

In contrast, the contemporary figuration of the 'homosexual' as the 'LGBT' may seem to be uncontroversially positive. Many 'homosexuals' welcome the opportunity to inhabit the image of the 'LGBT rights holder' because of how it appears to signify both normality and progress. At the same time, other contemporary 'homosexuals' find the image of the 'LGBT rights holder' too constraining. Their objections center on how the 'LGBT' is produced by and is productive of institutions, structures of understanding, and practical orientations that value only what they describe as hetero/homonormative ways of being 'homosexual' (in marriage, the military, and consumption) and devalue what they describe as queer ways of inhabiting one's sexuality (Duggan 2003), illustrating a tension between IR conceptualizations of norms as uniformly beneficial (e.g., Finnemore and Sikkink 1998) and (antinormative) queer critiques of norms/normalization. As for Neuwirth/Wurst, by both embracing and exceeding hetero/homonormativities, his/her performative figuration complicates both the 'LGBT' and a 'hetero/homonormative versus (antinormative) queer' dichotomy.

These illustrations suggest figurations are never stable. For every performance of a figuration depends upon innumerable particularities, including historical circumstances, geopolitical context, spatial location, social/psychic/affective/political dispositions, and perceived/attributed traits (racial, religious, sexual, classed, gendered, [dis]abled) of individuals in relation to the figurations they are presumed to inhabit, an individual's success, failure or jamming of their assigned/assumed figuration as they performatively enact it, and how these performativities are received and read by others. Because no two performative enactments are ever identical (Butler 1999), every repetition and inhabitation introduces some, even tiny, amount of difference. What this means for figurations of the 'homosexual' is they are never completely frozen, for they are always only distilled forms or images that change—even in small ways—through their every iteration and inhabitation. Therefore, institutional arrangements of power/knowledge/pleasure—be they described as heteronormativities and/or homonormativities—are likewise less stable than they appear to be.

All of these aspects of performativity—in combination with how tropes and temporalities are deployed—combine to produce the final element of figuration—worlding (in IR, see Agathangelou and Ling 2004). Worlding 'map[s] universes of knowledge, practice, and power' (Haraway 1997, 11). In the cases of the Victorian 'homosexual', the Obama administration's 'LGBT rights holder' and European debates over Neuwirth/Wurst, knowledge about these figurations, the way they are performatively put into practice, and the power relations running through them combine so differently in each case that it is sometimes difficult to remember that we are speaking about the same general figure—the 'homosexual'.

The sometimes extreme differences in how the figure of the 'homosexual' is worlded emphasizes another of Haraway's points—the maps produced by worlding practices are as contestable as the figurations to which they give specific form (1997, 11). In Foucault's terms, this means neither understandings of the 'homosexual' nor the networks of power/knowledge/pleasure that produce this figure are ever frozen. Rather, they are products 'of the encroachment of a type of power on bodies and their pleasures . . . [that define] new rules for the game of powers and pleasures' (Foucault 1980, 48). These games are played not only in intimate relations but also in national, regional, and international relations.

Statecraft as Mancraft

Combining Foucault's insights about discourse and productive power with Haraway's Butlerian unpacking of figuration makes it possible to

offer a more nuanced account of the figuration of the 'homosexual.' If
we layer this analysis with Richard Ashley's 'statecraft as mancraft', what
comes into sharper focus is how states attempt to freeze meanings of the
'homosexual' when they enter international games 'of powers and pleasures' (Foucault 1980, 48).[9] Ashley argues it is impossible to understand
the formation of modern sovereign states and international orders without understanding how a particular version of 'sovereign man' is inscribed
as the *necessary* foundation of a sovereign state and how this procedure
of 'statecraft as mancraft' produces a specific ordering of international
relations. I unpack Ashley's argument by making two moves. I illustrate
Ashley's argument with reference to the 'homosexual' in Victorian and
in Obama administration discourse. I use the analyses above of Foucault,
Haraway, and Butler to argue that Richard Ashley's 'statecraft as mancraft'
both furthers understandings of figurations of the 'homosexual' generally
and provides specific IR research questions for analyzing figurations of
the 'homosexual' in sexualized orders of international relations.

Writing about international relations from a poststructuralist perspective, Ashley's arguments build upon Foucault's analysis of the constitution
and problematization of subjectivities. Yet Ashley adds Jacques Derrida's
deconstructive critique of logocentrism to this analysis, based upon his
reading of Derrida's texts from the 1970s and 1980s (e.g., 1977; 1981).

Logocentrism refers to how '*the* word'—indeed, a singular, specific
word signifying a specific presence—grounds all meaning in a linguistic system because of how it is positioned as a universal referent that is
located outside of history. In the classical age, 'God' was the most common example of a 'Logos' in a logocentric system. In the modern age, as
Nietzsche argued, 'man' displaced 'God' from this logocentric position.
Understood as 'a pure and originary presence—an unproblematic, extra-
historical identity, in need of no critical accounting' (Ashley 1989, 261),
'modern man' is now the figure who functions in modern discourse as 'an
origin, an identical voice that is regarded as the sovereign source of truth
and meaning' (Ashley 1989, 261).

Derrida argues that by identifying one word, one being, one presence
as an originary 'logos' from which all other meanings flow, logocentric

systems create conditions of possibility for both hierarchies in linguistic systems and specific narratives of history. Applying Derrida's ideas
to modern renderings of international politics and international theory
(especially to Kenneth Waltz's neorealist theory),[10] Ashley explains how
'the Logos' is the 'sovereign source of truth and meaning' in the manifestation and analysis of the modern nation-state and in specific renderings of
domestic and international orders.

Specifically, Ashley argues that in international relations theory and
practice, 'modern man' as sovereign man functions not only as 'the
Logos' of modernity in general but also as the foundation of the sovereign nation-state. This is because, since the move from monarchical to
popular sovereignty, it has been 'modern man' who has given the modern
nation-state its sovereign authority. The state's sovereign authority that had
previously been vested in the monarch—as transcendental, as reasonable,
as the interpreter of meaning—is now vested instead in 'modern man'. To
be sovereign, then, every sovereign nation-state inscribes a particular sovereign man as an always already existing domestic presence, as the foundation of its authority domestically and internationally, which emerges
from the complex interplay of domestic and international relations.[11]

What emerges from Ashley's analysis are three key points that I illustrate with reference to the Victorian 'homosexual' and to Clinton's gay
rights-holding 'homosexual'. First, because the modern sovereign
nation-state is intimately tied to 'modern man', the sovereign inscription
of the modern state is intimately tied to the sovereign inscription of 'modern man'. To put it in Ashley's terms, '*Modern statecraft is modern mancraft*. It is an art of domesticating the meaning of man by constructing
his problems, his dangers, his fears' (1989, 303). These are projected into
the dangerous realm of international anarchy that sovereign man with his
foreign policies attempts to tame. For example, Victorian modern man
as 'imperial man' required the dangerous, unruly, racially darkened, and
sexualized 'savage' as his 'colonial (perverse homosexual) subject' to justify both the reasonableness of Victorian 'sovereign man' and his imperial
rule. In contrast, some have argued (Rao 2012) that the Obama administration's modern man as 'neo-imperial man' requires the dangerous,

unruly, racially darkened, and sexualized 'post-colonial (perverse homosexual) state' to justify the reasonableness of an enlightened US 'sovereign man' who internationally proclaims gay rights as human rights to legitimize his neoimperial rule (also see Richter-Montpetit 2014b; 2014c). These examples illustrate why 'paradigms of man are themselves tools of power' (Ashley 1989, 300).

Second, this has implications for understanding how international relations are ordered. For, as Ashley argues, 'modern mancraft' does not just give rise to the modern sovereign state; it also gives rise to modern understandings of international order. For just as the 'logos' in Derrida's logocentric system makes it possible to establish hierarchies, the 'logos' of 'modern man' as the 'logos' of the modern state organizes international relations according to hierarchies as well.

These include reasonable man / pure danger, civilized/barbaric, security/danger, peace/war, domestic/international, and order/anarchy. In this logocentric system, whatever can be narrated from the point of view of 'the logos' and made to 'speak from a sovereign voice is what is valued and protected; what cannot be made to speak from a sovereign voice (e.g., anarchy and terror) must be violently opposed (Ashley 1989, 284). Specifying 'modern man' in the 'Malthusian couple' as their civilized, secure, domestic logos, Victorians narrated the deviant 'homosexual' as an intimate, national, and international source of barbarism, instability, and danger to 'modern man' (Stoler 1995). Expanding figurations of the 'normal couple' to include the 'LGB but not always T',[12] the Obama administration in contrast narrated those unreasonable *states* that do not recognize the gay rights of the 'LGBT' as sources of barbarism, instability, and danger to 'modern man', established neocolonial education policies to enlighten unreasonable state's leaders (e.g., by distributing 'LGBT' human rights tool kits to foreign embassies), and imposed sanctions on *some* states that failed to embrace gay rights as human rights (Clinton 2011). This is how 'modern man' as sovereign man authorizes the potential use of violence by the sovereign state on behalf of his presumed transcendental reason (Ashley 1989, 268).

Third, Ashley argues that none of these figurations—of 'modern man', of the modern state, or of international orders that we in IR understand as variations of order versus anarchy—are stable or ahistorical. For the reasonableness of 'modern man' can always be shown to be unreasonable, just as the order of domestic politics can always be shown to contain aspects of anarchy. To put it in Derrida's terms, the binaries that order domestic and international relations constantly deconstruct themselves, making them both unstable and (because unstable) unreliable. What this means is that various invested actors—from citizens to states to formal international institutions—constantly attempt to stabilize these unreliable hierarchies and the figurations that authorize them so they *appear to be* ahistorical, given, and true, so that they might more reliably function in domestic and international politics. The overdetermined labor that both the Victorians and the Obama administration employ(ed) to construct their opposed figurations of the 'homosexual'—often in the face of international resistances by colonial states (in the case of the Victorians; Stoler 1995) and by postcolonial and post-Communist states (in the case of the Obama administration; Puar 2007; Rao 2012; Wilkinson and Langlois 2014)—is a case in point. This in part explains why international politics is inscribed as dangerous by sovereign nation-states (Ashley 1989, 304). For by not ceding to the will of a particular national sovereign man, international politics (anarchy) always threatens to expose sovereign man and the sovereign order he guarantees as historical and contingent. That explains why the order/anarchy boundary is so highly policed, both in international practice and in international theory.

Ashley's Derridian analysis, like Foucault's and Haraway's analyses, suggests contemplating how figurations and the orders (and anarchies) they produce and that are produced by them are fixed and frozen as well as unfixed and unfrozen. But because Ashley's analysis is IR-focused, it additionally provides specific IR research questions that allow analysis of both how 'modern man' is figured as sovereign man on behalf of sovereign nation-states and how specific figurations of 'modern man' as sovereign man participate in the production of domestic and international orders. These research questions are the following:

- How does speaking 'the truth' about 'homosexuality' and the 'homosexual' participate in the organization and regulation of international relations?
- What ordering principles of sexuality generate and sustain—and are generated and sustained by—figurations of the 'homosexual', and how do they function in international relations?
- How do figurations of the 'homosexual' function as instances of 'statecraft as mancraft', and how specifically is this normality or perversion figured as 'the logos' of or against 'sovereign man'?
- How do these ordering principles of sexuality and figurations of the 'homosexual' as or against 'sovereign man' work together to order international relations?
- What do various practices of statecraft as mancraft make possible in world politics, and what contingencies are rendered necessary by and through these practices? (Ashley 1989; also see Hopf 2010)

From Statecraft as Mancraft to Queer Logics of Statecraft

The above research questions go some way toward elaborating queer IR research programs informed by a queer intellectual curiosity. Yet I suggest here that they are limited by Derrida's initial understanding of deconstruction and its relationship to the 'logos' and the 'plural'. In the texts Ashley consults, Derrida argues deconstruction is not something we bring to a text; rather, it is something that is inherent in a text. This is because meanings in a text (or, in Foucault's broader terms, a discourse) are always already plural. The logocentric procedure that tries to impose a singular meaning upon a text or a discourse, then, is always as political as it is impossible. This explains why politics—like the politics of statecraft as mancraft—endlessly loops through circuits in which states (or other political communities) attempt to impose order on anarchy. By critiquing the logocentric procedure as it functions in domestic and especially international politics, Ashley's analysis takes us some way toward understanding how 'paradigms of man are themselves tools of power' (Ashley 1989, 300), not just in specific times and places (as in, e.g., Kuntsman 2009; Puar and Rai 2002; Puar 2007), but more generally. For Ashley explains how these impossibly singular normal or perverse paradigms of sovereign man attempt to figure impossibly singular normal or perverse international orders in their own image. This is how actors attempt to impose order onto anarchy.

As powerful as this account is, I suggest it overlooks a crucial aspect of how figurations of sovereign man are mobilized to craft domestic and international orders. What is missing is an account of how *not just a singular logos but a plural logoi* potentially figures sovereign man and orders international politics in ways that *construct and deconstruct* these figures and orders. Why this matters in queer IR contexts is because this plural logoi can be understood as simultaneously normal *and/or* perverse as it is enacted through sexes, genders, and sexualities as well as through various registers of authority (something I will explain further with reference to Neuwirth/Wurst).

A plural logoi—especially a normal *and/or* perverse logoi—appears, on the face of it, to be counterintuitive. This is especially the case because of how Derrida initially sets up the 'logos' as the necessarily singular (and presumptively normal) 'word' that he opposes to the necessarily plural (and possibly perverse) 'text'.[13] Following Derrida, Ashley analyzes accounts of sovereign man as the necessarily singular (and presumptively normal) 'sovereign orderer' who is opposed to the necessarily plural (and presumptively perverse) 'anarchy'. While Ashley insists on the plurality of man,[14] he does not consider how this plural man might function as a *sovereign* man who might be necessarily plural. As a result, Ashley neglects to consider how the plural might be empowered not just because it is foundationally normal(ized) but because it is *also* foundationally perverse (perverted). Ashley's analysis therefore misses opportunities to investigate how the normal *and/or* perverse plural might function as a possible or even necessary foundation of meaning in a logocentric system, rather than always in opposition to the singular (presumptively normal) logos.

What might a plural logoi look like, and what might its implications be for understandings of statecraft as mancraft? My notion of a plural logoi comes from Roland Barthes's (1994 and 1976) description of the rule of the *and/or*. To explain what the *and/or* is and how it functions, I use illustrations of sexes, genders, and sexualities first to contrast the *and/or* with the more traditional *either/or* and second to pluralize the rule of the *and/or* itself.

The *either/or* operates according to a binary logic, forcing a choice of *either* one term *or* another term to comprehend the true meaning of a text, a discipline, a person, an act. For example, in the binary terms of the *either/or*, a person is *either* a boy *or* a girl. In contrast, the *and/or* exceeds this binary logic because it appreciates how the meaning of something or someone cannot necessarily be contained within an *either/or* choice. This is because sometimes (maybe even always) understanding someone or something is not as simple as fixing on a singular meaning—*either* one meaning *or* another. Instead, understanding can require us to appreciate how a person or a thing is constituted by and simultaneously embodies multiple, seemingly contradictory meanings that may confuse and confound a simple either/or dichotomy. It is this plurality that the *and/or* expresses.

According to the logic of the *and/or*, a subject is *both* one thing *and* another (plural, perverse) while *simultaneously* one thing or another (singular, normal). For example, a person might be *both* a boy *and* a girl while *simultaneously* being *either* a boy *or* a girl. This might be because a person is read as *either* a boy *or* a girl while also being read as in between sexes (intersexed), in between sexes and genders (a castrato), or combining sexes, genders, and sexualities in ways that do not correspond to one side of the boy/girl dichotomy or the other (a person who identifies as a 'girl' in terms of sex, as a 'boy' in terms of gender, and as a 'girlboy' or 'boygirl' in terms of sexuality). In these examples, a person can be seen as *and* while simultaneously being *or* because the terms 'boy' and 'girl' are not reducible to traditional dichotomous codes of sex, gender, or sexuality either individually or in combination, even though traditional *either/or* readings attempt to make them so.

While Barthes's rule of the *and/or* is derived from his description of the castrato's body that he reads as combining two sexes and two genders (1974), the plural that constitutes a subjectivity can also be *more than* one thing *and/or* another. For a subjectivity can be one thing *and* another *and* another, and so on, as well as one thing *or* another *or* another, in relation to sexes, genders, and sexualities, as there are multiple sexes, genders, and sexualities individually and in combination (Fausto-Sterling 1993). This suggests both the limitations of deploying Barthesian plural logics as if they expressed a singular rule of the *and/or* and the expansive possibilities of plural logics that pluralize the rule of the *and/or* itself.

This discussion makes two significant points. First, the singular choice we are forced to make by an *either/or* logic (e.g., boy or girl) excludes the plural logics of the *and/or*. Plural logics of the *and/or* contest binary logics, understanding the presumed singularity and coherence of their available choices (either 'boys' or 'girls', either normal or perverse), their resulting subjectivities (only 'boys' and 'girls'), and their presumed ordering principles (either hetero/homonormative or antinormatively disruptively/disorderingly queer) as the social, cultural, and political effects of attempts to constitute them as if they were singular, coherent, and whole. Therefore, it is only by appreciating how the (pluralized) *and/or* constitutes dichotomy-defying subjectivities and (anti)normativities that we can grasp their meanings. Second, when the (pluralized) *and/or* supplements the *either/or*, meanings are mapped differently. For in the (pluralized) *and/or*, meanings are no longer (exclusively) regulated by the slash that divides the *either/or*. Instead, meanings are (also) *irregulated* by this slash and by additional slashes that connect terms in multiple ways that defy *either/or* interpretations.

Importantly, Barthes does *not* argue that *either/or* logics are unimportant. He suggests it is both the *either/or* and the (pluralized) *and/or* that constitute meanings. Yet he stresses texts should not be reduced to an *either/or* logic, so we can 'appreciate what *plural* constitutes' a text, a character, a plot, an order (Barthes 1974, 5). 'Releasing the double [multiple] meaning on principle', the logic of the (pluralized) *and/or* 'corrupts the purity of communications; it is a deliberate "static", painstakingly elaborated, introduced into the fictive dialogue between author and reader, in short, a countercommunication' (1976, 9). The (pluralized) *and/or*, then, is a plural logic that the *either/or* can neither comprehend nor contain.

It is how the (pluralized) *and/or* introduces a kind of systematic, nondecidable plurality into discourse as 'that which *confuses* meaning, the norm, normativity [and, I would add, antinormativities]' (Barthes 1976, 109; Wiegman and Wilson 2015) around the normality *and/or* perversion of sexes, genders, and sexualities rather than just accumulating differences (as intersectionality sometimes suggests; Crewshaw 1991) that makes it a queer logic (Weber 1999, xiii). For a (pluralized) Barthesian *and/or* accords with Sedgwick's definition of queer as 'the . . . excesses of meaning when the constituent elements of anyone's gender, of anyone's sexuality aren't made (or *can't be* made) to signify monolithically' (1993, 8) as exclusively '*and*' or as exclusively '*or*'. Identifying these often illusive figurations, the now queer Barthesian *and/or* suggests how we should *investigate* queer figures. Barthes's instruction is this: read (queer) figures not only through the *either/or* but also through the (pluralized) *and/or*.

While Barthes offered this instruction in the context of reading literature (1974), his queer rule of the (pluralized) *and/or* applies equally to foreign policy texts and contexts. For 'sovereign man' as a plural logoi in a logocentric procedure can figure foreign policy and (dis)order international politics.[15] For example, as we will see in chapter 6, the case of the 2014 Eurovision Song Contest winner Tom Neuwirth and/as Conchita Wurst offers an illustration of how the 'normal *and/or* perverse homosexual' can function in logics of statecraft as mancraft as *both* a singular 'sovereign man' *and* a plural 'sovereign man'.

Debates about Neuwirth/Wurst as the 'normal homosexual', the 'perverse homosexual', and the 'normal *and/or* perverse homosexual' suggest that statecraft as mancraft is less straightforward than Ashley suggests. Because the logos/logoi of the logocentric procedure can be plural as well as singular by being normal *and/or* perverse around sexes, genders, and sexualities and around numerous important registers of international politics (like nationality, civilization, and religious and secular authority), sometimes statecraft as mancraft is (also) a queer activity that results in unusual sexualized orders of international politics. We cannot account for these queer instances of statecraft simply by adding the singular 'homosexual'—as either sovereign man or his foil—to our analyses. Rather, tracing how plural logics of the *and/or* function in global politics—the *queer* logics of statecraft—is to appreciate how the normal *and/or* perverse plural sometimes scripts sovereign figures, their adversaries, and the unusual orders these mixed figures produce and are productive of.

Queer logics of statecraft are evident in those moments in domestic and international relations when actors or orders rely upon a queerly conceptualized Barthesian *and/or*—an *and* that is at the same time an *or* in relation to sexes, genders, and sexualities—to perfomatively figure sovereign man, the sovereign state, or some combined version of the order/anarchy and normal/perverse binaries as normal *and/or* perverse. Analyzing international relations through a lens of queer logics of statecraft directs us, following and then extending Ashley's arguments, to categories that connect *and* break apart foundational binaries like order/anarchy and normal/perverse, by understanding the stabilizing 'slash' in these binaries as multiplying and complicating connections, figures, and orders rather than reducing and simplifying them. It leads us to ask how 'the plural' as 'a deliberate "static"' (Barthes 1976, 5, 9) is introduced into these binaries to *both establish and confound* their meanings and the meanings of 'men', 'states', and 'orders' as well as the meanings of 'sexes', 'genders', and 'sexualities' which are foundational to them. In a Butlerian vein, queer logics of statecraft require us to take seriously how the plural is performatively enacted, enabling a plethora of national and international figurations and logics that can be (queerly) inhabited (also see Weber 1998b). Following Sedgwick, we can observe that queer logics of statecraft are attentive to how sexes, genders, and sexualities that fail or refuse to signify monolithically are productive of and are produced by unexpectedly normal *and/or* perverse 'sovereign men', 'sovereign states', and sovereignly ordained and opposed orders and anarchies.

Queer logics of statecraft, then, do not just describe those moments when the performatively perverse creates the appearance of the performatively normal. Nor do they describe only the opposite, when the performatively normal creates the appearance of the performatively perverse, although those can be among their effects. Rather, queer logics of statecraft describe those moments in domestic and international politics when the logos/logoi as a subjectivity or the logos/logoi as a logic is plurally normal *and/or* perverse in ways that 'confound the norm, normativity [antinormativity]' (Barthes 1976, 109; Wiegman and Wilson 2015) of individually or collectively *singularly* inscribed notions of sovereign man, sovereign states, or sexualized orders of international relations.

This is not to say that queer logics of statecraft do not give rise to 'institutions, structures of understanding, and practical orientations' (Berlant and Warner 1995, 548 n. 2) that make 'sovereign men', 'sovereign states', and international orders appear to be singular, coherent, and privileged. In this respect, they can be akin to sexual organizing principles like heteronormativities and homonormativities (Berlant and Warner 1995, 548 n. 2; Duggan 2003, 50). For, by 'confusing the [singular] norm, normativity, [antinormativity]' (Barthes 1976, 109; Wiegman and Wilson 2015), queer logics of statecraft can produce new institutions, new structures of understanding, and new practical orientations that are paradoxically founded upon a disorienting *and/or* reorienting plural. This can make them more alluring, more powerful, and more easily mobilized *both* by those who, for example, wish to resist hegemonic relations of power and by those who wish to sustain them (Weber 1999; 2002; Puar and Ra, 2002; Puar 2007). Unlike heteronormativities and homonormativities, though, we cannot name in advance what these institutions, structures of understanding, and practical (dis)/(re)orientations will be. We cannot know if they will be politicizing or depoliticizing. To determine this, it is necessary to both identify the *precise* plural each particular queer logic of statecraft employs to figure some particular 'sovereign man', 'sovereign state', and international order, always asking, 'For what constituency or constituencies does this plural operate?'

The case of Neuwirth/Wurst is striking, as we will see, because it illustrates how Europeans leaders debated—albeit very briefly—a plural logoi as a possible ground for contemporary Europe, whether they recognized Neuwirth/Wurst as a plural logoi or not. In discussions about the 'new Europe', both sides in this debate employed Neuwirth/Wurst to construct and authorize their Eurovisioned hierarchies of order versus anarchy, as if they were true. In this way, Neuwirth/Wurst generated not only competing sexualized orders of contemporary Europe but also practically (dis)/(re) oriented and (de)/(re)railed any idealized contemporary European-wide vision of an already united Europe.

It is not surprising that in their mobilizations of Neuwirth/Wurst, European leaders attempted to claim him/her/them as either normal or perverse, for this is how traditional logics of statecraft as mancraft operate. Because European leaders failed to consider Neuwirth/Wurst through the lens of queer logics of statecraft, they generally failed to appreciate what plural(s) constituted him/her/them and how the plural *and/or* logic he/she/they embodies is what made their attempts to claim or disown—to normalize or to pervert—this normal *and/or* perverse figure both possible and impossible. Yet it is this very failure on the part of European leaders to read Neuwirth/Wurst through the plural(s) that constitute(s) him/her/them that suggests an additional set of research questions for international theory and practice, including the following:

- Can a paradigm of sovereign man be effective without being—as Ashley claims the ideal type of 'sovereign man' must be—'regarded as originary, unproblematic, given for all time, and, hence, beyond criticism and independent of politics' (Ashley 1989, 271)?
- What happens when a political community like a state or the EU considers grounding itself upon a pluralized *and/or* logoi?
- Under what conditions might this be desirable or even necessary, and what might it make possible or preclude?
- How might queer logics of statecraft affect the organization, regulation, and conduct of international politics?

The rest of this book puts both of these queer IR theoretical and methodological approaches to work. It does this by analyzing how the will to knowledge about the sexualities of the 'underdeveloped', the 'undevel-opable', the 'unwanted im/migrant', the 'terrorist', the 'gay rights holder', the 'gay patriot', and the 'Eurovisioned queer drag queen' functions in and matters intensively to intimate, national, regional, and international games of power around sovereignty.

The 'Perverse Homosexual' in International Relations

The 'Underdeveloped' and the 'Undevelopable'

Who is the 'perverse homosexual' in international relations? And how does the will to knowledge about the 'perverse homosexual' participate in the figuration of 'sovereign man'?

This chapter and the next argue that four figures that consistently appear in the discourse of 'Western' / global 'Northern' 'developed' states as perverse—the 'underdeveloped', the 'undevelopable', the 'unwanted im/migrant', and the 'terrorist'—are among the specific (if surprising) articulations of the 'perverse homosexual' in international relations. These particular figurations of the 'perverse homosexual' matter for transnational/global queer studies and international relation because they make possible (by being opposed to) specific figurations of 'sovereign man' as '(neo) imperial man' and as '(civilizationally) developed man'.

All of these figurations of or against 'sovereign man' appear to arise out of and in turn produce what Berlant and Warner call heteronormativity, 'the institutions, structures of understanding, and practical orientations that make heterosexuality seem not only coherent ... but also privileged' (1998, 548 n. 2). By tracing where, when, and how these 'perverse homosexuals' are spoken of in past and ongoing colonial, imperial, and developmental heteronormative discourses that incite them as a concern, stabilize them as a problem, and regulate solutions to the problems they raise through specific policies, these chapters analyze how figurations of the 'perverse homosexual' are made to function as instances of 'statecraft as mancraft' (Ashley 1989). In these discourses, the 'perverse homosexual' is figured as that threat to 'sovereign man' who enables the production of (and is produced through) specific order-versus-anarchy binaries. These *either/or* binaries participate in the regulation of international politics because they establish sexualized orders of international relations.

To be clear, I am *not* arguing that the figure of the 'homosexual' as the 'underdeveloped', the 'undevelopable', the 'unwanted im/migrant', and the 'terrorist' *alone* explains all sovereign statecraft as sovereign mancraft. Rather, I am suggesting that if we dig down into the evolutionary theories that produce figurations of and opposed to 'sovereign man', what we find is that these theories depend upon understandings of civilization and its relationships to evolutionary time and geopolitical space that are deeply racialized, (dis)ableized, classed, sexed, gendered, and sexualized.[1]

This is by no means a new proposition, either empirically or theoretically. For example, even a cursory reading of (neo)imperial discourses and their supporting discourses of racialization makes it explicit that various precursors to and variations of the 'underdeveloped' owe their temporal and spatial figurations as perverse in part to how they are coded as perversely sexed, gendered, and sexualized. Institutions and cultural understandings of encumbered versus unencumbered sexuality (Mead 1928), whiteness versus blackness (Fanon 1967), orientalism (Said 1978), savagery and coloniality (Stoler 1995 and 2002), and postcoloniality and imperialism (Spivak 1988) have fueled imaginaries of what came to be known as the 'underdeveloped'. We see this in figures such as the 'noble savage' unencumbered by sexual prohibition in modern Western anthropology (Mead 1928), the 'barbaric savage' and the 'colonial' in Victorian discourse (Stoler 1995 and 2002), the 'blackman' marked by race in white colonialism and psychoanalysis (Fanon 1967), 'the black female body' (hooks 1982; Hammonds 1999; Spillers 2003), 'the illiterate peasantry, the tribals, the lowest strata of the urban sub-proletariat' called the 'subaltern' in imperial discourse (Spivak 1988, 283), and 'the timeless oriental who does not advance with modernity' in Western discourse (Said 1978), for example.

While international relation scholars are increasingly aware of how these figures are produced through complex networks of racialization, (dis) ablization, gender, class, indigeneity, and empire (beginning with Roxanne Doty's [1996] seminal international relation study of 'imperial encounters'), they are just beginning to grasp how these figures are also implicated in and produced by complex networks of power/knowledge/pleasure in relation to the figure of the 'homosexual'. Yet as V. Spike Peterson has long argued (1992, 1999, 2010, 2013, 2014a, 2014b) in her groundbreaking international relation analyses of gender and sexuality, figures like the 'heterosexual' and the 'homosexual' are foundational to international relation conceptualizations of states, nations, and international politics more widely. My contention in this set of chapters is that figurations of the 'homosexual' in Western discourses of statecraft as mancraft and the sexualized organizations of international relations to which they give rise are *among* those modalities of power/knowledge/pleasure that are the least examined such networks that *in part* underwrite international relation theories to this day. My suggestion is that to ignore these moves is to not fully understand how international relation theories and practices function, how they can be improved, and how they can be resisted.

THE 'UNDERDEVELOPED' AND THE 'UNDEVELOPABLE'

The figure of the 'underdeveloped' is a relatively recent arrival to international relation theory and practice. The 'underdeveloped' was incited in post–World War II popular and institutional discourse as a potentially threatening figure emerging out of crumbling Western colonial empires. From a Western perspective, the 'underdeveloped' could threaten the 'West' if he were to denounce his ties to his former colonizers and align himself instead with the newly emerging Soviet bloc.[2] This thinking placed the 'underdeveloped' at the crossroads of a choice between global capitalism and global communism, which—if made incorrectly—could imperil Western international order and throw international politics into dangerous anarchy.

To woo the 'underdeveloped' away from communism was to maintain him within the Western capitalist bloc; the 'underdeveloped' was stabilized in international relation theory and practice as a specific problem that the Western bloc of sovereign states urgently had to address. This was done by figuring the 'underdeveloped' as socially, psychologically, economically, and politically primitive through modernization and development theory, 'the latest manifestation of a Great Dichotomy between more primitive and more advanced societies' (Huntington 1971, 285). Borrowing primarily from the structural-functionalist evolutionary sociology of Talcott Parsons (1966) and the stages of growth evolutionary economic analysis of Walt Rostow (1960), comparative and international relation theorists created systems theories (Easton 1957; 1967) and development theories (Almond and Powell 1966) that stabilized the 'underdeveloped' as a primitive ignorant species-life whose political socialization and political development required Western guidance. This guidance invariably recommended implanting the 'underdeveloped' with a desire for the right kind of development and then placing him on a civilizing course from decadence to decency that mapped exactly to a political and economic progression from irrational, local tribalism toward modern Western capitalism and (usually) political liberalism (exceptionally, see Huntington 1969). In this way, 'The bridge across the Great Dichotomy between modern and traditional societies [became] the Grand Process of Modernization' (Huntington 1971, 288). At the same time, the modernization and development process identified the 'undevelopable' as those who would not or could not achieve Western-style development and who were accordingly cast as pure threats to Western global security.

By adapting the Great Dichotomy to international political theorizing, comparative and international relation theorists stabilized all those understandings found in the Great Dichotomy and refined them for political analysis and public policy. Their 'sovereign man' and his opposite were precisely those of the Great Dichotomy—civilized, rational, modern, often imperial, presumptively Christian and always 'developed man' in his singular, ahistorical abstraction opposed to potentially dangerous, plural, uncivilized (or uncivilizable), irrational, traditional 'underdeveloped' or 'undevelopable man' mired in (while often excluded from modern) history. These theorists organized these figures into an order-versus-anarchy dichotomy that hierarchized 'developed' over 'underdeveloped' and 'undevelopable' populations and territories and designated 'developed' populations and states as a form of Western sovereign man who should be aspired to by 'underdeveloped' postcolonial populations as the foundation of their newly emerging sovereign nation-states. They located these figures within the linear, progressive logic of modernization, albeit at different moments (the beginning of the modernization process for the 'underdeveloped'; not a part of the modernization process for the 'undevelopable') and in different geographic locations (the 'non-West' or the 'South' vs. the 'West' or the 'North'). And they understood the process of modernization as a mechanism for implanting a desire for capitalist development in 'underdeveloped' populations and newly emerging sovereign nation-states, as a way to solve the Western bloc's problem of the 'underdeveloped' as a global security issue.

Finally, the 'underdeveloped' and the 'undevelopable' were regimented in a diverse array of foreign policies. US foreign policies offer some examples. President Harry Truman's policies, which encouraged modernization as a function of nation building as a way of containing communism while avoiding direct wars (Merrill 2006), and President Kennedy's establishment of the Peace Corps (Almond 1970a, 23) are but two illustrations. Such policies were often less focused on having the 'underdeveloped' much less the 'undevelopable' achieve the end goal of development than they were with maintaining the 'underdeveloped' and the 'undevelopable' in systems of biopolitical surveillance, administration, management, and constant correction and securitization, first in support of and supported by a globalized liberalism and later by a globalized neoliberalism (Doty 1996; Duffield 2007).

For the 'undevelopable', the biopolitical management of life gave way to the necropolitical management of death (Mbembe 2003), since the

'undevelopable' not only could not be assimilated through the development process, but constituted a pure threat to the development process
itself. Sometimes this occurred directly through violent wars (in Korea and
Vietnam, for example); other times it occurred through the 'defensive' con-
tainment of dangerous difference. For example, before he became secretary
of state, Henry Kissinger claimed, 'We must construct an international order
before a crisis imposes it as a necessity' (1966, 529). This claim is rooted in
Kissinger's observation that 'the instability of the contemporary world order
may . . . have at its core a philosophical schism' between the 'West' and the
'new countries', which 'have retained the essentially pre-Newtonian view
that the real world is almost completely *internal* to the observer' (1966, 528),
making Western-style development and its accompanying domestic political structures and international diplomacy unattainable (also see discussion
in Said 1978, 46–47). As secretary of state, Kissinger acted on this claim to
oppose 'revolutionary states' and their 'prophetic' leaders in Vietnam (1966).

Through each of these sometimes very different foreign policies, modernization became a securitizing system of management and rule to be
imposed by the 'developed' on the 'underdeveloped' and the 'undevelopable' to tame or to destroy their dangerous anarchy that—if left unmoni-
tored, unmanaged, and unmodernized—threated Western capitalist states
and Western civilizational order itself (Doty 1996).

The 'Great Dichotomy between more primitive and more advanced
societies' and its figuration of the 'underdeveloped' and the 'undevelopable' did not originate in international relation theory. Rather, it 'has been
a common feature of Western social thought for the past one hundred
years' and more (Huntington 1971, 285). Variously described as traditional
versus modern, uncivilized versus civilized, or underdeveloped versus
developed, this Great Dichotomy places the 'underdeveloped' and the
'undevelopable' on the lesser side of its dominant imperial spatial hierarchy. It is able to do so largely because it temporalizes this hierarchy
through its use of nineteenth- and twentieth-century understandings of
time such as those found in evolutionary biological, psychological, social,
and political development. In these ways, the 'underdeveloped' and the
'undevelopable' are figured as perversions in/of evolutionary time.

From a post–World War II Western perspective, what is at stake in the perverting of evolutionary temporality is the very security of the 'West' itself. For modernization and development is always both a theory and a practice aimed at securing the West against the other great modern theory of development undergirded by its own understandings of evolutionary time—Marxism. What this means, then, is that precisely *how* the 'underdeveloped' and the 'undevelopable' are temporally figured and what makes their figurations as temporally perverse possible has had direct significance for how post–World War II international relation theory is conceptualized and practiced. Furthermore, how understandings of the 'underdeveloped' and the 'undevelopable' are frozen, refigured, and remobilized to figure contemporary understandings of the 'unwanted im/migrant' and the 'terrorist' means that their significance continues to this day (e.g., see Soguk 1999; Berman 2003). It is for these reasons that I spend the rest of this chapter analyzing precisely how the 'West' figured the 'underdeveloped' and the 'undeveloped' as perversions in/of their conceptualization of evolutionary time.

To do this, I focus on how the tropes of degeneracy and decadence performatively figure the 'temporally perverse underdeveloped' and 'undevelopable' and participate in the worlding of specific *sexualized* orders of international relations though their organization of modern/modernizing and developed/developing spaces, times, and desires. These international orders are *sexualized* orders because—as Neville Hoad shows in relation to Freudian psychoanalysis and I show in relation to Gabriel Almond's modernization and development theory—figurations of sexuality are so intimately intermingled with the tropes of degeneracy and decadence that the figuration of the 'temporally perverse underdeveloped' and 'undevelopable' is always/also a figuration of the 'temporally perverse homosexual'.

Following Hoad, I read how the 'temporally perverse underdeveloped' and 'undevelopable' are figured in evolutionary biological, psychological, social, and political development narratives through two dominant temporal tropes—degeneracy and decadence. As Neville Hoad explains, 'Decadence and degeneracy ... are both developmental tropes; degeneracy implying a falling back into an earlier time, an anxious space of the past in the future, and decadence connoting a bringing into the present of some very late, perhaps never-to-be reached state, an anxious space of premature death' (2000, 137).

The evolutionary trope of degeneracy gives rise to a figuration of the 'underdeveloped' as suffering from 'arrested' development, while the evolutionary trope of decadence gives rise to the 'undevelopable' as developmentally nonfunctional. The first of these figurations is found in Sigmund Freud' psychoanalytic theory (see Hoad 2000), while the second is found in the structural-functionalist modernization and development theory of Gabriel Almond (Almond and Powell 1966; Almond 1970a; 1970b).[3]

What I suggest here is that both Freud's and Almond's figurations of the 'temporally perverse underdeveloped' rely either explicitly (in Freud's case) or implicitly (in Almond's case) upon the figuration of the 'homosexual' as temporally perverse. For Freud, this is because he links sexual development to civilizational development through his reading of 'homosexual sex' and of the 'homosexual'. For Almond, it is because his understanding of political development owes fundamental debts to Talcott Parsons's structural-functionalist understanding of 'heterosexual sex' and the 'heterosexual' as presumably practiced by and embodied in the procreative nuclear family. For Parsons, the presumptively procreative heterosexual nuclear family drives social development because it drives biological and therefore social reproduction. In contrast, 'homosexual sex' and the 'homosexual' have no developmental function in society because they have no reproductive function in biology (Parsons 1966).

The 'Degenerate Homosexual' as the 'Degenerate Underdeveloped'

Who is the 'degenerate homosexual'? And how does the will to knowledge about the 'degenerate homosexual' participate in the figuration of 'sovereign man'?

These two figures and their relationships are rooted in the 'key tropes of Darwinian evolutionary theory' and how these tropes 'permitted an imbrication of race, gender, nation and class [and ableist] categories in the constitution of knowledge of the body of the "invert" and the subsequent "homosexual" ' (Hoad 2000, 133). Mobilizing the Great Dichotomy, nineteenth- and twentieth-century biologists, sexologists, and psychologists fused understandings of sexual degeneracy and decadence with understandings of civilizational degeneracy and decadence. In their analyses, the male 'homosexual' was figured as both sexually and civilizationally 'primitive'.

Sex, gender, and/or sexuality figured the 'homosexual' as degenerate in biological and medical discourses that equated the female sex and feminized gender with the male 'homosexual'. Just as the 'female' was understood as the biologically degenerate sex in relation to the 'male', the 'homosexual' appeared in medical discourse as biologically degenerate in relation to the 'heterosexual' (Hoad 2000, 136). For example, the 'homosexual body' was equated with 'the retarded female fetus' that developed more slowly than the male fetus and was described at a metabolic level as having inert, passive, anabolic cells rather than energetic, progressive, katabolic cells (Hoad 2000, 136; also see Conway 1972; Geddes and Thomson 1889).

Narratives regarding the sexed, gendered, and/or sexualized retardation of the 'homosexual' were merged with narratives of civilizational retardation, culminating in the claim that 'homosexual sex' was itself primitive. For example, 'homosexual sex' was cast as 'more ritualized and primitive [because more promiscuous] than its heterosexual counterpart' (Hoad 2000, 140). This led nineteenth-century anthropologists to posit 'homosexual sex' as 'the initial state of human social organisation', to be followed by progressively more advanced forms of socio-sexual organization that culminated in 'the civilized family' (Hoad 2000, 140). In this way, promiscuity became 'a defining attribute of those deemed primitive, whether primitive in the sphere of phylogeny—the savage, or primitive in his individual psychosexual development—the gay man' (Hoad 2000, 140).

These understandings were supported by additional evolutionary narratives that placed the not-properly civilized 'homosexual' on a racialized gender continuum, which described him as a part male, part female sexual 'half-breed' similar to racial 'half-breeds' who might display civilized

behaviors because they were good at 'adapting themselves to circumstances with perfect ease' (Edward Carpenter, cited in Hoad 2000, 136; for
a detailed discussion, see Somerville 2000).

These figurations of the 'homosexual' as sexually and civilizationally
primitive were accompanied by legal and popular narratives of the times
that figured the 'homosexual' as decadent as well. The example of the 1861
Oscar Wilde trial offers one example. In convicting Wilde for homosexual offenses, this trial was important for two reasons. On the one hand,
it refigured the dandy—who until this time had been read as possessing
surplus masculinity—into an effeminate figure, thus further equating the
'homosexual' with degeneracy. On the other hand, by criminalizing the
dandy, it marked this type of male 'homosexual' as not (only) degenerate
but decadent (Hoad 2000, 136).

These figurations of the 'homosexual' as sexually, racially, and temporally degenerate and decadent figured the 'homosexual' as a developmental
primitive who had more in common with the 'racialized uncivilized savage'
than he did with the 'white civilized European'. This had three effects. First,
it figured 'cultural [civilizational] difference in [natural] biological terms'
(Hoad 2000, 133) through various figurations of the 'perverse homosexual'.
In so doing, it, second, figured the 'white European sexual primitive' and
the 'nonwhite sexual savage' as the dominant, overlapping nineteenth-/
twentieth-century European images that the 'perverse homosexual' could
performatively inhabit. Finally, because these figurations of the 'perverse
homosexual' overlapped, they highlighted a fundamental contradiction
in how nineteenth-/twentieth-century Europeans gave an account of their
own historical development. This account idealized ancient Greek and
Roman civilizations as the roots of European civilization, even though the
ancient Greeks and Romans viewed 'homosexuality' as normal, while their
European descendants viewed 'homosexuality' as perverse.

As Hoad explains, this put evolutionary narratives under strain and raised
a series of troubling questions: 'Can the primitive and the decadent occupy
the same sequential position? Can socially sanctioned "homosex uality"
co-exist in the backward savages of the present and in the advanced cultures of Europe's past?' (2000, 137). What was at stake in these questions

was the figuration of the 'white heterosexual European' as a superior, imperial developed 'sovereign man'. For if the 'backward savage' was so like the 'ancient European' on a sexual/civilizational spectrum, then might that mean the 'evolved heterosexual European' was less evolved than he thought himself to be? Furthermore, from an international relation perspective, might this also mean that justifications for European domestic and imperial rule that were grounded upon the 'white civilized European sovereign man' as the natural, rational logos of European sovereign nation-states would unravel as well?

Hoad explains that while some evolutionary theories latched onto this problem to evidence how homosexuality caused the downfall of ancient civilizations, Sigmund Freud's theory of psychoanalysis—which was itself implicated in 'imperial discursive networks on race and sexuality' (Hoad 2000, 140)—offered a specific solution to this problem (Hoad 2000, 140–142). Freud's solution consisted in making three moves. First, Freud decoupled homosexuality from individual decadence. Second, he spatialized 'homosexuality' in relation to the Great Dichotomy of civilized versus uncivilized. And, third, he temporalized civilized versus uncivilized spaces of 'homosexuality'. Let me explain each of these moves in turn.

Freud decoupled homosexuality from decadence in his famous 1935 letter to an American mother of a homosexual son. Writes Freud:

> Homosexuality is assuredly no advantage, but it is nothing to be ashamed of, no vice, no depredation, it cannot be classified as an illness, we consider it to be a variation of the sexual function produced by a certain *arrest* of sexual development. ... In a certain number of cases, we succeed in developing the blighted germs of heterosexual tendencies which are present in every homosexual. (Cited in Hoad 2000, 141)

This passage does several things. It destigmatizes homosexuality on moral and medical grounds, by insisting it is neither a vice nor a depredation nor an illness. It puts 'homosexuality' on a developmental scale from 'homosexuality' to 'heterosexuality', where 'homosexuality' signifies a pause, a halting, a delay in one's sexual development but also a kind of 'force' that blights 'heterosexual tendencies'. In so doing, it establishes 'heterosexuality' as the ideal endpoint on a normal sexual progression toward which the 'homosexual' individual has failed to progress.

Freud's second move is to spatialize homosexuality by locating it on both sides of a civilized versus uncivilized binary. This occurs in his *Three Essays on the Theory of Sexuality*, as part of his explanation for why 'inversion' (which later came to be known as 'homosexuality') is not degenerative. As Freud explains,

> If we disregard the patients we come across in our medical practice, and cast our eyes around a wider horizon, we shall come in two directions upon facts which make it impossible to regard inversion as a sign of degeneracy:
>
> (a) Account must be taken of the fact that inversion was a frequent phenomenon—one might almost say an institution charged with important functions—among the peoples of antiquity at the height of their civilization.
>
> (b) it is remarkably widespread among many savage and primitive races, whereas the concept of degeneracy is usually restricted to states of high civilizations (cf. Block); and, even amongst the civilized peoples of Europe, climate and race exercise the most powerful influence on the prevalence of inversion and upon the attitude adopted towards it. (Freud 2005, 285, cited in Hoad 2000, 142)

In this passage, it would appear that Freud's insistence that 'homosexuality' is not a sign of degeneracy hinges upon his assertion that 'savage and primitive races' cannot degenerate—cannot fall back to an earlier time. This is because their primitiveness already locates them at the earliest moment of development. If this is the case, then what begins to emerge here is a distinction between how individual versus collective 'homosexuality' can be described in civilized versus uncivilized spaces. In civilized spaces—those racial and climatic spaces that Freud implies are associated with what we now call the 'North' and here expresses both something akin to the 'global North' as well as the 'European North'—'homosexuality' can be understood as the arresting of a particular individual's sexual development in a larger population of civilized heterosexuals. In uncivilized spaces (the 'global South' as well as the 'European South'), in contrast, 'homosexuality' describes the status of entire populations whose sexual and civilizational development has yet to begin and therefore cannot be arrested (Hoad 2000, 142).

These ideas foreshadow Freud's final and arguably most important move, the temporalization of space. For it is this move that allows Freud to preserve both the 'European self' as sexually and civilizationally developed and maintain reproductive heterosexuality as the privileged 'evolutionary motor of species-life' (Hoad 2000, 142). This final move occurs in Freud's *Beyond the Pleasure Principle*. Here, Freud argues that 'contemporaneous non-European cultures are understood as representatives of Europe's past' (Hoad 2000, 142; also see McClintock 1995 on 'anachronistic spaces'). What Freud is arguing here is that 'primitive homosexuality' is a stage of sexual *and civilizational* development that modern Europeans have already passed through. This becomes clearer if we rewrite Freud's statement like this: 'Contemporaneous non-European ['primitive homosexual'] cultures are understood as representatives of ['civilized'] Europe's ['homosexual'] past' (Hoad 2000, 142).

In making this claim, Freud is suggesting that there is only one universal temporal trajectory of development—which describes both the evolution of sexuality and the evolution of cultural organization (Hoad 2000, 142)—*and* that this universal temporal trajectory is being lived at two different yet contemporaneous moments in the civilized world and in the uncivilized world. In the uncivilized world, 'homosexuality' is so widespread because the 'uncivilized' are at the beginning of this temporal trajectory. In the civilized world, some individuals experience moments of 'arrested development'. But on the whole, 'we' civilized have already passed through this starting point of sexual and cultural development marked by widespread 'homosexuality'. For 'us' the civilized, that moment was the birth of our culture in ancient Greece and Rome.

By making this claim, Freud not only makes 'homosexual sex' 'a precondition for civilization' (Hoad 2000, 141) by equating the evolution of
sexuality with the evolution of cultural organization (Hoad 2000, 142).
He also makes progress a place—an always respecifiable 'North' (or
'West') where linear, evolutionary time has delivered all 'Northerners' (or
'Westerners') except the degenerate 'homosexual' to mature, heterosexual,
and civilizational development. In so doing, Freud confirms Hoad's observation that 'what the [degenerate] shares with the primitive is a position
on the fringes of the normative evolutionary narrative. Neither can exist
in the present' (2000, 137).[4]

By arguing that ' "we", the "civilized", have already been the "primitive" ' (Hoad 2000, 142), Freud's specific temporalization of space allowed
twentieth-century Europeans to retain their esteem for ancient European
civilizations, to continue to figure their contemporary 'homosexuals' as
'underdeveloped', and to combine their sexual and civilizational narratives
in ways that preserved their evolutionary thinking. It also allowed them
to further justify in the name of their white, cisgendered, heterosexual,
ableized, Christian, bourgeois, imperial, developed 'sovereign man' their
contrasting modes of regulation, securitization, correction, and rule of/
over the 'homosexual'. For example, it was in part thanks to how developmental temporalities were racialized (Stoler 1995) and spatialized (Hoad
2000; also see McClintock 1995; Said 1978) that it was possible for the
whitened Western European 'homosexual' to be put on a course of progressive correction so he could live *within* Victorian society (albeit often
contained within corrective spaces, including the psychiatrist's office and
the prison), while figurations of whole populations of colonial subjects
racialized as nonwhite endlessly oscillated between the irredeemable
"nonprogressive homosexual" and the redeemable "morally perfectible
homosexual" (Bhabha 1994, 118), both of whom must live *under* Victorian
imperial rule.

By combining the Great Dichotomy of primitive versus civilized
with his figuration of the 'homosexual' through the temporal trope of
degeneracy, Freud not only mapped a contestable world of civilizational
development as sexual development, but in so doing he also produced a

sexualized order of international relations, by first sexualizing and then temporalizing intimate, European/North American, and international order-versus-anarchy dichotomies.

The 'Decadent Homosexual' as the 'Decadent Undevelopable'

Who is the 'decadent homosexual'? And how is he related to the 'decadent undevelopable'?

While in developmental terms the 'degenerate homosexual' cannot exist in the present, the 'decadent homosexual' barely exists at all.[5] This is because, unlike the 'degenerate homosexual', who is on an evolutionary trajectory from 'homosexuality' to 'heterosexuality', the 'decadent homosexual' is on no such trajectory. For he is biologically vestigial, figured as that remainder from the evolutionary process who exists but has no function. This makes the 'decadent homosexual' not just a temporal perversion *within* the developmental process, but also a temporal perversion *of* the developmental process itself. This is why his temporality is described as decadent, for it brings into the present something that the evolutionary process long ago discarded. This means that when he does appear, he does so as 'an anxious space of premature death' (Hoad 2000, 137).

In this section, I trace how the 'decadent homosexual' is produced though specific understandings of temporality, the family, and the development process to figure him as the 'decadent undevelopable'. These understandings of temporality, the family, and the development process arise in Talcott Parsons's account of the development of social systems and are taken up by Gabriel Almond in his modernization and development theory to explain political development. By combining Parsons's understanding of the 'decadent homosexual' with his own understanding of political development and underdevelopment, Almond figures the 'decadent homosexual' as the 'undevelopable' because this figure has no function in political development. In sketching out this argument, I examine how Parsons and Almond understand development as functionalist, evolutionary, and teleological and how they take the presumptively Christian (and ideally Protestant; Turner 2005), procreative, white, cisgendered, able-bodied bourgeois, heterosexual nuclear family (hereafter the 'reproductive cisgendered heterosexual family' or 'couple') as their foundation of social and political development.

Functionalism is 'a conceptual scheme which involves the analysis of social institutions in terms of the functions they perform in some larger system, and/or the analysis of the functions which must be performed in any system if it is to persist' (Rothman 1971, 244). For a social or political system to persist—to survive—its specific functional requirements must be met. Functional subsystems exist precisely to maintain the system, to keep it functioning through time.

Temporality in Parsonian structural-functionalist sociology is evolutionary and teleological. As Nancy Kingsbury and John Scanzoni explain, 'Parsons argued that just as organisms adapted to external forces, and thus changed in order to survive, this same process of evolution takes place within social systems' (1993, 204; also see Parsons 1964 and 1966). Evolutionary biology is not just an analogy for Parsons; it is what ensures the survival and maintenance of any social system. The subsystem that performs this biological function on behalf of the system as a whole is the nuclear family, understood as the 'socially sanctioned co-habitation of a [cis]man and [cis]woman who have preferential or exclusive enjoyment of economic and sexual rights over one another and are committed to raise the children brought to life by the woman' (Pitt 1964, 56). The nuclear family ensures the survival of the social system as a whole by fulfilling its function of producing children and socializing them to embrace the dominant norms and values of the society's culture.

The nuclear family itself is maintained because of role differentiation between the man and the woman in this subsystem, with the man protecting the family from 'general disequilibrium' and the woman protecting the family from 'emotional disequilibrium' (Parsons et al. 1955, 23). If this is accomplished, Parsons argues, equilibrium is achieved and the social system is maintained (Kingsbury and Scanzoni 1993, 196). In this way, 'The family, organized around a *unique and unalterable type of role structure*, operates or *functions* for something larger than itself' (Kingsbury and

Scanzoni 1993, 197). If, however, family members deviate from their roles by introducing disequilibrium into the family (e.g., by not having children, by having children outside of marriage, by not raising their children together, by not identifying with the sex and/or gender they were assigned at birth), this leads to 'family disorganization', which in turn leads to the disorganization of society as a whole. Deviance, then, is something to be punished and overcome so that sexuality can remain functional for the social system as a whole (Parsons 1951, 206).

Reproductive heterosexuality as performed within the nuclear family, then, is foundational to Parsonian structural functionalism.[6] What is not function is deviance from familial, reproductive, cisgendered heterosexuality. Mechanisms of social control can '*counteract* a tendency to deviance' (Parsons 1951, 206) and restore heterosexual sex to its social function. What do not have functions in Parsons's system is trans* or homosexual sex.[7] Homosexual deviance or, as later Parsonian sociologists called it, 'alternative' or 'other' lifestyles 'may have disfunctions for children and society' because 'they represent something besides "The Family"' (see Kingsbury and Scanzoni 1993, 205).

Taken together, Parsonian teleological accounts of social development and of the role the 'reproductive cisgendered heterosexual couple' has in ensuring the survival of social systems figure the 'reproductive cisgendered heterosexual couple' in heteronormative terms, as normal, coherent, whole, and privileged (Berlant and Warner, 1998, 548 n. 2). While particular 'heterosexuals' may deviate from their function in the subsystem of the nuclear family, their reproductive function can be restored through mechanisms of social control. The 'homosexual' (like the 'trans*'), in contrast, has no social function because the 'homosexual' is erroneously figured as someone who is not involved in either biological reproduction or in childrearing. As such, the 'nonreproductive homosexual' is figured as the nonfunctional opposite of the functional 'reproductive cisgendered heterosexual couple'. Temporally, this locates the 'reproductive cisgendered heterosexual couple' as the necessary foundation of social development on the teleological trajectory of social evolution. At the same time, it locates the 'nonreproductive homosexual' outside of developmental time altogether, for he has no role to play in the development of society because he has no role to play in the nuclear family. Worse still, as a temporal perversion of the development process itself, this evolutionary remainder figured as the 'decadent homosexual' becomes 'an anxious space of premature death' (Hoad 2000, 137) for the social system and for social development itself.

Almond drew upon Parsonian structural-functionalist sociology to give a functionalist account of political development. For Almond, political development describes changes in traditional societies from traditional to modern. Almond's modernization and development theory, which was a 'manifestation of the Great Dichotomy between more primitive and more advanced societies', claimed that 'the bridge across the Great Dichotomy ... was the Grand Process of Modernization' (Huntington 1971, 285, 288). Modernization occurred when social and political changes in traditional societies converted their 'particularistic, ascriptive and functionally diffuse norms and structures' that characterized their political systems in 'universalistic, achievement, and functionally specific norms and structures' that characterized modern political systems (Rothman 1971, 242). Through the grand process of modernization, political systems became more differentiated, with specialized structures being created to perform particular functions. In other words, traditional political systems that modernized came to resemble the classic separation of powers ideally found in European and American political systems.

While the complexities and utility of Almond's theory were the subject of intense debate (Rothman 1971; Huntington 1971; Groth 1970), what was indisputable was Almond's foundational debts to Parsons. Indeed, as Almond put it himself in one of his many reformulations of modernization and development theory, 'Parsons contributed in basic ways to our ability to compare whole societies and their subsystems and to discriminate between modern and premodern systems. Many of his notions have become almost as common as the air we breathe' (Rothman 1971, 23–24). Among the atmospheric aspects of Parsonian sociology that Almond breathed in were Parsons's debts to evolutionary biology, to teleological temporality, and to his figuration of the 'reproductive cisgendered hetero-sexual couple' as the engine of social development.

What drives political development for Almond is a biologically derived understanding of systems evolution, which he lifted wholesale from Parsons's account of social systems. Stanley Rothman elaborates on how this biological analogy operates in Almond's general theory of development.

> The general theory implicitly draws upon biological analogies. Societies begin as one-celled (primitive) creatures and gradually differentiate. They develop specialized roles and structures (cells and organs), such as judiciaries, specialized organs of communication, etc. for dealing with particular problems. As they do so their capacity to deal with their environment increases, although problems of coordination become more pressing, entailing the creation of a more complex 'bureaucratic (nervous?) system' (Rothman 1971, 238; see Almond and Powell 1966, 229–332).

Similarly, Rothman points to the 'teleological quality' in Almond's specific theory of development, which 'assumes the mobilized modern state as the inevitable outcome of development' (1971, 251; as Almond and Powell 1966, 217). Developmental evolution, then, inevitably converts traditional political systems into modern ones.

While Almond identifies a number of subsystems and their functions that drive the evolutionary process, among the most important processes that Almond identifies for 'political stability and development' is political socialization (Almond and Powell 1966, 65). As Almond and his coauthor Bingham Powell write, 'Political socialization is the process by which political cultures are maintained and changed' (1966, 64), and changes in political culture effect changes in political systems. Among the key influences on an individual's political socialization is the family. As Almond and Powell explain, 'The family unit is the first socialization structure encountered by the individual. The latent and manifest influences inculcated at the early stages in life have a powerful and lasting influence. Among the many important latent influences, perhaps the most distinctive is the

shaping of attitudes toward authority' (1966, 66). Because Almond and
Powell define a political system as 'all those interactions which affect the
use or threat of legitimate physical coercion' (Almond and Powell 1966,
17–18), how an individual is socialized to think about authority directly
impacts the development of a political system.

As in Parsons sociological model, then, the family in Almond's theory is a
structure with a particular function, political socialization. It is not the only
political socialization structure in a political system. Nor does its socialization of children into the political system go unchallenged or unchanged as the
child grows and encounters additional structures of political socialization (in
school, in the media, through direct political experience), especially if these
structures present conflicting messages. Yet the family remains the primary
structure through which children are socialized into the political system
(Almond and Powell 1966, 63–72). As such, the family plays a foundational
role in the development of the political system because it has a major role—if
not the most important role—in the political socialization of children.

Almond never speaks of the 'family' in any more specific terms. He does
not refer to the 'nuclear family', much less to the 'reproductive cisgendered
heterosexual couple.' Yet because his understanding of the structure and the
function of the 'family' is taken directly from Parsons, Almond's family is
Parsons's family, albeit with both a social and a political socialization function. As such, Almond's family is the presumptively procreative cisgendered
heterosexual nuclear family that drives social and political development
because it produces children and socializes them into both the social system
and the political system.

By importing Parsons's nuclear family into his theory of modernization and development, Almond by default also imports Parsons's figuration of the 'decadent homosexual.' While Parsons explicitly names and
theorizes the 'decadent homosexual', Almond does not. Yet the 'decadent
homosexual' lurks in Almond's theory as an unnamed specter. He haunts
Almond's account of political development in the same way he stalks
the 'reproductive cisgendered heterosexual couple' in Parsons's account
of social development. As this aberration appears in modernization
and development theory, the 'decadent homosexual' is the minoritized

dysfunctional remainder of the development process. He is a perversion of biological species-life that can take individual, social, *and*—thanks to Almond—political form.

As he is figured through Almond's fusion of Parsonian sociology with modernization and development theory, the 'decadent homosexual' is not the 'underdeveloped'. He is not on the teleological trajectory toward development. He does not hold within himself the promise of modernization and development. Instead, he is the 'undevelopable', who promises the 'premature death' (Hoad 2000, 137) of the conversion of traditional societies and political systems into modern ones. In other words, he promises the death of political development itself.

By combining the Great Dichotomy of primitive versus civilized with his implicit figuration of the 'homosexual' through the temporal trope of decadence, Almond—like Freud—has produced a sexualized order of international relations. Yet because Almond ties the 'homosexual' to decadence rather than degeneracy, his sexualization and temporalization of the order-versus-anarchy binary is different from Freud's. Unlike Freud's 'degenerate homosexual', Almond's 'decadent homosexual' is not the precondition for civilizational development. Quite the contrary. Now minoritized and stigmatized as the 'undevelopable', the 'decadent homosexual' has three functions in modernization and development theory and practice (even if Almond would never have described them in this way).

First, the 'decadent homosexual' reasserts the centrality of the 'reproductive cisgendered heterosexual couple' and its supporting structures of heteronormativity in achieving modernization and development. Second, as the minority figure beyond development, he implants in the majority 'developing' the knowledge that he, the 'decadent homosexual', marks the limits of the development process itself. As a result, his third function is to serve as the scapegoat whose existence in traditional societies explains why social and political development has failed to take place. This makes the 'homosexual' less a figure of the biological management of developmental life (as he is in Freud's theory) than a figure of the necropolitical management of developmental death (Mbembe 2003). For by threatening the development process itself with death, the 'decadent homosexual' can justifiably be left to die.

The 'Temporally Perverse Homosexual' as the 'Temporally Perverse Underdeveloped' and the 'Temporally Perverse Undevelopable'

The 'temporally perverse homosexual' is not as easily divided into the 'underdeveloped' and the 'undevelopable' as I have suggested here. This is because—as they are employed by Freud and by Almond—the temporal tropes of degeneracy and decadence that create these figures overlap. As Hoad points out, Freud's homosexual is both degenerate and decadent. In spite of his efforts to decouple 'homosexuality' from decadence by putting all individuals and civilizations on the same, universal continuum from underdeveloped to developed, Freud nevertheless minoritizes and stigmatizes 'homosexuality' as decadent. This is because Freud posits 'heterosexuality' as the ideal endpoint of normal sexual and civilizational progression (Hoad 2000, 140). Similarly, we find degeneracy in Almond's imported account of the Parsonian nuclear family. For Parsons's nuclear family is the very endpoint of the universal normal sexual progression that Freud describes. It is the 'civilized family' found in nineteenth-century evolutionary anthropology (Hoad 2000, 140), the heteronormative endpoint of universal familial progression that minoritizes the 'homosexual' as nonfunctional difference.

That the universalized figure of the 'underdeveloped' and the minoritized figure of the 'undevelopable' may seem to be distinct and possibly contradictory is an illusion. These figures are but different points of emphasis—different moments of imagined time—in the same heteronormative network of power/knowledge/pleasure that gave us the 'temporally perverse homosexual'. This should come as no surprise to either queer studies theorists or international relation theorists. That universalizing and minoritizing discourses 'while contradictory, have both continued to coexist simultaneously as explanatory frameworks for homosexuality' (Summerville 2000, 21, summarizing Sedgwick 1990, 44–48, 86–87) is a point Eve Sedgwick made in *Epistemology of the Closet*. That the universal and the particular compete with while codetermining one another in international relations is a point R. B. J. Walker made in *Inside/Outside* (1993).

The crucial issue for transnational/global queer studies and international relation theorists, then, is *not* to determine which 'temporally perverse homosexual' is the correct one. Rather, what matters is how one, the other, or both of these accounts appear to be true; how they emerge from and participate in putting sex into discourse through networks of power/knowledge/pleasure; what the specific sexualized orders of international relations are that they enable or disable; what conditions, understandings, and strategies have to be put in place for one of these figures and their sexualized order to become dominant at a particular place and time while making other figures and orders recede into 'political amnesia' (Rogin 1990); [8] and how it is possible to recall a dormant—even discredited—figure and its order so that it might reorder or even disorder international relations.

This last issue is particularly important for international relation scholars precisely because the figures of the 'underdeveloped' and the 'undevelopable' and the discourses that generated them are so thoroughly *discredited and persistent*. On the one hand, Freud's civilizational account of sexuality has been repudiated by a whole host of intellectuals, including queer studies theorists and modernization and development theorists (Hoad 2000; Banuazizi 1987). On the other hand, Almond's functionalist account of modernization and development stands out as the most discredited approach to development of its time (Wiarda 1989–1990).[9] So, too, are the explicit and implicit connections Freud and Almond drew between 'homosexuality', the 'homosexual', and the processes of civilization and modernization.[10] *And yet the figurations of the 'underdeveloped' and the 'undevelopable' as the 'temporally perverse homosexual' persist.* Their persistence has several important effects on contemporary international relations.

They participate in the following:

- The figuration of the 'reproductive cisgendered heterosexual couple' as the logos—the singular authoritative origin—of social and political development (Peterson 1992; 1999; 2010; 2013; 2014a; 2014b)

- The legitimation of international relation's governing dichotomy of order versus anarchy and its expression through 'the Great Dichotomy between more primitive and more advanced societies' and states (Huntington 1971, 285)

- The understanding of order versus anarchy, advanced versus primitive, civilized versus uncivilized as not just normal versus perverse but as a sexualized understanding of normality against a sexualized understanding of perversion

- The creation of sexualized orders of international relations based upon racialized, (dis)ableized, classed, sexed, gendered, and sexualized understandings of evolutionary biology, supported by specific codings and arrangements of time, space, and desire

- The marking off of the civilizationally and sexually 'developable' from its presumed opposite, the 'undevelopable'

- The legitimation of specific securitizing techniques of intimate, national, and international biopolitical and necropolitical management and rule of the 'developable', the 'undevelopable', and the 'underdeveloped' through contemporary development policy (e.g., Gibson-Graham 1996; Bedford 2005; 2007; 2009; Bedford and Rai 2010; Lind 2009; 2010; Bergeron 2010)[11]

Taken together, what this means is that these figurations of the 'perverse homosexual' not only position the white(ned), Christian, bourgeois, ableized 'reproductive cisgendered heterosexual couple' as the privileged 'evolutionary motor of species-life' (Hoad 2000, 142), but also figure this couple as the engine of the production of 'sovereign man' as '(neo)imperial man' and/or 'developed man', who grounds the Western sovereign nation-state's authority nationally and internationally.

All of this, I am suggesting, is in some part supported by the figuration of the 'underdeveloped' and the 'undevelopable' as the 'temporally perverse homosexual' in international relations theory and practice. If this claim strikes readers as anachronistic—if it seems to be the preserve of only nineteenth- and twentieth-century imperial discourses—then a cursory reading of contemporary development policy with its debts to heteronormativities should be enough to persuade them otherwise. These debts are evident, for example, in the post–World War II Bretton Woods economic system, which made 'the regulation of sex . . . a critical—if generally unrecognized—component of social and economic development policies' (Gosine 2005, 3). This regulation of sex has continued through, for example, World Bank policies that make 'couplehood between a [cis] man and a [cis]woman . . . a key informal institution necessary for reformulated development' (Bedford 2009, 211; and see World Bank 2000 and 2001).

Figurations of the 'temporally perverse homosexual' not only are foundational to contemporary development policies. They also inform contemporary figurations of the 'unwanted im/migrant' and the 'terrorist', as well as many of the policies that inform the regulation of these figures. It is to figurations of the 'unwanted im/migrant' and the 'terrorist' that I now turn.

The Out-of-Place and On-the-Move 'Perverse Homosexual' in International Relations

The 'Unwanted Im/migrant' and the 'Terrorist'

Who is the 'perverse homosexual' that Western discourses describe as out of place or on the move? And how does the will to knowledge about this 'perverse homosexual' participate in the figuration of 'sovereign man'?

My focus in this chapter is on the 'unwanted im/migrant' and the 'terrorist' as the out-of-place and on the move 'underdeveloped' or 'undevelopable'. More specifically, I analyze the 'unwanted im/migrant' who is sometimes racialized as Latino (as he is in contemporary US discourses) but who is more broadly racialized as Arab/Muslim/Sikh in US and European discourses. Especially since the terrorist attacks of September 11, 2001, the Arab/Muslim/Sikh 'unwanted im/migrant' has been known in these discourses as the modeler, breeder, or conductor of al-Qaeda terrorism (Puar and Rai 2002; Puar 2007; also see Weber 2002). The 'al-Qaeda terrorist', then, is the specific figuration of the 'terrorist' that I examine in this chapter.

As figures understood as lagging or lacking in their development, these particular figurations of the 'unwanted im/migrant' and the 'al-Qaeda terrorist' are expressions through which the thoroughly discredited links among culture, civilization, sexuality, and psychological, social, and political development discussed in chapter 3 persist. As such, when they are understood through what Berlant and Warner (1998) describe as heteronormativities, these figures constitute contemporary figurations of the 'temporally perverse homosexual' in whom what Michel Foucault calls 'the frozen countenance of the perversions' (1980, 48) has been implanted. What these figures additionally express—and what is the primarily focus of this chapter—are Western fears and anxieties that these 'temporally perverse homosexuals' can no longer be held within the containers modernization and development theory crafted for them, either spatially, temporally, or in terms of their desires. This is because the 'unwanted im/migrant' and the 'al-Qaeda terrorist' do not just embody sexual perversions of developmental temporality; they embody sexual perversions of developmental temporality *on the move*. It is how the sexually perverse 'underdeveloped' and 'undevelopable' *move* within and beyond their assigned spaces in Western developmental discourses that incite their refigurations by Westerners as the sexually perverse 'unwanted im/migrant' and 'al-Qaeda terrorist'.

THE 'UNWANTED IM/MIGRANT' AND THE 'TERRORIST': FROM CULTURAL, CIVILIZATIONAL, AND SEXUAL CHALLENGES TO MOBILE SECURITY THREATS

The 'underdeveloped' and the 'undevelopable' were always imagined in Western developmental discourses as inhabiting the emerging sovereign nation-states of the global South. It is their geopolitical movements from South to North that from World War II onward incited them as civilizational, sexual, and political threats to the 'West'.[1]

These threats were stabilized by inscribing the moving/migrating 'underdeveloped' and 'undevelopable' as geopolitical and '*cultural*' outsiders known as the 'unwanted im/migrant' and the 'terrorist'. US anthropological accounts of 'culture' were mobilized to specify the unique 'national character' of 'the people of a nation' and to 'separate[e] out the irredeemably foreign from the domestic' (Palumbo-Liu 2002, 112). As US anthropologist Margaret Mead described it in her famous World War II attempt to identify 'American character', 'national character' was understood as 'an abstraction, a way of talking about the results in human personality, of having been reared by and among human beings whose behavior was culturally regular' (Mead 1942, 21; cited in Palumbo-Liu 2002, 112). Mead suggested that the study of national culture itself was 'a form of applied science, by which skills developed in the field work on primitive, preliterate societies were used for rapid diagnostic study . . . [to] provide some kind of prediction of the probable behavior of the members of a given national group' (Mead 1961, 15–16, cited in Palumbo-Liu 2002, 112). In this way, Mead mobilized 'the Great Dichotomy' (Huntington 1971, 288) to presumably distinguish a fixed American character from 'seven other cultures' (Mead 1942, 260–261).

Of course, who could become an American was always meant to be flexible. Indeed, 'The liberal definition of American national character stressed an *ethos* to which theoretically anyone could subscribe: Hence, immigrants could adopt that ethos if they did so in good faith and in so doing become Americans' (Palumbo-Liu 2002, 112; my italics). But as Mead's cultural coding of American character asserted, 'This required first separating out *the irredeemably foreign from the domestic*' (Palumbo-Liu 2002, 112; my italics). In making these assertions, then, Mead's brand of cultural anthropology affirmed both the possibility and the necessity for the wartime US state to sort the 'desirable immigrant' from the 'unwanted im/migrant'.

If Mead's account of the 'irredeemably foreign' and the necessity for the World War II US to defend itself against the 'irredeemably foreign' sound familiar to IR scholars, it is because Mead's schematic was imported wholesale into IR by Samuel Huntington.[2] Just as in Mead's account, what Huntington identified as 'irredeemably foreign' in relation to the United States was the 'cultural other', whom Huntington attempts to fix as the 'civilizational other'. Huntington defines a civilization as 'the highest cul-tural grouping of people and the broadest level of cultural identity people have short of that which distinguishes humans from other species' (1996, 43). Ostensibly offered as an explanation for why the great conflicts in the post–Cold War world would occur not between nation-states or through ideological conflicts, Huntington's clash of civilizations thesis suggests that future great conflicts will be between the world's seven or eight clash-ing civilizations. It is foreign civilizations, Huntington argues, that pose the biggest threat to the 'West', a 'civilization' he ultimately equates with the United States (Huntington 1996, 305).[3]

Part of what makes foreign civilizations a threat to the 'West' is their (pre-sumed) rejection of Western ideas (e.g., Western modernity and Western development), which has led them to reestablish themselves upon their own 'native traditions' (1996, 95). In other words, 'foreign cultures' have increasingly become 'irredeemably foreign civilizations'. In Huntington's view, the United States has to defend itself against these 'civilizational oth-ers' in both domestic and international affairs. Huntington's account of the 'civilizational other' has been influential in US and European insti-tutional and popular discourses in stabilizing the 'unwanted im/migrant' as the domestic enemy within nonnative (Western) civilizations and the 'terrorist' as the enemy of civilization itself. This stabilization is rooted in Huntington's geopolitical placement of civilizations and his understand-ing of the out-of-place 'civilizational other' who is a threat to 'Western civilization' as the out-of-place 'underdeveloped' or 'undevelopable'.

Huntington literally maps civilizations in geopolitical space, indicat-ing the places where civilizational bodies belong—geopolitically and individually—in the contemporary world (1996, 26). This mapping allows Huntington to make two arguments. One is that civilizational borders are the historic locations of great conflicts. More importantly for our purposes is Huntington's second argument. This is that out-of-place civilizational bodies are threats to the nonnative (Western) civilizations in which they are located. The 'unwanted im/migrant' and the 'terrorist' are such bodies.

Huntington describes the 'unwanted im/migrant' as a challenge, before designating him as a threat to the survival of Western civilization. As he puts it, 'Western culture is challenged by groups within Western societies. One such challenge comes from immigrants from other civilizations who reject assimilation and continue to adhere to and propagate the values, customs, and cultures of their home societies' (1996, 304). For Huntington, the 'Hispanic' is one such 'unwanted im/migrant' (Huntington 2004a; 2004b). Huntington claims that the 'Hispanic' living in the United States is not properly 'American'—even when he is a US citizen—because 'the civilizationally Latin American Hispanic' does not fully accept 'civilizationally Western' US liberal capitalist values, what Huntington calls 'the American Creed' (Huntington 2004a, 41). Instead, 'the Latin American Hispanic' living in the United States lives by 'Latin American civilizational values' and is therefore less like a 'Western' Anglo-American (who is the type of US American who produced and upholds 'the American Creed') and more like a diasporic ethnic (Palumbo-Liu 2002, 120–121). As a diasporic ethnic, the 'Latin American Hispanic' is an out-of-place 'underdeveloped' or 'undevelopable' who remains connected to and culturally, politically, and religiously aligned with his Latin American homeland (Huntington 2004).

What this means is that the 'unwanted im/migrant' is both *civilizing development on the move* and *civilization on the move*. For by crossing geopolitical civilizational boundaries, the 'unwanted im/migrant' brings his unfinished civilizing developmental process with him. Not only that, he brings with him a type of civilizing development that is not (necessarily) delivering him to either Western modernity or Western development. In the case of the 'Latin American Hispanic' living in the United States, these double movements figure him as an out-of-place developmental and civilizational figure who deprives 'the developed West/North' 'of precisely that particular fundamental cultural identity to which all civilizations must hold if they are to survive' (Palumbo-Liu 2002, 119–120). This makes the 'unwanted im/migrant' not just an 'outsider, inside the State' (Ceyhan and Tsoukala, cited in Bigo 2002, 66). More specifically, he is in Mead's terms an 'outsider, inside the Culture' and in Huntington's terms an 'outsider, inside the Civilization'. In all of these ways, the 'unwanted im/migrant' is figured as a carrier of 'irredeemable foreignness' inside the state/culture/civilization who puts the 'developed West/North' itself at risk. In so doing, the 'unwanted im/migrant' is constructed as a figure of unease (Bigo 2002),[4] whose management by Western statist policies range from regulating immigration by surveilling, sorting, and excluding 'potentially dangerous minorities' (Bigo 2002, 82) to administering ever-more-complex citizenship naturalization (Fortier 2013b; in progress) and denaturalization (Nyers 2009; 2010) processes. This is how the 'unwanted im/migrant' is regimented in Western statist developmental and civilizational discourses.

'The terrorist' is also stabilized as an out-of-place civilizational figure in Huntington's account. This is not because the 'terrorist' represents a specifically non-Western civilization and a non-Western style of civilizing development that are inside the 'West/North'. Rather, it is because the 'terrorist' is out of place in any civilization. He is the opposite of civilization. For the 'terrorist' is a pure form of 'civilizational barbarism' (Huntington 1996, 321). As such, the 'terrorist' is both undevelopable and uncivilizable.

This does not mean that the 'terrorist' cannot be claimed on behalf of a civilization or on behalf of a civilizing developmental process. He can, and he frequently is. This was most evident in the wake of the September 11, 2001, terrorist attacks on the United States, about which President George W. Bush declared, 'This is civilization's fight' (September 20, 2001). For Bush, this civilizational fight was between the West (the United States) and 'Islam', which Bush, like Huntington, describes as both a religion and a civilization (Huntington 1996, 95). Cast in these terms, what is so frightening from a US perspective about this 'civilizational fight' is how it puts *civilizational barbarism on the move*, not just by generally moving out of its assigned geopolitical spaces but by explicitly targeting the US state and the 'West' and infiltrating the Western homeland. This understanding of the 'terrorist' regiments him as a 'figure of unease' much further up the risk continuum than the/other 'unwanted im/migrant(s)' (Bigo 2002). Western statist policies to the problem of the 'terrorist' therefore are designed not just to restrict his movements but to render him incapable of moving at all. This has been the aim of US and broader Western policies ranging from the US-led 'War on Terror' to policies of Homeland Security.

In these ways, civilizing development on the move and civilizational barbarism on the move are constituted as threats to the 'Western homeland' through the figures of the 'unwanted im/migrant' and the 'terrorist', understood as the out-of-place 'underdeveloped' and 'undevelopable'. This is what a typical IR reading of these figures and their relationships to the 'state' as the 'homeland' demonstrates. What this IR reading neglects, however, is how these figures also embody *sexual development on the move* through the figure of the 'unwanted im/migrant' and *sexual barbarism on the move* through the figure of the 'terrorist'.

Sexual development and sexual barbarism on the move are rarely discussed in IR. This is because, as noted above, IR tends to see sexuality as the domain of the 'home' (the family) rather than as the domain of the 'homeland' (the state). Yet the home and the family are as essential to IR as is homeland; indeed, they cannot be dissociated from one another, as IR scholar V. Spike Peterson has long argued (1999; 2010; 2013; 2014a; 2014b). We saw this in chapter 3, in how Gabriel Almond's modernization and development theory imports Talcott Parsons's conceptualizations of home and family into IR. And we see it here in Mead's and Huntington's attempts to define national character as national culture and/or as civilization.

For example, Mead's claim that there is something called 'national character' hinges upon her ability to link activities in the family home with the identity of the nation. This is clear in how she defines 'national character' as 'an abstraction, a way of talking about the results in human personality, *of having been reared by and among human beings whose behavior was culturally regular*' (Mead 1942, 21; my italics; also see Mead 1928 on 'sexual mores'). Similarly, Huntington's civilizational discourse links activities in the home with the security of the homeland. For example, Huntington stokes US fears of the 'Latin American civilizational Hispanic' not just based upon this figure's geopolitical movements but also based upon this figure's sexual activities. Huntington writes, 'The most immediate and most serious challenge to Americans' traditional identity comes from the immense and continuing immigration from Latin America, especially from Mexico, *and the fertility rates of these immigrants*' (Huntington 2004,

32; my italics). This, for Huntington, is among the ways in which the 'Hispanic' 'adhere(s) to and propagates the values, customs, and cultures of their home society' (1996, 304).

It is this strange *emphasis and neglect* of home and its connection to homeland that typifies much of IR scholarship and accounts for its under-theorization of sexuality on the move. In contrast to most IR literatures, queer migrations literatures make sexual movements in the home and (in)between homelands their primary foci (e.g., Eng 1997; Ahmed 2000; Luibhéid and Cantú 2005; Luibhéid 2008; 2013; Fortier 2000; 2001; 2002, 2003; Gopinath 2005). In so doing, they offer a corrective lens through which to reconsider figures who are presumably on the move and out of place geopolitically, developmentally, *and* sexually.

The remainder of this chapter reconsiders the 'unwanted im/migrant' and the 'terrorist' from both an IR and a queer migrations perspective. It argues that complex connections among civilizing/civilizational movements and sexual movements in the home/land together do two things. First, they figure the 'unwanted im/migrant' and the 'terrorist' as the out-of-place 'underdeveloped' or 'undevelopable', whose movements in relation to space, time, and desire mark them as civilizationally and sexually out-of-place global Southerners who hold developmental and/or security risks for the 'developed' Western / global Northern home/land. Second, as instances of statecraft as mancraft, they give rise to sexualized orders of international relations that securitize the 'unwanted im/migrant' and the 'terrorist' so that white, Christian, bourgeois, heterosexual, cisgendered, ableized, 'developed' Westerners/Northerners can feel more at ease (Bigo 2002) and at home in their home/lands.

In order to bring civilizational and sexual figurations *and their movements* into greater relief, I attempt to disentangle these impossibly entangled narratives in my analysis of the 'unwanted im/migrant' and the 'terrorist'. This leads me to read the 'unwanted im/migrant' first as civilizing development on the move and then as (civilizing) sexual development on the move. Similarly, I first read the 'terrorist' in general terms and then specifically the 'al-Qaeda terrorist' as civilization barbarism on the move before rereading him as sexual barbarism on the move. I conclude by reflecting on how a queer migrations lens exposes the 'anxious labor' (Luibhéid 2008, 174) that Western discourses of statecraft as mancraft expend to attempt to create binary sexual figurations of and in the home and homeland that might sustain heteronormative sexualized orders of international relations.

THE 'UNWANTED IM/MIGRANT' AS CIVILIZING DEVELOPMENT ON THE MOVE

How is the 'unwanted im/migrant' known in Western discourses of statecraft as mancraft as the (as-yet) uncivilized out-of-place 'underdeveloped' and 'undevelopable'? And how does he put the Western / global Northern homeland at risk as civilizing development on the move?

My claim in this section is that the 'unwanted im/migrant' is the (as-yet) uncivilized out-of-place 'underdeveloped' or 'undevelopable', who both owes debts to specific understandings of space, time, and desire implanted into these figures and, at the same time, puts these understandings into flux as civilizing development on the move. To make sense of this claim, I will review how the 'underdeveloped' and the 'undevelopable' are figured in relation to civilizing space, time, and desire, before suggesting how the 'unwanted im/migrant' complicates these understandings by moving civilizing development from the global South to the global North.

As we saw in chapter 3, the civilizational figurations of the 'underdeveloped' and the 'undevelopable' arise out of the Great Dichotomy of more primitive versus more advanced (Huntington 1971, 285). Mobilized by nineteenth- and twentieth-century evolutionary biologists, psychologists, sociologists, and political theorists and by IR scholars who incorporated these understandings into theories of modernization and development, the Great Dichotomy produces developmental narratives around a series of subbinaries—uncivilized versus civilized, traditional versus modern, perverse versus normal, anarchy versus order. These binaries fashion specific international political understandings of civilizing development and of the place of the 'underdeveloped' and the 'undevelopable' in civilizing development.

Civilizing development is not just understood as a process that transforms the 'underdeveloped' into the 'developed'. It is also understood as a process that implants a desire for civilization as a desire for Western-style development in (post)colonial populations. If the 'developed' succeed in implanting a desire for civilization as Western-style development in (post) colonial populations, these populations are refigured as the 'underdeveloped'. If this process fails, these populations are refigured as 'undevelopable'.

Time as much as desire distinguishes the 'developed' from the 'underdeveloped' and the 'undevelopable' because civilizing development is understood as a temporal process. Development time is linear, progressive, and teleological, so long as the desire for Western-style civilization as development has been successfully implanted into (post)colonial populations. This means that the 'undevelopable' forever remains uncivilized because he never manages to begin the civilizing developmental process. In contrast, the 'underdeveloped' moves along this teleological trajectory toward civilizing development, modeled on a specifically classed, racialized, religionized, ableized, gendered, and sexualized understanding of Western-style political development, which itself marks the endpoint of the civilizing developmental process.

Yet this civilizing developmental process never ends for the 'underdeveloped' for two reasons. On the one hand, his class, race, ability, and sexuality always mark him as 'developing' rather than 'developed'. On the other hand, the 'underdeveloped'—like the 'undevelopable'—does not live his civilizing developmental process just anywhere. He lives it in a very specific place. In the Western / global Northern geopolitical imaginary, this place is in the more primitive, uncivilized (post)colonial territories and emerging sovereign nation-states of the global South.

In this civilizing narrative of development, then, place and space are as important to understanding the 'underdeveloped' and the 'undevelopable' as are time and desire because two specific spaces are demarcated as the containers of civilizing developmental desire and the teleological civilizing development process itself. The universal space that contains civilizing developmental desire and time is the sovereign nation-state. For—whether in the global North or in the global South—civilizing development at one time or another is understood to have taken place within this space. But now that the global North is developed and civilized, the global South is the particular container of ongoing civilizing development. By designating the sovereign nation-state and the global South as the containers for civilizing development, 'the spatialization of [temporalized, desiring] identity'—as 'the [as-yet] uncivilized global Southerner' versus 'the civilized global Northerner'—is accomplished through 'the ontologizing of [temporalized, desiring] space'—'the global South' versus 'the global North' (Gilroy 2000, 122; also see Gilroy 1994). All of these designations of space, time, and desire, then, combine to mark where the 'underdeveloped' and the 'undevelopable' belong, where they are regarded by Westerners / global Northerners as in (their) place.

This very (neo)imperial Western / global Northern narrative of civilizing development depends not only upon specific understandings and organizations of space, time, and desire, but also upon specific understandings of orderly international movement. From a Western perspective, orderly movements are imperial movements in which Western imperial subjects move into Southern colonial territories to provide (post)colonial populations with 'civilization' and to provide the West with markets and military outposts. Disorderly movements are postimperial movements in which Southern (post)colonial populations move their (as-yet) uncivilized selves into the developed West/global North in order to settle. It is when the 'underdeveloped' and the 'undevelopable' put their civilizing development in motion from South to North that they are refigured in Western / global Northern development and security narratives as the 'unwanted im/migrant'.

As the out-of-place 'underdeveloped' and 'undevelopable', the 'unwanted im/migrant' carries traces of these civilizing developmental understandings of space, time, and desire in himself, while complicating them because of how the 'unwanted im/migrant' has been or is in the process of moving between spaces, times, and desires and, in so doing, putting civilizing development on the move.

For example, the 'unwanted im/migrant' is a figure in whom the desire for civilizing development has successfully been implanted. But how the 'unwanted im/migrant' lives this desire departs from a Western / global Northern vision of how the 'underdeveloped' *should* live this desire. This is because the 'unwanted im/migrant' lives his desire for civilizing development by seeking development *not* in his underdeveloped or undevelopable Southern (post)colonial territory or state but in an already developed Western / global Northern state. What the 'unwanted im/migrant' desires, then, is not to undergo civilizing development in his (as-yet) uncivilized homeland but to live development in the place he believes he really belongs, the already civilized, developed world that in his view should be his new homeland. For—as the failures of the development project in the global South have taught him—it is only in the already civilized, developed world that the 'unwanted im/migrant' can truly achieve individual, familial, social, and political civilizing development. It is this desire for civilized development in the Northern civilized developed world that sets the 'unwanted im/migrant' and his civilizing development in motion.

This (misplaced) desire multiplies the spatial (dis)locations in which the 'unwanted im/migrant' can be found. Geographically, he may be located in the global South, where his desire for the civilized developed North begins to cleave him from his (as-yet) uncivilized homeland and to set him on a course toward development in the developed North. He may be located in a diasporic space (Brah 1996), between his location of residence (his former [as-yet] uncivilized homeland) and what he views as his location of belonging (the civilized developed North). Or he may be located in the civilized developed North (his new homeland), into which he carries with him traces of his (as-yet) uncivilized former homeland. In all of these locations, the 'unwanted im/migrant' is marked as an outsider, inside the state/culture/civilization.

It is the misplaced desire of the 'unwanted im/migrant' for civilized development in the wrong place (the civilized developed North) that also makes him difficult to place temporally. For as a global Southerner in the global North, the 'unwanted im/migrant' lives two temporalities simultaneously. These are the Southern time of the 'never-quite-finished developing' or the 'undevelopable' and the Northern time of achieved development. What this suggests is that the 'unwanted im/migrant's' arrival in the North does not (yet) mark him as 'developed', because of how his arrival at 'developed' is endlessly deferred in Western / global Northern developmental discourses since his race, religion, class, ability, gender, and sexuality always mark him as inferior in this discourse.[5] In this respect, the 'unwanted im/migrant' seems to live in a kind of developmental diasporic time (Fortier 2001, 97–98; 2008),[6] in which he is caught somewhere between leaving un(der)development and (never quite) arriving at development.

What this discussion suggests is that the 'unwanted im/migrant' is not only the out-of-place 'underdeveloped' or 'undevelopable' spatially, as a traveler who has crossed or is crossing from the global South to the global North. He is also out of place temporally and in relation to his developmental desires. This in part explains why the 'im/migrant' as the 'underdeveloped' or the 'undevelopable' is unwanted by those in the 'developed' North. For as a figure who is out of place in Western developmental discourses spatially, temporally and in terms of his civilizing developmental desires, he not only corrupts Western / global Northern development projects by moving civilizing development out of the global South and into the global North. In so doing, he also corrupts post–World War II Western / global Northern developmental security projects (Duffield 2007), which arose as much to combat Cold War communism in the 'developing world' as they did to guard against the unwanted im/migration of '(as-yet) uncivilized developing' populations into the 'civilized developed' North.

As a figure moving between a partly disavowed (as-yet) uncivilized homeland in the 'developing world' and a desired civilized homeland in the 'developed' world, the 'unwanted im/migrant' is marked in Western / global Northern development and security discourses as a potential carrier of dangerous anarchy. This is because he is understood as introducing '(as-yet) uncivilized underdevelopment' or an inability to (continue to) become civilized and developed into the Western / global Northern order of the 'developed world'. In so doing, the 'unwanted im/migrant' directly threatens modernization and development projects and the Western (neo) imperial 'sovereign, civilized, developed man' who licenses them to contain 'developing man' in the global South. This is how the 'unwanted im/

migrant' puts the Western / global Northern homeland at risk as civilizing development on the move.

THE 'UNWANTED IM/MIGRANT' AS SEXUAL DEVELOPMENT ON THE MOVE

How is the 'unwanted im/migrant' known in Western discourses of state-craft as mancraft as the (as-yet) sexually immature out-of-place 'underdeveloped' and 'undevelopable'? And how does he put the Western / global Northern 'home/land' at risk as sexual development on the move?

My claim in this section is that the 'unwanted im/migrant' is the (as-yet) sexually immature out-of-place 'underdeveloped' or 'undevelopable', who both owes debts to specific understandings of space, time, and desire implanted into these figures and, at the same time, puts these understand-ings into flux as sexual development on the move. To make sense of this claim, I will review how the 'underdeveloped' and the 'undevelopable' are figured in relation to sexual spaces, times, and desires, before suggest-ing how the 'unwanted im/migrant' complicates these understandings as sexual development on the move.

The sexual figurations of the 'underdeveloped' and the 'undevelop-able' arise out of the Great Dichotomy of more primitive versus more advanced, which produced a civilizing narrative of development that was also a sexual narrative of development. In this narrative, a primi-tive versus advanced civilizational binary is understood to also express a homosexual versus heterosexual binary. Together these binaries produce specific international political understandings of civilizing development as sexual development and of the place of the 'underdeveloped' and the 'undevelopable' in the civilizing sexual development process.

Like civilizing development, sexual development describes a process that presumably transforms the sexually 'underdeveloped' into the sexu-ally 'developed'. On the one hand, this is understood as a natural process, whereby the sexually 'underdeveloped' naturally blossoms into the sexu-ally 'developed', thereby delivering him into both sexual and civilizational maturity. On the other hand, this is understood as a social, psychological, and/or political process, whereby a desire for sexual maturity is implanted into the sexually 'underdeveloped' so that he can begin his sexual and civilizing processes of development. As they appear in Western / global Northern development narratives, it is the modern, white, Christian, bourgeois, able-bodied Western cisgendered heterosexual who is the normalized, mature figure of sexuality and of sexual practice. If this sexually developed figure succeeds in implanting a desire for civilizing as sexual development in (post)colonial populations, these populations are refigured as the civilizationally and sexually 'underdeveloped'. If this process fails, these populations are refigured as the civilizationally and sexually 'undevelopable'.

As in any development narrative, this narrative of civilizing sexual development is temporalized. Figured through the trope of degeneracy, the civilizationally and sexually 'underdeveloped' is described as 'arrested' (see Hoad 2000) and put on a linear, progressive trajectory toward development. This is in contrast to the 'undevelopable', whose temporal and sexual perversions figure him as nonfunctional in any developmental process. As such, he is described through the trope of decadency (see Hoad 2000; Parsons 1966).

For those 'underdeveloped' figures for whom it is presumably possible, civilizing development as sexual development is not just about their modeling 'developed' heterosexuality. It is also about heteronormative institutions harnessing the 'unwanted im/migrant's' heterosexuality on behalf of social and national developmental projects.[7] For this to be accomplished, sex must be cisgendered, heterosexual, procreative, and, most importantly, in the service of the home/land, where the home is understood as the domain of the procreative heterosexual nuclear (Parsons 1966) as well as the national (Peterson 1999; 2010; 2013; 2014a; 2014b) and civilizational family and where the homeland is understood as one's place of national origin. In this way, the home emerges as the place—indeed, the universal container—in which civilizing sexual development takes place, while the homeland emerges as the particular container in which one's home is properly located.

This discussion shows how the Great Dichotomy of heteronormative sexuality—in this case homosexual versus heterosexual—is joined up with the Great Dichotomy of civilization—more primitive versus more advanced—to figure the proper places of the 'underdeveloped' and the 'undevelopable' in (neo)imperial Western / global Northern developmental discourses spatially, temporally, and in relation to their desires. As we saw in the previous section, once these figures move out of place, they are refigured as the 'unwanted im/migrant'. What I want to suggest here is that by embodying a combination of civilizing and sexual development, the 'unwanted im/migrant' not only puts civilizing development on the move, but also puts sexual development on the move. In so doing, he unsettles civilizing sexual developmental narratives and their understandings of space, time, and desire. To make sense of precisely how space, time, and desire are unsettled by the 'unwanted im/migrant' as sexual development on the move, it is important to identify the specific ways in which civilizing sexual development moves with/as the 'unwanted im/migrant'.

As he appears in Western / global Northern developmental discourse, the 'unwanted im/migrant' personifies two forms of disorderly movement simultaneously. The 'unwanted im/migrant' first embodies disorderly movement as the (post)colonial Southern who moves his (as-yet) uncivilized self into the developed West / global North in order to settle (as we saw in the previous section). In his reversal of the proper direction of (neo)imperial travel, the 'unwanted im/migrant' puts civilizing development in motion. Because civilizing development is also sexually developing, this South-to-North movement by the 'unwanted im/migrant' also puts sexual development in motion. This makes the 'unwanted im/migrant' a carrier not only of presumably (as-yet) uncivilized development into the global North, but also of presumably (as-yet) sexual immaturity. This has the effect of complicating how space, time, and desire are coded in these developmental narratives.

As in the civilizing developmental narrative, it is the 'unwanted im/migrant's' misplaced desire for civilized development in the global North that sets him and his sexual development in motion. Once in motion, the 'unwanted im/migrant' carries with him those temporal and spatial traces of un(der)development that were implanted in him through his figuration as the 'perverse homosexual'. This means that he bears traces of arrested and decadent sexuality within himself, making him either not-yet functional or forever nonfunctional within the sexually developed North. For example, his presumed promiscuity marks him as sexually uncivilized, in the image of the promiscuous homosexual, and his homosexuality—variously figured as the precondition for sexual and civilizational development (see Hoad 2000) or as nondevelopmental altogether (Parsons 1966)—figures him as sexually primitive.

As a result, the 'unwanted im/migrant's' sexual place in the joint projects of civilizational, familial, societal, and political reproduction are questionable. This is because he is (at best) a promiscuous sexual primitive on a developmental trajectory from homosexuality to heterosexuality and (at worst) forever nonfunctional because he is forever homosexual. Either way, this means the 'unwanted im/migrant' has no (legitimate) reproductive function in the heteronormatively structured home. This also means he has no function in the heteronormatively structured homeland (Peterson 1999; 2010; 2013; 2014a; 2014b). Overall, this makes it difficult to locate the 'unwanted im/migrant' as sexual development on the move within either the static spatial containers of home, family, society, state or the global South, or within the unidirectional trajectory of linear, progressive developmental time that he is meant to occupy in Western developmental discourses.

What else makes the 'unwanted im/migrant' as sexual development on the move difficult to locate is his embodiment of a second type of disorderly movement, what Michael Warner calls queer movement. Queer movement for Warner does not reverse the direction of travel (from South to North, for example). Rather, queer movement is 'a movement aslant, sideways' (Warner, book cover of Patton and Benigno Sánches-Eppler 2000). In other words, it is a stepping out of place that is also a stepping out of line or out of alignment with where and when developmental narratives attempt to place their sexual subjects. Sexually, this might involve rejecting the arbitrary homosexual versus heterosexual binary and instead embracing a nonbinary queer understanding of sexuality as 'sexuality on the move', because 'sexuality is not only not essence, not timeless, it is also not fixed in place' (Patton and Benigno Sánches-Eppler 2000, 2).

This queer understanding of sexuality confounds developmental narratives of desire that necessarily track sexual development from homosexual to heterosexual or from promiscuously heterosexuality to civilized heterosexuality. In so doing, this queer understanding of sexuality also confounds temporal designations of sexual development. For when he takes a (queer) step off this temporal trajectory (Luibhéid 2008, 170), the 'unwanted im/migrant' cannot be described temporally as 'arrested' or as the precondition for civilizational development (see Hoad 2000). Nor can he be described as developmentally 'decadent' in the derogatory terms this designation is meant to convey (Parsons 1966). This is because his temporal decadence is (or at least may be) an intentional decadence—an intentional opting out of developmental time—that might better be described in the terms Jack Halberstam describes it, as a 'queer *art* of failure' (2011; my italics; also see Muñoz 1999; 2009; and Halberstam 2005).

This also places the 'unwanted im/migrant' askew in relation to his home and homeland. In the familial home, the now figuratively queer 'unwanted im/migrant' cannot be described as a sexually prefunctional, immature heterosexual nor as a nonfunctional homosexual, both of whom have no (legitimate) reproductive role in the family, society, or the nation. Because he has stepped outside of the developmental narratives that allow these terms to meaningfully describe him, the figuratively queer 'unwanted im/migrant' becomes a sexual outsider, inside the home (Fortier 2001; 2003; also see Brah 1996; Eng 1997; Ahmed 2000; Gupta 2004; Gopinath 2005; Chavez 2009; 2010). As such, he potentially throws presumably fixed understandings of sexuality and sexual development into flux, by demonstrating that 'heterosexuality is an unstable norm ... which requires anxious labor to sustain' (Luibhéid 2008, 174). Because sexual development is so intimately tied to civilizing development, the figuratively queer 'unwanted im/migrant' also demonstrates the freighted labor in the home *and in the homeland* that civilizing development requires. Through his queer sideways movements that problematize heteronormative developmental discourses, then, the 'unwanted im/migrant'

effectively denaturalizes gendered and sexualized nationalisms and internationalisms (Fortier 2001, 409; also see Peterson 1999; 2010; 2013; 2014a;
2014b) *and the 'sovereign men' who presumably ground them.*

This double movement of the 'unwanted im/migrant'—his reverse
movement from the geopolitical South to North and his simultaneous
sideways movement in relation to sexual developmental understandings
of space, time, and desire—produces some unlikely figurations of the
'unwanted im/migrant' that cannot easily be dealt with by heteronormative Western / global Northern developmental discourse.

On the one hand, the usual developmental figurations of the 'unwanted
im/migrant' as the out-of-place 'underdeveloped' or 'undevelopable'
persist. In these figurations, the 'unwanted im/migrant' remains prefunctional or nonfunctional in relation to normalize heteronormative
procreation inside the family. At the same time, though, additional sexual
figurations of the 'unwanted im/migrant' proliferate. For example, the
'overly reproductive heterosexual immigrant family' that bears traces of
how the 'perverse homosexual' in raced, classed, gendered, sexualized,
and disabled to make him a threat to social and national heteronormativities is a persistent trope (e.g., in Huntington 2004, 32; also see Luibhéid
2008; 2013). So, too, is the reproductive homosexual family before it is
homonormativized and homonationalized (processes I will discuss in
chapter 5; see Duggan 2003; Puar 2007; Luibhéid 2008; 2013; Peterson
1999; 2010; 2013; 2014a; 2014b).

These impossible figures with 'impossible desires' (Gopinath 2005;
Luibhéid 2008) become additional figurations of the 'unwanted im/
migrant' as a figure of 'unease' (Bigo 2002). For as figures understood
in Western / global Northern developmental discourses of statecraft
as mancraft as both outsiders inside the state/culture/civilization *and*
'outsider[s] . . . inside the home' (Fortier 2001, 134), these 'unwanted im/
migrants' are not only potential carriers of dangerous (as-yet) uncivilizing
development into the Western / global Northern homeland. At the same
time, they also threaten to bring 'the violence of the world we live in *at
the heart of the home,* at the heart of the national self' (Fortier 2008, 60;
also see Ahmed 2000; Salecl 2004, 24; and Žižek 1998). In so doing, they

directly threaten the sovereign nation-state and the 'sovereign man' as 'civilized, developed man' who grounds the state. This is how the 'unwanted im/migrant' puts the Western / global Northern home/land at risk as sexual development on the move.

THE 'AL-QAEDA TERRORIST' AS CIVILIZATIONAL BARBARISM ON THE MOVE

How is the 'terrorist'—and more specifically the 'al-Qaeda terrorist'[8]—known in Western discourses of statecraft as mancraft as the civilizationally barbaric out-of-place 'undevelopable'? And how does he put the 'Western / global Northern homeland' at risk as civilizational barbarism on the move?

Civilizational barbarism is, by its very definition, out of place in any civilizational discourse, Western or otherwise. This is because civilizational barbarism is the dangerous opposite to the civilizational homeland (Huntington 1996, 321), which is understood as the universal space in which a desire for one or another type of civilization is formed in populations that either matches or clashes with that of another civilization. Because it is a perversion of any type of desire for civilization, civilizational barbarism has no proper place. In this sense, civilizational barbarism is home(land)less. This does not mean that Western / global Northern discourses do not assign civilizational barbarism a place or that Western policies do not try to keep civilizationally barbaric figures in their place. They do—spatially, temporally, and in relation to desire. In this section, I analyze the predominant contemporary figuration of the 'terrorist' in IR—the 'al-Qaeda terrorist'. I explain how the 'al-Qaeda terrorist' is assigned to specific places in Western discourses and how his movements complicate Western understandings of where the 'undevelopable' ought to be placed, in ways that figure the 'al-Qaeda terrorist' as a known risk to the 'Western / global Northern homeland'.

Spatially, even though the 'al-Qaeda terrorist' has no proper place in any civilization, he is assigned two points of origin in Western discourse.

The first of these is religious, which understands the 'al-Qaeda terror-ist' as originating from within a radical, indeed fanatical, pathological Islam. According to this narrative, it is the religious radicalization of the 'al-Qaeda terrorist' that displaces his proper desire as the 'underdeveloped' to become 'developed' and replaces it with a psychopathologized desire to become 'the fanatical Islamic jihadist'.[9] As a jihadist, the 'al-Qaeda terror-ist' becomes civilizationally barbaric by embracing a violent incivility that he expresses through acts of cruelty against communities of nonbelievers, especially populations in or adhering to the values of 'Western civilization'.

In this religious narrative, part of what accounts for the misplaced desire of the 'al-Qaeda terrorist' is his relationship to time. Temporally, the 'al-Qaeda terrorist' acts in historical, earthly time in order to preserve God's laws on earth. This situates him in the eschatological temporality of religious devotion, where his earthly life is a fleeting moment on his path toward his eternal reward in the afterlife. As a primarily eschatologi-cal temporal figure whose pathological devotion to God's laws makes him impervious to the implantation of a modern, Western desire for earthly development, the 'al-Qaeda terrorist' eschews the progressive temporality of civilizing development that promises to deliver him into one or another form of more advanced civilization. What he desires, instead, is to enforce God's righteous traditions on earth by illuminating (through religious con-version where possible) or eliminating (through terrorism where neces-sary) nonbelievers who pervert God's laws through their commitments to modernization and development. This makes the 'al-Qaeda terrorist' not just nonfunctional and undevelopmental in any civilizational schema of historical development, but also the pure enemy of modernity itself, fig-ured in Western discourses as 'diabolical', as a 'henchman', a 'dirtbag', a 'monster', 'a shadow of evil' who is 'the opposite of all that is just, human, and good' (Puar and Rai 2002, 118; also see Rutenberg 2001). It is his patho-logical piety that puts his civilizational barbarism on the move, as a reli-gious crusader against all nonbelievers and against 'Western civilization' itself (see Carroll 2004).

In Western discourse, the point from which the 'al-Qaeda terrorist' stages his crusade is necessarily geopolitical. This is because every religion and every so-called civilization in every part of the globe has religious fundamentalists, some of whom are violent. This is why Western discourses spatialize the 'al-Qaeda terrorist' a second time, locating this figure who is racialized as nonwhite in the 'global South'. Huntington's division of the world into seven or eight civilizations that places each civilization in a distinct global territory offers one illustration of this move (Huntington 1996, 26).

By freezing this nonwhite, fanatical 'civilizational other' in its place in the postcolonial world, the 'West' to some degree succeeds in its own terms in demarcating dangerous 'Islamic fundamentalists' from innocuous, white 'Western' ones.[10] But it nevertheless fails to keep the 'al-Qaeda terrorist' in his civilization of origin—rhetorically or practically. This is because the 'al-Qaeda terrorist' does not (primarily) put his civilizational barbarism on the move at what Huntington calls 'the bloody [territorial] borders' between the West and the Rest (Huntington 1996, 254–259). The 'al-Qaeda terrorist' puts his civilizational barbarism on the move through a network of terrorist cells. In so doing, he utterly unravels Western attempts to contain him spatially or temporally.

Spatially, the 'al-Qaeda terrorist' is postnational in ways Huntington's 'Western civilization' never was. As I have argued elsewhere (Weber 2002), this is because al-Qaeda operates more like an international firm in the contemporary neoliberal global order than like a territorial state. For example,

Just as a KFC franchise succeeds by enticing customers through efficient service and with products that their competitors have yet to think of, so too does al-Qaeda seem to function by providing a product (an Islamic fundamentalist ideology turned terrorist) to meet customer demand through technological efficiency (training programs that enable 'employees' to perform one or more specific tasks in the 'production process') and forward thinking (transforming Hollywood-like scripts [like flying planes into buildings] into actual events).

Like other global corporations, when circumstances sour on the ground, making operations from one locale unattractive (e.g.,

unfavorable terms from host governments), al-Qaeda just moves its
ground operations to more welcoming sites. These places include
not only Afghanistan and parts of the [so-called] Arab world, but
Germany, Britain, Canada, and [the United States of] America.
And these are just the ground operations. Not only is al-Qaeda, this
time like a 'dot.com' business, located everywhere; it is also located
nowhere. It exists as a mobile network of connections of cash and
carriers accessible from just about anywhere but locatable almost
exclusively as mere network nodal points. (Weber 2002, 142–143)

While this does not stop Western leaders from associating the
'al-Qaeda terrorist network' with a sovereign nation-state—as President
George W. Bush equated Osama bin Laden and his al-Qaeda network with
Afghanistan's Taliban government (Bush 2001)—such correlations inevitably fail. The al-Qaeda network of cells cannot be pinned down within a
territorial nation-state because it is elliptical, fluid, and changeable. Today
it is one thing, like a free-flowing dot.com company. Tomorrow it is something else, with its terrorist cells as neoliberal global franchises springing
into action as 'civilizational (anti)heroes' on US domestic airliners (Weber
2002, 143).

As al-Qaeda cells multiply and divide, appear and disappear, their geographical and 'civilizational' origins shift. The end result is figures that
were previously unimaginable in Western fantasies about the 'al-Qaeda
terrorist'—like the civilizational outsider ('the al-Qaeda terrorist') who
was the civilizational insider ('the Western civilizational citizen') who is
now inside Western civilization as 'irreducible foreignness'. It was as this
confused figuration of the 'al-Qaeda terrorist' that British-born Muslims
fighting US and British coalition forces in Afghanistan were reported to
have become the first 'foreign' casualties in the War on Terror.[11] What this
means, then, is that the 'al-Qaeda terrorist' has no civilizational home
front because he does not reside in nor can he be placed, much less kept
in place, within a civilizational homeland. This makes him all the more
anarchical, unruly, and illusive as the pure enemy of 'Western civilization'
and 'civilized, developed sovereign man'.

Temporally, the 'al-Qaeda terrorist' is just as confounding of Western narratives as he is spatially. He is an actor who understands himself to be located in God's eschatological time that is for the moment being played out in man's historical time. But his civilizational barbarism is enacted by mixing so-called traditional and modern temporalities in ways that make a mockery of the Great Dichotomy's developmental temporality designating more primitive versus more advanced. For the 'al-Qaeda terrorist' is a presumably primitive, traditional eschatological subject whose actions are made possible because he is plugged into a savvy high-tech network as an anonymous nodal point. And these actions themselves are understood as undevelopable civilizational barbarism that have developed future fictions (like novelist Tom Clancy's idea of flying planes into US government buildings as suicidal terrorist acts; Clancy 1994) into contemporary historical actions.

Taken together, all of this explains how the 'al-Qaeda terrorist' puts the Western / global Northern homeland at risk as civilizationally barbaric 'antisovereign man' on the move. The 'al-Qaeda terrorist' is such a risk to Western civilization's 'civilized, developed sovereign man' that the 'al-Qaeda terrorist's' dangerous mobility must be stopped. The 'West' tries to immobilize his civilizational barbarism on the move in three ways—by keeping him outside of Western civilization (Bigo 2002), by keeping him inside containment facilities like those in Guantánamo Bay, Cuba, and finally by making him a necropolitical target of state policies who must be killed (preferably outside the Western homeland/culture/civilization) before he kills (inside) the Western homeland/culture/civilization (see Puar 2007; Kuntsman 2009; Haritaworn, Kuntsman, and Posocco 2013a and b).

THE 'AL-QAEDA TERRORIST' AS SEXUAL BARBARISM ON THE MOVE

How is the 'al-Qaeda terrorist' known in Western discourses of statecraft as mancraft as the sexually barbaric out-of-place 'undevelopable'? And how does he put the 'Western / global Northern home/land' at risk as sexual barbarism on the move?

Like civilizational barbarism, sexual barbarism is definitionally out of place in any narrative of normalized sexuality. This is because sexual barbarism is the dangerous opposite of civilizational sexuality. Sexually barbaric figures will not naturally mature into sexually civilized beings. Nor can they be successfully implanted with a desire for civilized mature sexuality through social, psychological, or political processes. For sexual barbarism describes a modality of sexual conduct that is so violently uncivilized and cruel that it cannot be recuperated by any moral narrative of civilizing or civilized sexual development. This makes the sexual barbarian a freak of both nature and culture, the monstrous sexualized 'half-human, half-animal' that Foucault (1997) writes about, whose monstrosity, as Jasbir Puar and Amit Rai explain (2002, 119), is as racialized and culturalized as it is sexualized. As such, it has no proper place in the nuclear family (Parsons 1966), understood as the civilizing site of sexual development for the nation (Peterson 1999; 2010; 2013; 2014a; 2014b) and/or for the civilization (Huntington 1996; 2004). Sexual barbarism, then, is a form of civilizational barbarism that is presumptively homeless.[12]

This does not mean that Western discourses do not assign sexual barbarism a place or that Western policies do not try to keep those they figure as sexually barbaric in their place. Just as they do in discourses on civilizational barbarism in general, these discourses use specific codings of space, time, and desire in their attempts to contain civilizationally and sexually barbaric figures.

Spatially, Western discourses assign the civilizationally and sexually barbaric 'al-Qaeda terrorist' a home of origin—'the Islamic civilizational home' (Said 1978; also see Razack 2004; Lewis 2006; Fortier 2008). Understood as the home in which the 'al-Qaeda terrorist' is reared, this home lies at the heart of civilizational barbarism itself, which (as we saw in the previous section) the Great Dichotomy locates in psychopathological, fanatical Islam and in a primitive Islamic homeland in the global South. The 'Islamic civilizational home' is not that of the white Christian bourgeois nuclear family that Parsons describes (1966), in which reproductive cisgendered heterosexuality is modeled by the able-bodied, matured, white Christian bourgeois figure and harnessed on behalf of society (Parsons 1966) and the nation-state (Almond and Powell 1966; Peterson 1999; 2010; 2013; 2014a; 2014b). It is instead a specific perversion of this home, in which a racialized, religiously sanctioned patriarchal polygamy is modeled, matured, and harnessed on behalf of 'Islamic civilization' (Huntington 1996). It is this 'Islamic civilizational home' that is known in Western discourses to be the universal space for sexual development within 'Islamic civilization'.

As measured against the white Western bourgeois nuclear familial home, this 'Islamic civilizational home' is perverse because it folds a selfish male desire for sexual pleasure with multiple partners into the family home. As it is understood in Western discourse, this selfish sexuality is a specifically Islamic modality of primitive male heterosexual promiscuity that bears traces of primitive male homosexual promiscuity (see Hoad 2000). As such, it legitimizes a deviant form of private male hyperheterosexuality that oppresses women and girls in the home, which reflects public forms of male hyperhomosociality that oppress women and girls in the wider 'Islamic civilization'. While not always scripted as sexually barbaric in Western discourses, the 'Islamic civilizational home' was regimented as such in Western discourses on the War on Terror, in part to justify the US-led war in Afghanistan on the purported grounds of rescuing women and girls from civilizationally and sexually barbaric Islam (e.g., see Cloud 2004; Weber 2005; 2006). This fermented the idea that the 'Islamic civilizational home' was dangerously over(re)productive in two senses—as the private sexual site of the public perversion of social relations in 'Islamic civilization' and as the illiberal breading ground of the 'al-Qaeda terrorist's' private sexual perversions.

Reared in this always primitive civilizational home, the 'al-Qaeda terrorist' in Western discourse is a figure into whom male license for selfish sexual satisfaction has been implanted. At the same time, he is a figure who has failed to mature into the normative (in Western descriptions of 'Islamic' terms/perverse in Western terms) sexuality required to reproduce the 'Islamic civilizational home'. Western discourse explains the 'al-Qaeda terrorist's' (failed) uptake of 'Islamic civilizational sexuality' temporally. On the one hand, the 'al-Qaeda terrorist's' embrace of a fanatical form of Islamic homosociality is rooted in his temporal failure to develop sexually. This makes him the decadent homosexual found in Freudian psychoanalysis (see Hoad 2000), albeit one with no prospect of ever becoming sexually developed. As such, the 'al-Qaeda terrorist' is the frozen countenance of perversion Foucault describes as the 'perverse homosexual' (1980, 48). On the other hand, because he is a civilizational barbaric who lives more in God's time than in man's time, the 'al-Qaeda terrorist' is described as being less interested in harnessing his perverse sexual desire on behalf of reproducing the earthly Islamic family romance than he is in claiming his heavenly reward for martyring himself in jihad—some sixty to seventy virgins (Puar and Rai 2002, 124). This confirms his undevelopable, nonfunctional status in the family home, making him a sexual outsider, inside the 'Islamic civilizational home'.

All of this figures the 'al-Qaeda terrorist' as a civilizational and sexual barbaric who is hyperheterosexualized while also being hyperhomosexualized and hyperhomosocialized. In Puar and Rai's terms, this is why the 'al-Qaeda terrorist' appears in Western (and especially post-9/11 US terrorist) discourses as a psychologized monstrous creature who—marked in part by his failed heterosexuality—is a 'monster-terrorist-fag' (2002, 124, 139). For he is an abomination of normality (monster), an undevelopable and uncivilizable threat to the Western home/land and to Western civilization (terrorist), and a figural 'homosexual' (fag). In rendering him sexually barbaric, Western discourses posit the 'al-Qaeda terrorist's' perverse desires—which they decree to be religiously inspired and politically irrelevant (Khalil 2001, cited in Puar and Rai 2002)—as the motivation for his movements. How he moves as a civilizational barbaric (as we saw in the previous section) is as a civilizational outsider who eschews any civilizational homeland. How he moves as a sexual barbaric is as a sexual outsider who eschews any civilizational home. In combination, these movements further complicate Western encodings of the 'al-Qaeda terrorist' spatially and temporally, while proliferating his threats to the Western / global Northern home and homeland.

Spatially, the 'al-Qaeda terrorist' remains more attached to the terrorist cell than to the 'Islamic civilizational family'. Because this attachment is both civilizationally barbaric and sexually barbaric, this attachment does not just denote a violent entrepreneurial *productivity* (modeled on one or another type of international firm in the contemporary neoliberal global order; Weber 2002). It connotes a dangerous *reproductivity*, in relation to both 'the (already dangerously reproductive) Islamic civilizational family' and to civilization itself. Making sense of this dangerous reproductivity requires looking again at how Western discourses position the 'al-Qaeda terrorist' temporally and what this positioning does.

As a figure whose earthly activities are eschatologically directed (toward the nonreproductive afterlife) rather than historically directed (toward reproducing life), the 'al-Qaeda terrorist' breaks the link between familial/social reproduction and civilizational reproduction when God's laws demand it, making him a sexually nonfunctional decadent in relation to the civilizational family. Yet I would suggest that the 'al-Qaeda terrorist's' designation in Western discourses as sexually decadent is not primarily based upon his decision to (sometimes) opt out of sexual reproductive time, which Western discourses never actually allow him to do (Puar and Rai 2002; Puar 2007). Rather, the 'al-Qaeda terrorist's' sexual decadence results because his eschatological existence as a devout, fanatical Islamic jihadist causes him to move 'aslant, sideways' (Warner, back cover of Patton and Benigno Sánches-Eppler 2000), by being out of step and out of line with the civilizational family and with familial/social/civilizational reproduction. This queer movement leads him to substitute one kind of reproduction (the heterosexual reproduction of the family) for another (the homosocial reproduction of the terrorist cell) as the privileged site of reproductive activity and to substitute one figure (the child) for another (the monster-terrorist-fag) as the privileged result of his homosocial reproduction.

This makes the primary brand of reproduction belonging to 'al-Qaeda terrorist' *asexual*, even though it is characterized in Western discourse as being sexually motivated. More than a hyperheterosexual or hyperhomosexual figure, then, the 'al-Qaeda terrorist' is both beyond sex and driven by sex at the same time. As such, he is a kind of sanctified turned zealous Islamic neuter, who functions in civilizational discourses on family, home, and homeland as a deliberate static (Barthes 1976, 9) that plays havoc with norms, normativities and antinormativities (Wiegman and Wilson 2015) of the kind expressed in heteronormativities (Berlant and Warner 1998) and in homonationalisms (Puar 2007) on all sides of supposed civilizational divides. For like his civilizational barbarism, the sexual barbarism of the 'al-Qaeda terrorist' is all over the sexual and civilizational map. This proliferates his figurations in Western discourses and the risks his civilizational and sexual barbarism on the move create in/for the 'Western / global Northern home/land'.

For example, the 'al-Qaeda terrorist' remains the 'monster-terrorist-fag' when his movements violently assault the 'West'. But he is also any racially darkened 'cultural' figure whose 'irredeemable foreignness' (Palumbo-Liu 2002, 112) might be seen by the 'West' as emanating from the 'Islamic civilizational home'. These cultural turned civilizational others—including but not limited to so-called Arabs, Muslims, and Sikhs (Puar and Rai 2002; Puar 2007)—might have settled in the 'West' generations ago and taken a Western citizenship. Or they might be newly settling im/migrants to the 'West'. Either way, their misassociation with how Western discourses describe the 'Islamic civilizational home' transforms them into 'unwanted im/migrants', with all that conveys in terms of their civilizational development and sexual development on the move *and* with all that conveys in terms of their association with the 'al-Qaeda terrorist'.

Read through this Western lens, these 'unwanted im/migrants' are forever those 'diasporic ethics' (Palumbo-Liu 2002, 120–121) in whom the 'American Creed' (Huntington 2004, 41) or some more generalized Western creed of modernization and development has not and cannot be implanted. This is because they model the wrong type of civilizational family in the geopolitical West/North and harness this civilizational family for the wrong types of reproduction. By this reading, they are not 'Westerners' or 'Northerners', nor can they become 'Westerners' or 'Northerners'. They are infiltrators of the 'Western / global Northern home/land' who deprive the 'West' of the cultural and civilizational purity it understands itself to require in order to survive (Palumbo-Liu 2002, 119–120). More than any-thing else, then, these 'unwanted im/migrants' as modelers, breeders, or conductors of al-Qaeda terrorism bring 'the violence of the world we live in *at the heart of the home*, the heart of the national self' (Fortier 2008, 60). These are among the ways the 'al-Qaeda terrorist'—as a mobile figure or the 'unwanted im/migrant' settled in the 'West'—is figured as a known threat to the 'Western / global Northern home/land' because of how he puts sexual barbarism on the move.[13]

The extreme uneasiness the 'al-Qaeda terrorist' causes Westerners is used in Western discourses to justify a Huntingtonian revival of a Western wartime footing of the sort Mead's cultural defense of the 'American national character' justified during World War II. In this War on Terror discourse, the 'al-Qaeda terrorist' as 'civilizationally barbaric, undevel-opable, antisovereign man' is such a risk to 'Western civilization' that his dangerous mobility must be stopped. The 'West' tries to immobilize his civilizational barbarism on the move in three ways—by keeping him outside of Western civilization (Bigo 2002), by keeping him inside con-tainment facilities like those in Guantánamo Bay, Cuba, and finally by making him a necropolitical target of state policies who must be killed (preferably outside the Western homeland/culture/civilization) before he kills (inside) the Western homeland/culture/civilization (see Puar 2007; Kuntsman 2009; Haritaworn, Kuntsman, and Posocco 2013a and b).

CONCLUSION

In their analyses of queer migration and queer diaspora, queer migrations scholars demonstrate how any attempt to posit home and homeland as secure ontological places is confounded by encounters with movement *and queerness* inside the home/land (Eng 1997; Ahmed 2000; Fortier 2001; 2003; Luibhéid 2002; 2008; 2013; Luibhéid and Cantú 2005; Luibhéid, Buffington, and Guy 2014). As this chapter demonstrates, their conclu-sion is as true in IR as it is in queer migration studies. For the (some-times) queer movements of the 'unwanted im/migrant' and the 'al-Qaeda terrorist'—as civilizational and sexual development on the move and as civilizational and sexual barbarism on the move—occur across, between, and within heteronormatively understood homes, homelands, and sexualities in ways that expose these foundational sites of national/civilizational reproduction as irregular, indeterminate, and transposable.

Western responses to these irregularities—to these intricately produced anarchies—are rooted as much in the desires of Western populations for ease in the homeland as they are in their desires for ease in the home. This is why Western (post)developmental (Bigo 2002) and security narratives reoppose to the 'Islamic civilizational family' their figuration of the 'Western civilizational family' as the foundation of national/civilizational sovereignties. This is why these discourses contrast the properly patriotic and cultural attachments to nation, culture, and home/land of the 'Western civilizational family' with the improper attachments of the 'Islamic family' to nation, culture, and home/land (Puar and Rai 2002; Puar 2007). And this is how these discourses fix the 'unwanted im/migrant' and the 'al-Qaeda terrorist' as the necessary civilizationally and sexually perverse figures who are called upon to normalize Western individual, familial, and national/civilizational figures and attachments to 'civilized, developed sovereign man' and the sovereign orders he authorizes as rational, reasonable, and just.

These 'homing desires' (Brah 1996, 187)—these desires 'to feel at home achieved by physically or symbolically (re)constituting spaces which provide some kind of ontological security in the context of migration' (Fortier 2000, 163)—are usually understood to be the desires of im/migrating or diasporic subjects. What this analysis suggests is that the civilizational and sexual movements of figures like the 'unwanted im/migrant' and the 'al-Qaeda terrorist' implant homing desires in Western subjects. These homing desires take practical form in Western (post)developmental and security discourses that attempt and fail to 'manage unease' in the homeland (Bigo 2002) *and also in the home* by figuring a Western 'civilized, developed sovereign man' as the manager of their unease by being the manager of their security. In so doing, they expose the 'anxious labor' (Luibhéid 2008, 174) Western discourses expend to create binary sexual figurations of and in the home and homeland that might sustain heteronormative sexualized orders of international relations (also see Peterson 1999).

Chapters 3 and 4 on the 'underdeveloped', the 'undevelopable', the 'unwanted im/migrant', and the 'terrorist', considered together, suggest that these 'homing desires' have long been a feature of how Western heteronormativities put sex into discourse in intimate, national, and international relations. The tropes of home and homeland participate in creating these four figurations of the 'perverse homosexual' as the primary performativities that (post)colonial subjects can inhabit. These tropes tie the 'underdeveloped', the 'undevelopable', the 'unwanted im/migrant', and the 'terrorist' to specific places, times, and desires that establish specific figures—the normal sovereign versus the perverse antisovereign—who guarantee various *either/or* anarchy-versus-order binaries as perverse-versus-normal binaries. And these tropes mobilize these binaries to create specific (albeit unreliable) mappings of the world to contain the movements of these 'dangerous figures' in that world, which no amount of determined work can contain geopolitically or sexually. In all of these ways, then, heteronormative Western discourses script the 'underdeveloped', the 'undevelopable', the 'unwanted im/migrant', and the 'terrorist' as 'perverse homosexuals' who are foundational to traditional *either/or* Western logics of statecraft as mancraft and Western sexual organizations of international relations.

What we will see in chapter 5 is how this freighted labor is mobilized again, this time through homonormativities, in ways that both reply upon and disavow figurations of the 'perverse homosexual' in order to birth a very specific figuration of the 'normal homosexual'.

The 'Normal Homosexual' in International Relations

The 'Gay Rights Holder' and the 'Gay Patriot'

Who is the 'normal homosexual' in international relations? And how does the will to knowledge about the 'normal homosexual' participate in the figuration of 'sovereign man'?

This chapter argues that two figures that have recently been introduced into IR theory and practice as normal—the 'gay rights holder' and the 'gay patriot'—are among specific articulations of the 'normal homosexual' in international relations. These particular figurations of the 'normal homosexual' matter for IR because they make possible (by being included in) specific figurations of 'sovereign man' as '(neo)imperial man' and as '(civilizationally) developed man'.

In the dominant transnational/global queer studies literatures, these figurations of 'sovereign man' as the 'normal homosexual' seem to arise out of and in turn produce what Lisa Duggan calls homonormativity, 'a new neoliberal sexual politics' that 'does not contest dominant heteronormative assumptions and institutions, but upholds and sustains them, while promising the possibility of a demobilized gay constituency and a privatized, depoliticized gay in domesticity and consumption' (2003, 50). Figurations of the 'normal homosexual' are made to function in (neo)colonialist/(neo) imperialist homonormative discourses as instances of 'statecraft as man-craft' (Ashley 1989). In these discourses, it is 'the disorderly, pathological state' that refuses or fails to recognize 'gay rights as human rights' that is figured as the threat to 'sovereign man'. It is this threat to the 'normal homosexual' that produces (and is produced through) specific order-versus-anarchy binaries. These *either/or* binaries of the 'normal state' versus the 'pathological state' participate in the regulation of international politics because they establish sexualized orders of international relations.

In contemporary international relations, answers to the question, Which states are 'normal states' and which states are 'pathological states'? are increasingly tested against a specific figure in international relations—the 'gay rights holder'. Drawing largely on the work of (transnational/global) queer studies scholars Lisa Duggan (2003), Jasbir Puar (Puar and Rai 2002; Puar 2006; 2007; 2010; 2013), Adi Kuntsman (2009), and Neville Hoad (2002) and (queer) IR scholars Anna Agathangelou (2013) and Rahul Rao (2014) as the point of departure, this chapter focuses on how the 'gay rights holder' is figured so he can be known as the 'normal homosexual' in some Western homonormative discourses on human rights. In these discourses, the 'gay rights holder' is a variation of the entrepreneurial neoliberal subject who is (re)productive in/for capitalism on behalf of the nation (Duggan 2003).[1] This situates this particular 'gay rights holder' firmly within neoliberal economics and within neoliberal cultures of tolerance and diversity. It can also situate 'gay rights holders' within national discourses of patriotism as 'docile patriots' (Puar and Rai 2002) and 'gay patriots' (Puar 2006; 2007; also see Kuntsman 2007; Richter-Montpetit 2014a). In these cases, the 'gay patriot' is the 'gay rights holder' mobilized explicitly on behalf of the 'nation' and against threatening anarchical, pathological, national and international 'others'. This chapter focuses on how one Western state—the United States under the Obama administration—figures the 'LGBT' as the 'gay rights holder'.

The discursive production of the 'LGBT rights holder' as the 'normal homosexual' by Western states like the United States does not mean there are no longer 'homosexuals' figured as perverse in international relations discourse, even by these very same states. Rather, it means that the figure of the 'perverse homosexual' in contemporary international relations is a figure whose unruliness and irrationality can be cast as threatening national patriotisms and national and international (neo)liberalisms. Thus, the 'underdeveloped', the 'undevelopable', the 'unwanted im/migrant', and the 'terrorist' continue to be feared, excluded, and sometimes killed by Western states, while the 'gay rights holder' and the 'gay patriot' are celebrated by these states, even though these 'normal homosexuals' are only selectively included and protected (Agathangelou, Bassichis, and Spira 2008; Haritaworn 2008a; Haritaworn, Kuntsman, and Posocco 2013; 2014a; 2014b).

To illustrate how the 'gay rights holder' and the 'gay patriot' are explicitly crafted through a will to knowledge that sets these figures in opposition to some 'perverse homosexuals' like the 'underdeveloped', the 'undevelopable', the 'unwanted im/migrant', and the 'terrorist' in contemporary Western discourses of statecraft as mancraft and to demonstrate how all of these figures might compose complex versions of homo(inter)nationalism (Puar 2006; 2007; Nath 2008) as sexualized orders of international relations, I offer a close reading of Hilary Clinton's 'Gay rights are human rights' speech, which she delivered at a UN meeting in Geneva on Human Rights Day in 2001, when she was President Obama's secretary of state. First, though, I put the 'gay rights holder' and the 'gay patriot' into context, showing how the 'gay rights holder' and those states that do not protect the rights of the 'gay rights holder' are incited as problems for Western states. I then outline the four moves Western states might make to address these problems before showing how these four moves appear in Clinton's speech. I also explain in detail how homonormativity and homo(inter)nationalism can be mobilized to solve these problems.

THE 'GAY RIGHTS HOLDER'

Human rights have long been a feature of Western liberal discourses, which confer political rights onto those subjects whom a political community (often the state) recognizes as human. Initially, the category of the 'human' had been the sole reserve of the white, male, usually Christian, bourgeois heterosexual. Throughout history, this category has expanded to include women, children, religious minorities, and ethnic and racial minorities because those whom Western discourses deem to be 'different' have engaged in lengthy political struggles first to be recognized as human and then to be granted their rights as human members of a political community. This historical struggle is a feature of gay, lesbian, bisexual, trans*, queer, and intersexed individuals and groups as well, which has been variously marked by key events in LGBTQI history like Stonewall or the activities of ACT UP in the face of the HIV crisis as well as by the day-to-day institutionalized work of organizations like Human Rights Watch, the International Gay and Lesbian Human Rights Commission, and numerous regional LGBTQI organizations (e.g., Gould 2009; Garcia and Parker 2006; Schulman 2013).

It is in the context of this historical struggle for LGBTQI human rights that the 'gay rights holder' emerges as a politically contested figure in international relations. The 'gay rights holder' is incited as a problem before various Western states not only because he exposes the illiberalism of liberalism, which Foucault persuasively argued is a necessary feature of both Kantian philosophy (Foucault 1980) and biopolitics (Foucault 2004; and on necropolitics, see Mbembe 2003). The 'gay rights holder' also poses a dilemma for Western modernization and development and/as security discourses that depend upon various inscriptions of the 'underdeveloped', the 'undevelopable', the 'unwanted im/migrant', and the 'terrorist' as 'perverse homosexuals' who in part underwrite continuing (neo)liberal, (neo) imperial, and (neo)colonial sexualized organizations of international relations.

How, then, to solve this dilemma? How might Western states include the 'homosexual' as a normal human in their liberal political communities while simultaneously preserving various figurations of the 'homosexual' as perverse? And how might this move be accomplished so that this new figuration of the 'normal homosexual' continues to underwrite (neo)liberal sexualized organizations of international relations?

Western states—and particularly the United States—have attempted to solve this dilemma by making four moves. First, they abandon same-sex sexual desires as the axis that differentiates the 'normal' sexualized subject from the 'perverse' sexualized subject. The *universal* figure of the 'perverse homosexual' implanted with the perversions of 'homosexuality' whom Foucault described as emerging out of the Victorian era is abandoned. This figure is no longer *necessarily* considered to be an 'alien strain' (Foucault 1980, 42–43) because his desire for same-sex relations is not *necessarily* seen as a perversion. What matters in this discourse is whether or not his sexual desire is tied to specific (neo)liberal values.

This brings us to the second move. Western discourses rely upon institutions and cultural understandings of what Lisa Duggan calls 'homonormativity' to express what these (neo)liberal values should be in the context of sexuality. As noted earlier, Duggan describes homonormativity as 'a new neoliberal sexual politics' that 'does not contest dominant heteronormative assumptions and institutions, but upholds and sustains them, while promising the possibility of a demobilized gay constituency and a privatized, depoliticized gay in domesticity and consumption' (2003, 50). To unpack this claim, let me return to how Berlant and Warner describe heteronormativity. Heteronormativity refers to those 'institutions, structures of understanding, and practical orientations that make [normative sexualities like] heterosexuality seem not only coherent—that is, organized as a sexuality—but also privileged' (Berlant and Warner 1998, 548 n. 2). As we saw in chapters 3 and 4, heteronormativity divides sexualized figures into normal and perverse. The normal sexualized figure is in or on its way to maturing into a (usually) white, Christian, bourgeois, ableized, cisgendered, heterosexual, reproductive family that functions as the biological and social engine of reproduction for the Western state. Perverse sexualized figures stray from how normal sexuality is modeled, matured, and reproduced. Among these perverse figures is the 'perverse homosexual'.

Duggan argues that homonormativity expands the category of 'the normal sexualized figure' to include some figures who were previously understood by heteronormativity as sexually perverse *so long as they are properly attached to neoliberalism*. To be properly attached to neoliberalism means embracing neoliberal modalities of domesticity and consumption (e.g., Edelman 2004; Ahmed 2010; Berlant 2011; Halberstam 2011; Muñoz 1999; N. Smith 2015).

Proper domesticity is modeled on the normalized 'reproductive family' described above. This model of the family simply expands under homonormativity to recognize that *some* 'homosexuals' also mature into, model, and reproduce 'normal' domesticated familial relations on behalf of the neoliberal state. This is because these 'homosexual families' comprise two-parent monogamous couples who raise children together in ways that are intended to support social/national/civilizational reproduction (Peterson 2014a; 2015). All that is different about them is that the two parents are of the same sex. In every other way, they are a 'normal family' because, as Karen Zivi puts it, they embody 'repronormativity' (2014).

Duggan argues that being a 'normal family' includes having a proper attachment to neoliberal consumption.[2] Proper consumption is about engaging uncritically in the market as a private consumer, usually as part of or on behalf of the private family unit. This proper attachment means that any challenge to 'neoliberal policies of fiscal austerity, privatization, market liberalization, and government stabilization [that] are [the] pro-corporate capitalist guarantors of private property relations' locally, nationally and internationally are forfeited by same-sex individuals in the name of being (in) just another 'normal family'. Duggan argues that the 'normal homosexual' in or maturing into the 'normal neoliberal family' repudiates this progressive left agenda—an agenda many nonconforming (because undomesticated and improperly consuming) queers have historically embraced (see, for example, Muñoz 2009; Halberstam 2011)—because the 'normal homosexual' has been co-opted by 'the false promises of superficial neoliberal "multiculturalism"' (Duggan 2003, xx). Neoliberal multiculturalism is a form of 'equality disarticulated from material life and class politics to be "won" by definable "minority" groups' like LGBTQIs (Duggan 2003, xx). Duggan calls this type of equality 'Equality, Inc.' For it is a brand of equality that widens the realm of 'acceptable homosexuality' for some neoliberal 'homosexuals' while simultaneously remarking the boundary of 'unacceptable homosexuality' at a range of what Duggan reads as queer practices and queered figures[3] that/who do not fit in with a conservative understanding of domesticable sex, sexuality, consumption, and politics (Duggan 2003, chap. 3).

In all of these ways, homonormativity shifts the axis of perversion from same-sex sexual desires to desires around neoliberal domesticity and consumption. The 'homosexual' who shares these neoliberal desires, who organizes his life around them, and who becomes depoliticized as a result of living in proper domesticity and consumption is no longer perverse. What is perverse is a desire for a different political, economic, and social life that is incompatible with neoliberalism. 'The 'new normal' sexual subject in 'the new homonormativity', then, is the 'homosexual' whose desires for domesticity and consumption are the same as those of the 'straight' neoliberal subject.

Together, these first two moves make a third move possible. This is the refiguration of the normal subject who—in Hannah Arendt's terms—has the right to have rights (1994). This new normal subject is the multicultalized white(ned), ableized, domesticated, entrepreneurial subject who is (re)productive in/for capitalism, regardless of whether he is heterosexual or homosexual. By inscribing this particular figuration of the 'homosexual' as worthy of rights, homonormative discourses simultaneously figure which 'homosexuals' are *unworthy* of rights—racialized and disableized sexual, social, psychological, economic, and political 'degenerates' and 'deviants' who cannot or will not developmentally mature into this 'new normal sexual subject'. What this means, then, is that figurations of the 'underdeveloped', the 'undevelopable', the 'unwanted im/migrant', and the 'terrorist' persist as dangerous domestic and international forces to be opposed, who are joined in this categorization as dangerous by a new variety of 'deviants' and 'degenerates' the new homonormativity marks as 'perverse'.

By identifying a new developmental trajectory for the 'normal homosexual', Western homonormative discourses in particular reinscribe and indeed purify what it means to be modern for individuals and for states (Puar 2010; also see Rahman 2014), as if Western populations indeed embodied or were well on their way toward embodying this purified modernity (for critique, see Latour 1993).[4] Queer studies scholar Neville Hoad sums up that spatialized, temporalized developmental trajectory like this: 'We were like them, but have developed, they are like we were and have yet to develop' (2002, 148). This understanding of development consolidates a fourth move. This move now measures an individual's modernity *not* against his development from a 'perverse homosexual' into a 'normal heterosexual'; rather, it measures his modernity against that individual's desire for neoliberal domesticity and consumption, which, once embraced, bestows on the 'new normal homosexual' the right to have rights. A state's modernity is now measured against its recognition and (where necessary) its protection of the (potentially emerging) 'new normal homosexual' as a full and equal member of his political community who is part of a minority human population of human rights holders. This reinscription of modernity has international consequences. For it obligates 'enlightened' Western states to defend this 'new normal sexualized subject' where he is oppressed, even though these states do so selectively in practice (Rao 2014b; Wilkinson 2013; 2014).

Transnational/global queer studies scholar Jasbir Puar refers to as 'homonationalism' this 'constitutive and fundamental reorientation of the relationship between the state, capitalism and sexuality' that produces what she calls 'the human rights industrial complex' (2013, 337, 338; also see Puar 2006; 2007). In very general terms, homonationalism expresses a combination of homonormativity with nationalism that figures 'good homosexuals' who are worthy of the state's protection while preserving 'bad homosexuals' as threats to the state (Puar 2007).[5] All of this functions through what Puar calls 'the human rights industrial complex', which 'continues to proliferate Euro-American constructs of identity (not to mention the notion of a sexual identity itself) that privilege identity politics, "coming out," public visibility, and legislative measures as the dominant barometers of social progress' (2013, 338).

On Puar's reading, because this 'human rights industrial complex' narrative of gay rights as human rights is a 'narrative of progress for gay rights [that is] built on the back of racialized others, for whom such progress was once achieved, but is now backsliding or has yet to arrive', these 'gay-friendly' declarations by states are also inherently homophobic (Puar 2013, 338; also see Agathangelou 2013; Weiss and Bosia 2013a; Rao 2014b). In this context, Puar's political project is to mobilize the analytic of homonationalism as 'a deep critique of lesbian and gay liberal rights discourses and how those rights discourses produce narratives of progress and modernity that continue to accord some populations access to citizenship—cultural and legal—at the expense of the delimitation and expulsion of other populations' (2013, 337; also see Butler 2008).

Puar also mobilizes homonationalism to critique 'docile patriotism' (Puar and Rai 2002) and 'gay patriotism' (Puar 2006; 2007)—nationalist expressions of patriotism that bind 'straight' and 'homosexual' subjects to homonormative nationalist state policies, be they the extension of gay rights as human rights or the combating of international terrorism, for example. These homonationalist state policies function by dividing primarily national populations into unpatriotic and patriotic. Unpatriotic subjects are those sometimes monstrous perverts whose illiberalism threatens the security of the state. In specific times and places, they might be figured as the 'underdeveloped', the 'undevelopable', the 'unwanted im/migrant', or the 'terrorist'(as we saw in chapters 3 and 4). In contrast, 'straight' and 'homosexual' 'docile patriots' are those properly domesticated, properly 'white' or 'whitened', neoliberal, consuming, familial national subjects who are called forth by antinational, anti(neo)liberal racialized monsters like the homosexualized 'terrorist' to 'enact their own normalization—in the name of patriotism' (Puar and Rai 2002, 126). In other words, it is their patriotic opposition to unpatriotic threats to the nation/civilization that hetero/homonormativized 'docile patriots' embody.[6]

Within this neoliberal geopolitical and historical context that Puar describes, states like the United States, the United Kingdom, and Israel, for example, cynically promote LGBT bodies as representative of their (vision of) modernity and democracy (Puar 2013, 338). This type of cynical promotion of gay rights as human rights is what Puar—following a number of queer activist—calls pinkwashing.[7] In the contexts Puar has examined in the most depth, the US-led War on Terror and the Israeli occupation of Palestine, 'Pinkwashing works in part by tapping into the discursive and structural circuits produced by U.S. and European crusades against the spectral threat of "radical Islam" or "Islamo-fascism"' and 'is only one more justification for imperial/racial/national violence within this long tradition of intimate rhetorics around "victim" populations' (Puar 2013, 338).

Pinkwashing can also take the form of a kind of 'homointernational-ism' (Nath 2008). Through homointernationalism, gay rights as human rights are promoted as global rights for all 'LGBT people' by Western states in particular. But the obligation to defend the 'LGBT' is cynically called for by these states in relation to the global South, even though Western states enforce these standards less stringently if at all in rela-tion to Northern states (e.g., in relation to Russia, see Wilkinson 2013; 2014) and even though Western states themselves fail to measure up to the standards they impose upon the global South (Spade 2013).[8] This has led transnational/global queer studies scholar Momin Rahman to claim that this type of homointernationalism is 'homocolonialist' (Rahman 2014), because the West's defense of 'gay rights as human rights' is a 'tool of empire' (Rao 2012; see also Morgensen on settler homonationalism; Morgensen 2011; 2012).

As recent scholarship in queer IR and transnational/global queer stud-ies demonstrates, there are numerous ways to investigate local, national, and international relationships among various figurations of the 'gay rights holder' and the 'gay patriot' and hetero/homonormativities[9] and how they function in and in relation to 'global homophobias' (Weiss and Bosia 2013a). Among the most influential expressions of these rela-tionships is found in former US secretary of state Hilary Clinton's 'Gay rights are human rights' 2011 Human Rights Day speech. Given the power of this address and the US power behind this address, I will analyze Clinton's speech in some detail to highlight how it can be read as illus-trating the homonormative and homo(inter)nationalist moves discussed above (also see Agathangelou 2013).[10] It arguably does this by stabilizing one specific set of understandings of the 'normal homosexual' and the 'perverse homosexual' in international relations to craft Clinton's specific rendering of the 'normal homosexual' as that 'sovereign man' whom the

US deploys in its foreign policy to regiment a 'homocolonialist' (Rahman 2014) sexualized order of international relations.

Before I launch into this analysis, however, I want to offer two notes of caution. One has to do with the dangers of applying terms like homonormativity and its spin-off term homonationalism as if they described universal, reified institutional and structural arrangements. The second has to do with the dangers of assuming that (Western) calls for 'gay rights as human rights' are always made exclusively in support of a (neo)imperialism.

First, like the institutions, structural arrangements, and practical dispositions that compose heteronormativity, arrangements described as homonormativity and homonationalism are also both geopolitically and historically specific as well as malleable. This means that how they become intertwined with the 'homosexual' is complex and distinctive in specific times and places. Duggan, in particular, makes this case.

For example, in her articulation of homonormativity, Duggan takes pains to caution her readers against any universalist renderings of either capitalism or liberalism, two terms upon which her notion of homonormativity depends. She does this by reminding her readers that 'capitalism has never been a single coherent "system". Liberalism has therefore morphed many times as well, and has contained proliferating contradictions in indirect relationship to the historical contradictions of capitalism' (2003, x–xi). Furthermore, Duggan explicitly states that the analysis of neoliberalism that generates her understanding of homonormativity is historically specific. The neoliberalism she discusses 'developed primarily in the U.S., and secondarily in Europe' from the 1950s onward (2002, xi–xii), and she goes on to focus her analysis on neoliberalism 'within the U.S. specifically' (2007, xii) before explaining how a hegemonic United States institutionalized neoliberalism in international institutions like the World Bank and the IMF. Duggan also takes pains to remind her readers that this US-led neoliberal hegemonic world order is in crisis, having gone from boom to bust over the past four decades, suggesting that postneoliberalisms are or may be on the horizon (Duggan 2011–2012). In so doing, she emphasizes the malleability of neoliberal institutions, understandings, and practical orientations.

Likewise, Duggan carefully details how her conceptualization of 'the new homonormativity' arose in relation to her consideration of a historically and geopolitically specific set of practices, how the International Gay Forum's agenda of gay equality illustrated what she called their 'new neoliberal sexual politics' (2007, 50). While Duggan makes it clear that this 'new neoliberal sexual politics' is illustrative of what she calls Equality, Inc., her analysis is always grounded in specific examples. Yet as homonormativity has been taken up and applied by some scholars and activists, this geographical and historical specificity sometimes falls away, leaving us with universalized, reified understandings of neoliberalism and homonormativity that seemingly apply in the same ways across time and space.

Similarly, Jasbir Puar's related concept of homonationalism was developed to describe a very specific historical issue—how the 'gay patriot' as a biopolitical figure was opposed to the 'terrorist' as a racialized necropolitical figure in the United States during the War on Terror. More recently, Puar has argued that 'homonationalism is also an ongoing process, one that in some senses progresses from the civil rights era and does not cohere only through 9/11 as a solitary temporal moment' (2013, 337). In this vein, Puar later extended her analysis of homonationalism to the Israeli occupation of Palestine (e.g., 2010; also see Schulman 2012; Remkus Britt 2015), and others have taken up homonationalism and its 'queer necropolitics' as (if they were) global phenomena (e.g., Haritaworn, Kuntsman, and Posocco 2013a; 2013b; 2014; although exceptionally see Lind and Keating 2013; Fitzgerald 2014).

Since coining the term, Puar has cautioned scholars and activists against its 'reductive applications'. Homonationalism 'is not simply a synonym for gay racism, or another way to mark how gay and lesbian identities become available to conservative political imaginaries; it is . . . not another way of distinguishing good queers from bad queers, not an accusation, and not a position' (Puar 2013, 337). Rather, homonationalism is 'a facet of modernity' (Puar 2013, 337). 'To say that this historical moment is homonational, where homonationalism is understood as an analytics of power, then, means that one must engage it in the first place as the condition of possibility for national and transnational politics' (Puar 2013, 337).

Yet some of the reductiveness that Puar warns others against seems to be at the heart of the very concepts Puar herself mobilizes and extends. This is because the various literatures on homonormativity have a tendency to flatten the subjectivities they investigate—be they the 'gay rights holder' or the 'docile gay patriot'—by reading their formations and resistances through what are arguably monolith constructions of homonormativity, homonationalism, and especially 'the human rights industrial complex'. This has the effective of reifying not just homonormativities and homonormativized subjectivities but also the very binary *logic* of power (albeit in very different formations and with very different political commitments) that those deploying homonormativities understand themselves to be contesting.

Homonormativities reproduce *either/or* logics of power because they appear to know in advance what does and what does not count as meaningful resistance. Meaningful resistance is always antinormative, and antinormativities are understood in these discourses to be (part and parcel of) what it means to be 'queer' (Wiegman and Wilson 2015). [11] What this means is that at the heart of contemporary constructions of homonormativity is an antinormative-versus-normative binary logic that reproduces the very antinormative-versus-normative binary logic that theorists of these homonormativities investigate.

In her analysis of the incitement of the 'rights holder', Louiza Odysseos implicitly contests *either/or* logics as unidirectional and monolithic (as do Nash, 2015; Langlois 2001; 2012; 2014; 2015; and Zivi 2011; 2014, albeit in different registers), in ways that are useful for reflecting on homonormativities. Following Foucault's insights on counterconduct in *Security, Territory, Population* (2009), Odysseos contends that *either/or* logics can ignore inventive practices of subverting, redirecting, and resisting regulation that can emerge in the very process of embracing the tools of our governing (Odysseos 2016). Instead of an understanding of power as primary and resistance as secondary, Odysseos complicates *either/or* readings of the figuration and regulation of the 'human rights holder' with Foucauldian understandings of regulation that arise 'in the midst of, and in response to, anxieties, concerns and resistances about its functions; its evolution emerges in a co-constitutive and circular fashion as both a response to, and resulting in, distinct counter-conducts' (Odysseos 2016).[12]

What this discussion suggests, then, is that while homonormativity and homo(inter)nationalism can be and are useful guides for analyzing how human rights and patriotism can be related to the 'homosexual' and 'homosexuality', they can too quickly smooth over interesting and powerful contradictions and indeed overdetermine all engagements with some reified (neo)liberalism and/or some set of reified nationalist practices. For example, they can lead scholars to embrace constructions like Puar's 'human rights industrial complex' in ways that *remove* complexity from IR theory and practice on human rights rather than capture the multiple contradictions and complexities in human rights formulations and mobilizations. In so doing, they can narrow options for meaningful resistance to only those types of resistance that universally eschew (Western) (neo) liberalisms and nationalisms, thus potentially undercutting the very political purposes for which they were formulated.

This is not to say that concepts like homonormativity and homonationalism should not be mobilized in queer analyses of international phenomena. Rather, it suggests that—when doing so—scholars need to be attentive to how these concepts and their various applications potentially both *assist and limit* any analysis. These limitations might include a neglect to fully appreciate, for example, how market politics *and/or* moral politics in a wide array of combinations figure the 'homosexual' in international relations (e.g., Amar 2013, 16) and how redirection and improvement of regulation in addition to subversion itself can be embraced as a form of resistance (e.g., Odysseos 2016). This warning is especially important for IR scholars to heed, because they work in a field that generally accepts the uncritical importation of concepts and arguments into IR and the straightforward application of these imports to specific IR concerns and cases, when IR would benefit from a more critical engagement with these concepts and arguments.

This first caution is related to my second caution—that scholars must similarly be attentive to the dangers of assuming that all (Western) calls for 'gay rights as human rights' are made exclusively in support of a (neo) imperialism. Anthony Langlois (2012) nicely outlines the risks implicit in such a position. In general terms, Langlois argues against *either* choosing a naive universal account of human rights as necessarily leading to human emancipation *or* rejecting such accounts because human rights are always in the service of empire. Rather, he argues for a position on human rights 'which enables us both to take advantage of what is good—there can be no denying the value of the human rights discourse to many in their struggles against injustice—but also to be aware of what is ambivalent or perhaps even fundamentally counterproductive' (2012, 562; also see Nash, 2015). For Langlois, this means we must acknowledge that 'a politics of rights does construct its participants in certain ways, and that those constructions can undoubtedly mesh with other aspects of the contemporary global politico-economic systems in ways which make people extraordinarily vulnerable'. But that does not mean that 'all rights are oppressive and hierarchical' (2012, 562). On this point, Langlois spells out the analytical (and political) error that leads to this latter conclusion, which he rejects. As Langlois puts it,

> Subjectivities facilitated by the politics of human rights might "converge" with those needed for liberal imperialism, but this does not make them the culprit or cause. This demonstrates the problem with many of these critical approaches: such relationships are set in stone and made necessary. Human rights become necessary accomplices in the 'governmentalisation' of international politics, or guilt by association when it comes to the imposition of neoliberal 'solutions' in the global economy. Such an approach risks leaving those for whom human rights are genuinely emancipatory high and dry, with nowhere to go—and this would indeed be a crisis for human rights. (2012, 563; also see Odysseos 2016)

As applied to international analyses of 'gay rights as human rights', work by Amy Lind and Christina Keating (2013), Ryan Richard Thoreson (2014), Nico Beger (2009), and Langlois himself (2014; 2015; Wilkinson and Langlois 2014) illustrates how the particularity of such calls for human rights inevitably complicates a 'for or against' position on 'gay rights' and 'empire'. This work makes me hesitant to decry Clinton's call for 'gay rights as human rights'. This is the case for me even though I agree with Rahul Rao, who argues that the term in which Clinton articulates this call may well place those who embrace it on 'the wrong side of empire' (2012), and I agree with Jasbir Puar, who argues that narratives like Clinton's are often 'built on the back of racialized others' (2013, 338; also see Agathangelou 2013), are often homophobic while appearing to be gay-friendly, and can often rightly be described as pinkwashing. I also agree that Clinton's pronouncement of 'gay rights as human rights' figures the 'LGBT' in many of the terms Duggan describes as homonormative. My analysis of Clinton's speech that follows demonstrates each and every one of these arguments.

Why, then, do I hesitate to embrace analyses that suggest Clinton's call for 'gay rights as human rights' is *necessarily* (neo)imperial? I do so for two reasons. First, reading Clinton's call as necessarily (neo)imperial closes down consideration of what it would mean for the United States *not* to call for 'gay rights as human rights'. Would a US failure to make such a call be any less (neo)imperial? If not, then we have to ask what—if anything—the categorization of US policy as (neo)imperial offers to analyses of 'gay rights as human rights'.[13] Second, regardless of the terms in which Clinton made her call for 'gay rights as human rights', these terms do not define what this call might do in the world. This is because, 'as Wendy Brown argues, rights do not "simply set people free to make the world as they see fit" . . . , nor are they *just* a cipher for the totalizing power of the sinister agents behind "the enlightenment project"' (Langlois 2012, 561). Indeed, some of the political power of rights discourses—however problematic these discourses might be—comes out of those moments when rights are leveraged to exceed the racist, (neo)imperialist terms in which they may be offered. All of this makes me uncomfortable with the claim that there is such a thing as '*the* human rights industrial complex' (Puar 2013, 338; my emphasis) or '*the* neoliberal imperium' (Agathangelou 2013) on whose behalf '*the* human rights industrial complex' is seemingly mobilized.

One way to think about the excessive potential of rights is with respect to the performative potential of rights. As Karen Zivi puts it, 'Analyzing rights theory and practice from a performative perspective means . . . appreciating the extent to which our claims both reference and reiterate social conventions and norms, *and yet have forces and effects that exceed them'* (2011, 19; my emphasis; also see Gearty and Douzinas 2014; Nash, 2015; Odysseos 2010; 2016). Claiming gay rights as human rights, then, may practically and performatively exceed homonormativity, homonationalism, and (neo)imperialism. For none of these institutions, structures of understanding, practical orientations, or claims to rights are ever set in stone, no matter how much presumably (neo)imperial actors like Clinton may (or may not) intend them to be. My understanding of 'gay rights as human rights', then, cannot be captured through *either/or* logics either intellectually or politically. For it is only through *and/or* logics that the excessive intellectual and political potential of 'gay rights as human rights' can be explored and potentially realized.

In my analysis of Clinton's speech, I demonstrate how Clinton makes some of the homonormative moves that Duggan warns us about and how these moves are employed to construct and support a type of homonationalism and pinkwashing that Puar denounces. This analysis is valuable to the larger point this chapter is making because it demonstrates how the most widely recognized contemporary expressions of the 'normal homosexual' in international relations as the 'human rights holder' and the 'gay patriot' figure in procedures of 'statecraft as mancraft' and can be put to *one set of uses* in international politics. What this reading fails to do—because it is beyond the scope of this book—is to go on to analyze how the call for gay rights as human rights has been performatively enacted—as a political tactic in specific local, national, and international battles against injustices borne by the 'homosexual'—by those struggling to claim the right to have rights, both before and after Clinton's intervention. What such an analysis might demonstrate (as other analyzes have)[14] is both the *advantages and limitations* of wholly embracing or wrongly reifying concepts like homonormativity and homonationalism and their embedded *either/or* logics in comprehending 'gay rights as human rights' in specific historical and geopolitical settings. I am mindful of the possibilities as well as the limitations of my mobilization of homonormativity and homonationalism when I present my analysis of the figuration of the 'LGBT' as the 'normal homosexual' in Clinton's speech, which is at best partial and at worst overdetermined.

THE 'LGBT', HOMONORMATIVITY, AND HOMONATIONALISM

Who is the 'LGBT' in Hilary Clinton's 'Gay rights are human rights' speech? And how does Clinton's figuring of the 'LGBT' as the 'normal homosexual' with the right to have rights participate in the figuration of a US 'sovereign man'? How specifically does Clinton's speech draw upon homonormativity to elaborate a context of homo(inter)nationalism that figures the 'LGBT' as the 'normal homosexual' in international relations and to hold the 'perverse homosexual' in international relations in reserve? And how, together, do these figurations provide the foundation for a US foreign policy that divides states along moral grounds in ways that are (compatible with) (neo)imperialist grounds?

The key claim of Clinton's speech is that the 'LGBT' is a legitimate human rights holder. To support this claim, Clinton equates the 'LGBT' with 'the universal human', whom the 1947 UN Declaration of Human Rights (UNDRH) recognizes as the figure with the right to have rights. On the one hand, this equation seems to be unproblematic, especially in the liberal, Kantian terms it is expressed. Clinton, for example, embraces Kant's idea that 'the universal human' should be guided by universal moral imperatives. It is 'the moral imperative of equality' (Clinton 2011, 4)[15] that supports Clinton's claim that there is an 'immutable truth, that all persons are created free and equal in dignity and rights' (2011, 6). This allows Clinton to argue that 'because we are human, we therefore have rights' (2011, 1).

The problem for Clinton, in her terms, is not that all 'universal humans' do not deserve national and international protection of their 'inherent humanity and dignity [and rights]' (2011, 1). Rather, the problem is that sovereign states fall down in their duty to protect the human rights of all people, especially 'minorities' and 'marginalized groups' (2011, 1, 2). The challenge Clinton takes up in her speech is to persuade governments that 'LGBT people' are among those human minorities who deserve rights. Furthermore, because 'LGBT people' deserve rights, Clinton argues, governments have an obligation to protect the 'LGBT' as a human rights holder. Clinton makes her case by playing on a general same-versus-different dichotomy that she deploys spatially, temporally, and in relation to desire.

Spatially, Clinton contests three spatial dichotomies that have served to deny the 'LGBT' human rights. These are 'legitimate minority' versus the 'rogue individual', 'universal homosexuality' versus 'Western-only homosexuality', and 'universal values' versus 'particular values'.

First, Clinton takes on the spatial dichotomy of 'legitimate minority' versus the 'rogue individual'. Neither of these figures is named explicitly in Clinton's speech, yet it relies upon both to make sense. A member of a 'legitimate minority', Clinton implies, is a figure who individually or in a group is recognized as fully human because he abides by universal moral imperatives, behavior that gives him a right to have rights. The 'rogue individual', in contrast, is a figure who individually or in a group is *not* fully human because he does not abide by universal moral imperatives. As such, in Kant's terms and in Clinton's terms, this figure is rightly beyond the bounds of a legitimate 'human community' and therefore does not deserve human rights. This, Clinton seems to suggest in her speech, is how many governments view the 'LGBT', a view that enables them to argue that 'gay rights' are not human rights but are akin to 'special rights' (Clinton 2011, 2). What might evidence their position, Clinton again implies, is that the 'LGBT' is not a protected figure named in the UNDHR.

Clinton challenges this position by reminding her audience that throughout history, many groups now recognized as legitimate minorities are unnamed in the UNDRH, including indigenous people, children, and people with disabilities (2011, 2). Clinton explains:

Yet in the past 60 years, we have come to recognize that members of these groups are entitled to the full measure of dignity and rights, because, like all people, they share a common humanity. This recognition did not occur all at once. It evolved over time. And as it did, we understood that we were honoring rights that people always had, rather than creating new or special rights for them. Like being a woman, like being a racial, religious, tribal, or ethnic minority, being LGBT does not make you less human. And that is why gay rights are human rights, and human rights are gay rights. (2011, 2)

This, Clinton tells her audience, is not just the view of the Obama administration on whose behalf she is speaking. As evidence, Clinton reminds her audience that 'at the Human Rights Council in March [2011], 85 countries from all regions supported a statement calling for an end to criminalization and violence against people because of their sexual orientation and gender identity' (Clinton 2011, 5), which amounts to these governments implicitly recognizing that gay rights are human rights.

The second dichotomy Clinton challenges posits 'universal homosexuality' against 'Western-only homosexuality'. Clinton employs her claim that there is a 'universal human' across time and space to dispel the idea that 'homosexuality' is particular to Western populations and to those who are influenced by the 'West'. This is important because 'some seem to believe [homosexuality] is a Western phenomenon, and therefore people outside the West have grounds to reject it. Well, in reality, gay people are born into and belong to every society in the world. They are all ages, all races, all faiths' (Clinton 2011, 2). Based upon this reality, Clinton argues that 'being gay is not a Western invention; it is a human reality' (3). It is, in other words, universal because the 'human' is universal. By listing what she calls 'non-Western' nations like South Africa, Colombia, Argentina, Nepal, and Mongolia that are 'protecting the human rights of all people, gay or straight' (3), Clinton evidences both how widespread 'homosexuality' is and how widespread international recognition of gay rights as human rights is (becoming) outside the 'West'.

The final spatial dichotomy Clinton contests is 'universal values' versus 'particular values'. Here, Clinton takes on the idea that particular cultural and religious values (values located just here—in one culture or religion) should be and often are opposed to her universal valuing of gay rights as human rights (values located everywhere—in all cultures and religions). 'Rarely,' Clinton claims, 'are cultural and religious traditions and teachings actually in conflict with the protection of human rights. Indeed, our religion and our culture are sources of compassion and inspiration toward our fellow human beings' (Clinton 2011, 3), including 'LGBT people'. Among the values that culture and religion teach us is how to practice love through our families and by caring for others. 'And caring for others is an expression of what it means to be fully human. It is because the human experience is universal that human rights are universal and cut across all religions and cultures' (3).

By dismantling spatial dichotomies that serve to place the 'LGBT' as the 'homosexual' in the category of the nonhuman or as a particular perversion of the 'human' who has no right to claim rights, Clinton primes her audience to be receptive to her fundamental claim about the desires of the 'LGBT'—that they are just like those of straight people. Clinton can make this unconventional claim (for her audience) by making two moves. First, she erases the 'homosexual' from her speech altogether. The 'cringeworthy' figure of the 'homosexual' (Peters 2014) who conjures up notions of 'perverse homosexuality' appears nowhere in the text of Clinton's speech. In its place, as we have seen, is the 'LGBT', who floats (somewhat more) freely from its perverse bond with 'homosexuality'. This allows Clinton to harness the 'LGBT' to a type of 'homosexuality' that resembles 'perverse sexuality' less than it does 'normal love'.

Clinton both reinscribes 'homosexuality' as 'normal love' and makes this type of 'normal love' just as natural and fixed as heterosexual 'normal love' presumably is when she calls upon presumably straight subjects to empathize with the plight of the persecuted 'LGBT'. 'We need to ask ourselves, "How would it feel if it were a crime to love the person I love? How would it feel to be discriminated against for something about myself that I cannot change?"' (Clinton 2011, 4). In this way, Clinton makes the 'LGBT' and the 'LGBT' practice of 'homosexuality' as 'normal love' unthreatening because it is nonsexual. In so doing, Clinton goes some way toward explaining to her audience why today's youth hold this simple belief: 'All people deserve to be treated with dignity and have their human rights respected, no matter who they are or whom they love' (2011, 6;).

By invoking the youth of today, Clinton implicitly makes reference to a kind of temporality she explicitly discusses throughout her speech—progressive temporality. Progressive temporality is one of three primary temporalities that Clinton employs to make her case that 'gay rights are human rights' (2011, 2)—universal temporality, progressive temporality, and historical temporality.

Universal temporality and its conveyance of human rights to all people is the temporality that undergirds Clinton's entire argument. Just as Clinton argues that 'gay rights are human rights' in all places, she also claims that 'gay rights are human rights' *at all times*. This universal temporality is fundamental to her claim (discussed above) that gay rights are not special rights. Speaking about the gradual recognition by states of 'gay rights as human rights', Clinton explains, 'We were honoring rights that people *always had*, rather than creating new or special rights for them' (2011, 2; my emphasis). By making this statement, Clinton is claiming that human rights are and always have been temporally universal. The problem is that governments—including the US government on whose behalf Clinton speaks (2)—have been slow in recognizing the temporal (and spatial) universality of 'gay rights as human rights' (1). Yet, Clinton claims, states are making progress on this score. This is how she introduces progressive temporality into her speech.

This progressive temporality is evolutionary. As Clinton points out, 'This recognition [of gay rights as human rights] did not occur all at once. It evolved over time' (2011, 2). Clinton mobilizes the progressive, evolutionary time of the universal acknowledgment and protection of gay rights as human rights to do three things. One is acknowledge that the United States has been on the same evolutionary trajectory in its recognition of gay rights as human rights that other nations find themselves on. But, as noted earlier, Neville Hoad argues the United States imagines itself as at or near the end of this process in its development (2002, 148). A second purpose is to outline the practical ways through which progress has been and will continue to be made—by entering into difficult conversations on the topic, by passing legislation to protect the 'LGBT' and 'LGBT' rights because 'it is often the case that laws must change before fears about change dissipate' (2011, 4), and by practicing empathy toward the 'LGBT' by 'being willing to walk a mile in someone else's shoes' (2011, 4). The final reason Clinton mobilizes progressive, evolutionary time is to tie it to historical time.

Historical time refers to the long view of history, the perspective from which peoples and nations are morally judged for their actions. History has a 'right side' and a 'wrong side'. 'The right side of history' is always the side of the progressive implementation of universal moral imperatives; 'the wrong side of history' is the side of obstructing such progress. Clinton makes all of this explicit in her speech, in her attempt to rally governments to support gay rights as human rights. It is worth quoting Clinton at length on this point.

> There is a phrase that people in the United States invoke when urging others to support human rights: 'Be on the right side of history'. The story of the United States is the story of a nation that has repeatedly grappled with intolerance and inequality. We fought a brutal civil war over slavery. People from coast to coast joined in campaigns to recognize the rights of women, indigenous peoples, racial minorities, children, people with disabilities, immigrants, workers, and on and on. And the march toward equality and justice has continued. Those who advocate for expanding the circle of human rights were and are on the right side of history, and history honors them. Those who tried to constrict human rights were wrong, and history reflects that as well.
>
> I know that the thoughts I've shared today involve questions on which opinions are still evolving. As it has happened so many times before, opinion will converge once again with the truth, the immutable truth, that all persons are created free and equal in dignity and rights. We are called once more to make real the words of the Universal Declaration. Let us answer that call. Let us be on the right side of history, for our people, our nations, and future generations,

whose lives will be shaped by the work we do today. I come before you with great hope and confidence that no matter how long the road ahead, we will travel it successfully together. (2011, 6)

In these words, her closing comments, Clinton sweeps away all of the prior spatial dichotomies she contested and replaces them with the only dichotomy that ultimately matters—morally, temporally, and spatially— 'the right side of history' versus 'the wrong side of history'. Don't take my word for it, Clinton suggests to her audience. Look to history for the proof that what I have said here is 'the immutable truth', 'that gay rights are human rights and human rights are gay rights' (2011, 6, 2).

Taken together, this is a powerful set of claims that forcefully makes the case that the 'LGBT' is the 'normal homosexual' who has a right to claim rights and that national governments have a duty to promote and protect the 'LGBT' as a human rights holder. As important and welcome as these claims are, however, they are not unproblematic. For in the specific ways that Clinton figures the 'LGBT' as the 'normal homosexual' and insists upon the duty of care governments have to this figure as a human rights holder, she employs every one of the four homonormativizing and homo(inter)nationalizing moves discussed above. As noted, these four moves enable Western states to include the 'homosexual' as a normal human in their tolerant, multicultural liberal political communities while simultaneously preserving figurations of the 'perverse homosexual' that are compatible with or underwrite (neo)imperial sexualized organizations of international relations. Let me explain how Clinton makes each of these moves.

By reinscribing 'homosexuality' as 'normal love', Clinton effects the first of these moves. This move is to abandon same-sex sexual desires as the axis that differentiates the 'normal' sexual subject from the 'perverse' sexual subject. So long as the 'homosexual'—now the 'LGBT'— embraces specific (neo)liberal values and is properly regulated through (neo)liberal national and international governmentalizing schemes, then the 'homosexual' as the 'LGBT' is deemed in Clinton's speech to be normal.

Clinton evidences how the 'LGBT' embraces (neo)liberal values by demonstrating that, as 'our family, our friends, and our neighbors', 'LGBT people' are *productive* citizens in our communities. 'They are doctors and teachers, farmers and bankers, soldiers and athletes' (Clinton 2011, 2). And they are 'entrepreneurs who happen to be gay' (Clinton 2011, 3). Taking up the economic language of costs and benefits, Clinton makes the case for protecting these 'entrepreneurial gays':

> Now, some worry that protecting the human rights of the LGBT community is a luxury that only wealthy nations can afford. But in fact, in all countries, there are costs to not protecting these rights, in both gay and straight lives lost to disease and violence, and the silencing of voices and views that would strengthen communities, in ideas never pursued by entrepreneurs who happen to be gay. Costs are incurred whenever any group is treated as lesser or the other, whether they are women, racial, or religious minorities, or the LGBT. (2011, 3)

This language of costs and benefits is precisely the language that the World Bank has taken up to argue on behalf of development schemes that economically benefit from protecting and promoting the 'LGBT' (Bedford 2005; 2008; Lind 2010; 2014a; World Bank 2014). By suggesting that productive citizens are (neo)liberal citizens who add economic benefits to states, Clinton figures the 'LGBT' as the entrepreneurial neoliberal subject who is productive in/for capitalism on behalf of the nation (Duggan 2003). In so doing, Clinton effects the second move discussed above. This move is to situate the 'LGBT' within the institutions, cultural understandings, and practical orientations of homonormativity (Duggan 2003), thereby making the attachment of the 'homosexual' to (neo)liberalism the axis upon which his normality or perversion is (so often) determined.

So figured (and this is the third move), the 'LGBT' is a normal subject who has the right to have rights. While these rights include the right to be economically productive for the nation—to be 'the gay entrepreneur'—they also include the right to be protective of the nation and to be reproductive for the nation. Clinton's claim that the 'LGBT' can, like any other citizen, be protective of the nation is made through her reference to President Obama's repeal of the 'Don't Ask, Don't Tell' policy—a policy that effectively removed numerous 'homosexuals' from the US military. Since this policy was rescinded, Clinton explains, 'the Marine Corps Commandant, who was one of the strongest voices against the repeal, says that his concerns were unfounded and that the Marines have embraced the change' (2011, 4). The 'LGBT' citizen who is the 'LGBT' soldier does not imperil the nation; rather, Clinton suggests, he protects it.[16]

In her speech, Clinton never discusses the right of the 'LGBT' to be reproductive for the nation. But she strongly implies this right when she urges state's leaders to ensure 'that all citizens are treated as equals under your laws' (2011, 5). For Clinton's claim is made in three contexts that all favor providing the 'domesticated LGBT couple' with the same rights to have and raise a family as the 'domesticated straight couple'. These contexts are Clinton's 2007 public declaration in support of same-sex civil partnerships (Weiner 2013) and her later support of same-sex marriage (Griffin 2013), the US national fight for same-sex marriage that President Obama publically endorsed a few months after Clinton's speech and which was ongoing in 2011 when Clinton gave her speech (Wallsten and Wilson 2012; Zizi 2014), and 'the international diffusion of marriage equality'[17] (Picq and Thiel 2015; for specific discussion, see Weiss and Bosia 2013b) that was also ongoing at the time of Clinton's speech. As Clinton's position on same-sex marriage 'evolved',[18] Clinton always maintained her support for 'LGBT couples'. As she put it in 2007, 'I am absolutely in favor of civil unions with full equality . . . of benefits, rights, and privileges' for 'LGBT couples' (Weiner 2013). The 'domesticated LGBT couple' with its reproductive capacity for the nation, then, has long been the specific figure that Clinton has been championing publically, something of which her audience of states' leaders would be well aware.

When Clinton finally did announce her support for same-sex marriage in 2013, she couched that support in her understanding of marriage itself, stating that 'marriage after all is a fundamental building block of our society' (Griffin 2013). This statement assumes the reproductive potential of the domesticated couple, as the biological and social engine of the nation/civilization (as we saw in chapter 3).[19] In this way, Clinton hints at—without stating it in her speech—that the 'domesticated LGBT'—individually and as a couple—is both productive and reproductive for the nation/civilization. This is how Clinton completes her figuration of the 'LGBT' in homonormative terms, as the entrepreneurial neoliberal subject who is (re)productive in/for capitalism on behalf of the nation (Duggan 2003).

These homonormative terms are also specifically homo(inter)national. For, as Puar notes (Puar and Rai 2002; Puar 2006; 2007), they effectively and affectively invest the 'homosexual' as the 'LGBT' with specifically homonormative desires for freedom, liberation, and rights nationally and internationally. Facing inward, the 'LGBT' is biopolitically governmentalized as a member of the 'loving national family' who is reproductive on behalf of the nation/civilization and is invested in cultural and material capitalist accumulation. Facing outward, the 'domesticated LGB but not usually T' (Spade 2008; Richter-Montpetit 2014b; 2014c; Dawson 2015) protects and defends the nation from dangerous others—as either docile citizen patriots or as active citizen soldier who happens to be 'homosexual'. In so doing, the 'domesticated LGBT' enacts its 'own normalization—in the name of patriotism' (Puar and Rai 2002, 126).

To assuage any doubts that the 'domesticated LGBT' is the explicit figuration on whose behalf Clinton is speaking, Clinton evokes the 'LGBT in the shadows' as the specter of the costs of not recognizing gay rights as human rights. Clinton does this when she spells out the specific costs to 'the public' of not embracing the 'LGBT' as a human rights holder. She states, 'Former President Mogae of Botswana pointed out recently that for as long as LGBT people are kept in the shadows, there cannot be an effective public health program to tackle HIV and AIDS' (Clinton 2011, 3).

Here, Clinton inscribes the 'LGBT in the shadows' as that 'homosexual' who is not just the victim of homophobia (which is the presumed reason the 'homosexual' is in the shadows in Botswana). Clinton's 'LGBT in the shadows' is also inscribed as forever linked to HIV and AIDS as a carrier of disease and death, as he is so often still known in global public health discourses. Clinton's evocation of the 'LGBT in the shadows' is reminiscent of Russian-Israeli journalist and poet Boris Kamyanov's figuration of what queer studies scholar Adi Kuntsman calls 'the shadow by the latrine' (Kuntsman 2009, chap. 1). 'The shadow by the latrine' refers to a male in a Soviet prison or camp at the bottom of the criminal hierarchy—'the prisoner in a position of total subordination' (Kuntsman 2009, 40)—who is subjected to physical and sexual violence. In her queer critical analysis of this figuration, Kuntsman writes that 'the conjunction of same-sex relations, criminality and abuse takes us into … a past that is about much more than just the criminalization of male homosexuality under Soviet law. This is a past that includes many layers of violence—political, physical, sexual, affective and discursive' (2009, 40). Clinton's evocation of the 'LGBT in the shadows' as the carrier of HIV and AIDS takes us to a similarly layered and violent past that is about more than just the criminalization of male homosexuality; it is also about the political, physical, sexual, affective, and discursive violence done to this figure—by those opposing this presumed carrier of disease and death—in the name of protecting society and the state from this figure.[20]

Kuntsman demonstrates that the 'homosexual' figured as the 'shadow by the latrine' is, in Avery Gordon's terms, a haunting figure. Writes Gordon, 'The ghost is not simply a dead or a missing person, but *a social figure*, and investigating it can lead to that dense site *where history and subjectivity make social life* (1997, 8; my emphasis; quoted in Kuntsman 2009, 41). Clinton deploys the 'LGBT in the shadows' as a similarly haunting social figure to argue for a particular form of social life within the state. This social life is one that is safe from the unregulated and undomesticated 'perverse homosexuality' that the 'LGBT in the shadows' represents. For as that 'homosexual' who is forever understood as a carrier of disease and death, the 'LGBT in the shadows' is a figure that—if left unregulated by the nation and undomesticated in the family, we are led to believe—threatens 'public health' because he presumably practices unsafe sex. This, Clinton suggests, is the dark history of the practice of 'homosexuality' to which no nation wishes to return. This is the haunting history that the 'LGBT in the shadows' carries with it.

Because Clinton's speech figures the 'LGBT in the shadows' in this way, the idea that 'homosexuality' is unsafe because of unregulated and undomesticated 'perverse sexual practices' creeps into it. Indeed, 'perverse homosexuality' and the 'perverse homosexual' are the haunting anchors of a social and national history that no nation wants to (re)visit or (re)live. As such, these perverse fornicating figures who love 'homosexual sex' more than they love their nation are crucial to Clinton's ability to figure the properly loving 'domesticated LGBT' as the 'normal homosexual' who holds the promise of a brighter, happier future. By sneaking this specific understanding of the 'homosexual' into her speech, then, Clinton not only retains a figuration of the 'perverse homosexual' who practices 'perverse homosexuality' as a haunting historical and social figure, but also deploys this figure as her trump card to make her case for why the 'domesticated LGBT' as the 'normal homosexual' holds the promise of better social and national relations.

Among the most striking things about Clinton's comments on the 'LGBT in the shadows' is her move from a summary of former president Mogae's remarks to a wider comment about this figure: 'Former President Mogae of Botswana pointed out recently that for as long as LGBT people are kept in the shadows, there cannot be an effective public health program to tackle HIV and AIDS. *Well, that holds true for other challenges as well*' (Clinton 2011, 3; my emphasis). By adding this final sentence, Clinton both specifies the 'LGBT in the shadows' as a carrier of HIV and AIDS who lacks any beneficial and/or resistive potential and also leaves *unspecified* those 'other challenges' that figure the unregulated and undomesticated 'LGBT' as a shadowy risk to 'public health'. What might these 'other challenges' be? Which figurations of the 'perverse homosexual' might be deathly carriers of these 'other challenges'? Clinton cleverly never says. For by leaving these 'other challenges' unspecified, Clinton leaves open the possibility that these perverse figures could continue to be the 'underdeveloped', the 'undevelopable', the 'unwanted im/migrant', and certainly the 'terrorist'.

At first, this move seems to undercut Clinton's primary message—that the 'LGBT' is a legitimate human rights holder because the 'LGBT' is a minority member of the community of 'universal humans'. 'And that is why gay rights are human rights and human rights are gay rights' (Clinton 2011, 2). Yet there is no contradiction here, at least in the Kantian terms in which Clinton's message is cast. For by drawing a distinction between the regulated and (re)productive loving 'LGBT' who is a figure of life verses the unregulated and therefore dangerous fornicating 'LGBT in the shadows' who is a figure of death, Clinton has left open the possibility that the 'LGBT in the shadows' *who stays in the shadows by rejecting (neo)liberalism and its modes of domesticating governmentality* is outside the 'universal human community' because he threatens this 'human community'.

This move draws a line between the 'normal homosexual' as a human rights holder and the 'perverse homosexual' who has no right to have rights. The 'normal homosexual', by this account, has a right to have rights because he is a minority member of 'the universal human community'. The 'perverse homosexual' has no right to have rights because—by 'choosing' to remain outside the limits of good sexual, economic, and political practice—he places himself beyond the limits of the 'universal human community'. This is because he 'chooses' death over life, danger over security, perversion over normality. 'It is precisely within the interstices of life and death', Jasbir Puar argues, 'that we find the differences between queers subject who are being folded (back) into life and the racialized queerness' of the 'perverse homosexual' who is necessarily marked for exclusion and possible death (Puar 2007, 35; also see Rao 2012, 5). This move—what Puar describes as a 'queer biopolitics' for 'good queers' that relies upon a 'queer necropolitics' for 'bad queers'—is part and parcel of Puar's understanding of homonationalism (also see Haritaworn, Kuntsman, and Posocco 2013a and b; Richter-Montpetit 2014b; 2014c). For it divides primarily national populations into the patriotic 'LGBT' and the unpatriotic 'perverse homosexual'. By playing upon this matrix of inclusion and exclusion, life and death, Clinton makes it possible for Western states and particularly the United States to retain their figurations of those 'perverse homosexuals' who are *unworthy* of rights. In so doing, Clinton licenses Western policies of queer biopolitics and queer necropolitics (Puar 2007; 2010; Rao 2012).

It is on the back of these three moves that Clinton makes her fourth and final move. This move is to identify a new developmental trajectory in relation to the 'homosexual' and to use this new developmental trajectory to reinscribe what it means to be a modern 'homosexual' and to be a modern state. In so doing, Clinton combines homonationalism with homointernationalism (Nath 2008). A modern 'homosexual' is *not* one who has abandoned 'perverse homosexuality' for 'normal heterosexuality'. Rather, a modern 'homosexual' is one whose desire for domesticity and consumption figures him as the entrepreneurial neoliberal subject who is (re)productive in/for capitalism on behalf of the nation (Duggan 2003), bestowing upon him the right to have rights. A modern state is a state that recognizes and (where necessary) protects this particular figuration of the existing or emerging 'new normal homosexual' as a member of a minority human population of 'LGBT' human rights holders who also is and should be a full and equal member of the state's political community. As Clinton explains it in her speech, this modern state is the state that is 'on the right side of history' (2011, 6).

Because not all states are modern in this new sense of modernity that Clinton inscribes, she pledges the support of the US government to protect and defend the 'LGBT' worldwide.

> To LGBT men and women worldwide, let me say this: Wherever you live and whatever the circumstances of your life ... please know that you are not alone. People around the globe are working hard to support you and to bring an end to the injustices and dangers you face. That is certainly true for my country. And you have an ally in the United States of America and you have millions of friends among the American people. The Obama Administration defends the human rights of LGBT people as part of our comprehensive human rights policy and as a priority of our foreign policy. (2011, 5)

Queer IR scholar Rahul Rao has critiqued Clinton's call for states to be 'on the right side of history' (2011, 6) as a form of 'gay conditionality' (2012). Gay conditionality might explicitly link foreign aid to a recipient country's respect for the rights of the 'LGBT', as it does in David Cameron's British foreign policy (Rao 2012, 1). Or it might embody a more generalized project of liberal enlightenment by modern Western states of modernizing (post)colonial states, where the liberal impulse to protect and defend the minority 'LGBT' serves (neo)imperial purposes because 'enlightened modern states' again become the powerful enforcers of policy in 'modernizing states'. It is this latter form of gay conditionality—in which 'to be on the right side of history' means, for Rao, to be 'on the wrong side of empire' (Rao 2010; also see Haritaworn, Kuntsman, and Posocco 2013a and b; Rahman 2014)—that is found in Clinton's speech.

Puar spells out the mechanics of this gay conditionality by comparing the long-standing 'woman question' in liberalism to this newly emerging liberal 'homosexual question'. As Puar explains,

> Liberal feminism has long been accused of needing the oppression of the native woman in order to achieve its own liberatory trajectory. 'How well do you treat your women?' became a key measure of the ability of a colonised or developing country to self-govern. While 'the Woman Question' has hardly disappeared, we can now find its amendment in 'the Homosexual Question', or 'How well do you treat your homosexuals?', as a current paradigm through which nations, populations and cultures are evaluated in terms of their ability to conform to a universalised notion of civilisation. Rescue fantasies and projections about endangered homosexuality 'elsewhere' are aspects of liberal gay rights frames, functioning in order to support the predominance of gay and lesbian proper subjects 'here'. (2010)

This is how Clinton divides the world into good gay-friendly states and bad homophobic states. In these bad states, the 'LGBT' needs to be rescued, either by correcting or opposing bad homophobic states and their homophobic policies. Clinton's speech details some of the specific ways in which the Obama administration will not only befriend the 'LGBT' worldwide but also enlighten global governments to the value of the 'LGBT' as a human rights holder through its various foreign policies. In so doing,

she regiments US foreign policy in relation to the 'LGBT' and in relation
to how states treat the 'LGBT', by outlining specific US policies designed
to tackle the issue of 'gay rights as human rights' on a global scale. Clinton
explains,

> In our embassies, our diplomats are raising concerns about specific
> cases and laws, and working with a range of partners to strengthen
> human rights protections for all. In Washington, we have created a
> task force at the State Department to support and coordinate this
> work. And in the coming months, we will provide every embassy
> with a toolkit to help improve their efforts. And we have created a
> program that offers emergency support to defenders of human rights
> for LGBT people.
>
> This morning ... President Obama put in place the first
> U.S. government strategy dedicated to combating human rights
> abuses against LGBT persons abroad. Building on efforts already
> underway at the State Department and across the Government,
> the President has directed all U.S. Government agencies engaged
> overseas to combat the criminalization of LGBT status and conduct,
> to enhance efforts to protect vulnerable LGBT refugees and asylum
> seekers, to ensure that our foreign assistance promotes the protection
> of LGBT rights, to enlist international organizations in the fight
> against discrimination, and to respond swiftly to abuses against
> LGBT persons. (2011, 5)

Overall, then, by abandoning same-sex sexual desires as the axis that
differentiates the 'normal' sexual subject from the 'perverse' sexual subject, by employing homonormativity to shift the axis of perversion to
desires around neoliberal domesticity and consumption, and by combining these two moves to refigure the normal subject who has the right to
have rights as the 'LGBT' and the 'gay patriot' and to reinscribe what it
means to be modern for individuals and for states, Clinton achieves three
things. First, she maps a new developmental trajectory for this 'normal
homosexual'. Second, she ensures that this new developmental trajectory

for the new 'normal homosexual' does not cancel out the old developmental trajectory for the 'perverse homosexual' we analyzed in chapters 3 and 4. And, finally, she mobilizes these figures to construct a sexualized order of international relations that is (neo)imperialist or is compatible with (neo)imperialism.

CONCLUSION

By homonormativizing and homo(inter)nationalizing 'homosexuality' and the 'homosexual' in her 'Gay rights are human rights' speech, Hilary Clinton imposes a Western will to knowledge about the 'homosexual' to figure a new 'normal homosexual'. This is what allows her to craft the 'LGBT' as the 'gay rights holder', understood as that sexualized minority subject within the universal human community who—like every other human being—has the right to have rights. What Clinton leaves us with is a figuration of the 'LGBT' as the 'gay rights holder' who appears to exist everywhere, in any number of forms. This is because Clinton's 'LGBT' appears to have no particular home or homeland, no particular race, religion, nationality, gender, civilization, (dis)ability, or class. In other words, all of the particularity of the 'LGBT' appears to have been stripped away from this figuration so that it can function in global politics as a universalizable figure—*the* 'gay rights holder'.

But universal figures are never as universal as they may at first appear to be. For their figuration is always made possible through a particular discourse that attempts to understand itself as if it were free of all bias. That discourse in this instance is the Obama administration's discourse on human rights, which itself relies upon a Western Kantian interpretation of the 'human'—as masculine, as white, as bourgeois, as progressively productive, as a global ruler, as civilized, as territorialized, as modernity itself.

Clinton's will to know the 'LGBT' as the 'gay rights holder' does not make the debts of the 'LGBT' to this specific Kantian 'universal human' disappear, but it does make these debts more difficult to see. This is not surprising, given the universalizing and naturalizing function of homo(inter)nationalism. As Dipika Nath explains,

> Homonationalism and homointernationalism rely upon the discourse of naturalism to do their work. Arguments of 'naturalness' inevitably imply universalism because what is 'natural' is seen to be unaffected by what is cultural or learnt. As gay rights become globalized, being gay becomes naturalized and universalized: it is seen to be essentially the same set of desires, demands and dissatisfactions everywhere. The result is that gay people all over the world are cast as de-racialised, de-nationalised and de-gendered people, banded together in a global gay nation. In practice, however, we know that whatever claims to be universal is only a reflection of the dominant; the universal or global gay or lesbian is in fact coded white, privileged, able-bodied, slim, European or American, and their vision of the good consumerist life is coded as global gay liberation. (2008, 8)

It is on behalf of this *particular* albeit universalized and naturalized 'normal homosexual'—as the domesticated entrepreneurial embodiment of modernity who is (re)productive in/for capitalism regardless of his sexual orientation—that the Obama administration in part maps the world. By asking of and answering for all sovereign states this specific 'queer question'—How well do you treat your homosexuals?—the Obama administration categorizes racialized and sexualized (post)colonial states and to a lesser extent (post)communist states as either normal or pathological (Rao 2012; Agathangelou 2013). 'Normal states' are those that champion gay rights as human rights and fold the 'LGBT' into state and social institutions as a moral and legal equal. 'Pathological states' are those that deny human rights and state protection to the 'LGBT'.

Using its defense of the 'LGBT' as its rationalization to map the world into normal and pathological states, the Obama administration is yet again employing statecraft as mancraft—this time to know itself as it 'really is' by refiguring itself as *the* 'global champion of gay rights as human rights'. In its human rights discourse, this is what it means for the contemporary

United States to be 'enlightened man', 'developed man', 'modern man'. It is this figuration of itself as 'sovereign man' that the administration employs to justify two kinds of international policies. The first is a 'gay conditionality' (Rao 2012), which *claims* to make the international status and treatment of states by 'the international community' conditional upon their treatment of the 'LGBT'. Speaking for (while inventing) both the 'LGBT' and for some presumably singular 'international community' that speaks on behalf of the 'LGBT' (Weber 1995), the Obama administration takes upon itself the task of constantly monitoring other states for this condition. The second international policy this division of the world justifies is the correction, exclusion, and punishment of 'pathological states', should these gay conditions not be met, culminating in a justification for intervention according to which 'white straights save brown queers from brown straights' (Rao 2010, chap. 6).

Despite this rhetoric, in practice the Obama administration applies its new standard of gay-friendly enlightened modernity as selectively as it has selected the attributes of the 'LGBT'. This is evidenced by the significantly different US responses to homophobia in Russia, India, and Uganda, for example (see Weiss and Bosia 2013; Wilkinson and Langlois 2014; Rao 2012; 2014b). It is also evidenced by the administration's failure to universally apply its own standards of gay-friendly enlightened modernity at home, in either practice or in law (e.g., Cage, Herman, and Good 2014). This has led queer studies scholars like Dean Spade to conclude:

> Clinton's speech evinces a relatively new logic in U.S. imperialism: that the U.S., regardless of failures to protect queer and trans people from state violence at home, will now use gay rights to exert pressure on countries where the U.S. has some ulterior motive. Clinton uses lesbian and gay rights to bolster the notion that the U.S. is the world's policing arm, forcing democracy and equality globally on purportedly backward and cruel governments. Gay rights operates as a new justification for this imperial role—a justification that fits well within the anti-Arab and anti-Muslim framings that have been developed during the War on Terror and portray Arab and

Muslim countries as more sexist and homophobic than the U.S., European countries and Israel. . . . These declarations of gay rights aim to distract from and justify—to *pinkwash*—the brutal realities of U.S. politics and policy. (2013; my emphasis)

In making this case, Spade mobilizes how pinkwashing functions (e.g., Darwich and Haneen Maikey 2014; Puar 2007)—as always in the interests of state and/or corporate power.

Scholars within and between global queer studies and queer IR do not agree with one other as to whether or not Clinton's speech is (just) an illustration of pinkwashing—whether it only or merely or necessarily figures some US 'sovereign man' as '(neo)imperial man'.[21] Even so, these scholars do agree that Clinton's speech illustrates the sometimes concerted work that Western states like the US under the Obama administration undertake to figure the 'normal homosexual' as the 'LGBT' through their imposition of specific regimes of knowledge. Clinton performs this figuration by relying upon specific tropes (e.g., the 'universal human' and 'human rights') and temporalities (universal, progressive, historical) to figure the 'gay rights holder' and the 'gay patriot' as the specific figurations the 'normal homosexual' can performatively inhabit.

Crucially, this figuration of the 'normal homosexual' both relies upon and disavows the 'perverse homosexual' and its various figurations as, for example, the 'underdeveloped', the 'undevelopable', the 'unwanted im/migrant', and the 'terrorist'. As I have argued here, the Obama administration manages to normalize the 'LGBT' in international human rights discourse while preserving the 'perverse homosexual' as the dangerous, disorderly other 'LGBT in the shadows' who must be opposed for 'gay rights as human rights' to prevail. This particular 'perverse homosexual' is now figured through regimes of knowledge that understand him as dangerous because this racialized, disableized, sexualized, social, psychological, economic. and political degenerate and/or deviant cannot or will not developmentally mature into 'the new normal gay(-friendly) sexualized subject' and embrace proper domesticity and neoliberal consumption. It is the threat posed by this persistent yet always transforming 'perverse homosexual' that—from the standpoint of homonationalism—calls forth those self-normalizing straight and gay docile patriots to protect and defend the 'LGBT' worldwide as another means of protecting and defending the nation/civilization and indeed some form of a sexualized (neo) liberal hegemonic international order.

It is only by thawing *some* regimes of knowledge, *some* of what Foucault described as the frozen understandings of the 'homosexual' as perverse—by recircuiting 'homosexuality' through novel networks of power/knowledge/pleasure that in *some* places and at *some* times replaced 'perverse homosexual acts' with 'same-sex love' as the dominant understanding of 'homosexuality'—that Clinton could craft this new 'normal homosexual'. So figured, these *specific* understandings of 'homosexuality' and the 'homosexual' are what enable the Obama administration to create a particular understanding of itself as 'sovereign man' to justify its *specific* homonormative sexualized order of international relations, upon which *some* of its human rights foreign policy is conducted.

Knowing 'homosexuality' and the 'homosexual' through any and indeed all of the regimes of knowledge discussed in this chapter and the last two—be these regimes about some old or newly emerging 'perverse homosexual' or some new or newly emerging 'normal homosexual'—requires 'homosexuality' and the 'homosexual' to be knowable and placeable in a traditional *either/or* logic of statecraft as mancraft. One of the central arguments of this book is that this logic does not describe the full range of ways statecraft as mancraft functions in international relations.

In the next chapter, I investigate in detail one instance in which this *either/or* logic fails to understand 'homosexuality' and the 'homosexual'. This logic fails, I argue, because it demands that 'sovereign man' and 'sovereign communities' be reduced to and known in singular terms—as *either* one thing *or* another. But not every (potentially) 'sovereign man' or 'sovereign community' can be comprehended in singular terms, whether in the registers of sex, of gender, sexuality, and/or sovereign authority. This is because some (potential) 'sovereign men' and 'sovereign communities' present as *either* one thing *or* another while simultaneously presenting as one thing *and* another in these registers. To appreciate the possibilities and challenges these (queerly) plural figures present to the procedure of statecraft as mancraft and to a modernist understanding of sovereignty itself, we must leave behind the exclusively singular *either/or* logics discussed in this and the previous two chapters so we may investigate pluralized *and/or* 'sovereign men' and 'sovereign communities' through the lens of queer logics of statecraft.

The 'Normal *and/or* Perverse Homosexual' in International Relations

The 'Eurovisioned Bearded Drag Queen'

Who is 'the normal *and/or* perverse homosexual' in international relations? And how does the will to knowledge about the 'normal *and/or* perverse homosexual' participate in the figuration of 'sovereign man'?

A range of diverse figurations of 'homosexuality' and 'the homosexual' in international relations exceed categorization as exclusively normal or perverse in relation to sexes, genders, and sexualities. These figurations matter for IR because they participate in the organization and regulation of international relations and inform IR theory and practice by complicating sexualized orders of international relations that require the 'homosexual' to be *either* normal *or* perverse.

Queer IR and transnational/global queer studies scholars are producing a growing body of literature that investigates such figurations. Familiar to IR scholars might be how figurations of Thai 'ladyboys' function in international sex trafficking (Winter and King 2013) or how figurations of 'the asexual Japanese couple' inform domestic and international scenarios that link sexual and economic (re)production (Haworth 2013). Less familiar to

IR audiences might be analyses of less obviously sexualized and queered
IR figurations, including of 'the torturer' (Richter-Montpetit 2014a), 'the
slave' (Agathangelou 2013), 'the nationally bordered body' (Weber 1998;
Sjoberg 2014; Peterson 2015), 'the revolutionary state and citizen' (Weber
1999; Lind and Keating 2013), and the 'homosexual' more generally (Weiss
and Bosnia 2014).[1]

Discussing each of these IR figurations and their importance in IR is
beyond the scope of this chapter. Because my aim here is to illustrate how
the 'normal *and/or* perverse homosexual' functions as a (potentially) plural foundation (what I call in chapter 2 a 'queer logoi') in a queer logic
of statecraft, I limit my analysis to one case study. That is of the figuration of Eurovision Song Contest winner and the self-identified 'homosexual' Tom Neuwirth and/as the bearded drag queen Conchita Wurst
(Neuwirth/Wurst).

At least since winning the 2014 Eurovision Song Contest and announc-
ing in her/his/their acceptance speech, 'We are unity, and we are unstoppable', Tom Neuwirth and/as Conchita Wurst has been taken up by some
Europeans as a figuration who embodies *either* a positive *or* a negative
image of an integrated 'Europe'. This places Neuwirth/Wurst in an *either/
or* logic of statecraft as mancraft (Ashley 1989), in which the crafting
of a singular 'sovereign man' for 'the European Community' functions
through a traditional understanding of sovereignty as 'a complex practice
of authorization, a practice through which specific agencies are enabled to
draw a line' between who can legitimately be included and excluded from
the political community this 'European sovereign man' grounds (Walker
2000, 22; also see Walker 1993). In this traditional *either/or* logic of statecraft as mancraft, what is debated is whether or not Neuwirth/Wurst as
a proposed 'sovereign man' of 'the new Europe' is/should be licensed to
draw a line between 'properly integrated and normalized Europeans'
and 'improperly integrated and perverse Europeans' in a 'Europe' that
has been striving for integration in one form or another since the end of
World War II.

Understanding Neuwirth/Wurst in this way required 'Europeans' to
read Neuwirth/Wurst as a figure who is knowable and placeable along

an *either/or* axis—in relation to 'Europe' and in relation to traditional 'European' debates about 'European' integration. Yet, as I will argue, while Neuwirth/Wurst certainly seems to be making a call for some kind of unity from a platform that has traditionally promoted 'European' integration, Neuwirth/Wurst does so as a figure who defies traditional understandings of integration across multiple axes. These include (but are not necessarily confined to) sex, gender, sexuality, race, geopolitics, and secular and religious renderings of authority. This means that while Neuwirth/Wurst has been mobilized as a singular 'sovereign man' on behalf of an integrated 'European' statecraft as mancraft (as *either* a positive figuration of a new normal 'Europe' *or* as a negative figuration of a new perverse 'Europe'), Neuwirth/Wurst exceeds the singularity of these *either/or* claims. This is because Neuwirth/Wurst is both one thing *or* another (normal *or* perverse) and simultaneously one thing *and* another (normal *and* perverse), with respect to 'European' integration and with respect to integration more broadly. This makes Neuwirth/Wurst a potential plural *and/or* foundation of what I call a queer logic of statecraft, whose call for unity from a 'European' integration platform is far more complex than it might at first appear to be.

To unpack these complexities, I offer two readings of Neuwirth/Wurst. First, I read Neuwirth/Wurst's figuration of the 'Eurovisioned bearded drag queen' as one thing *and/or* another—as the 'normal *and/or* perverse homosexual' in the registers of sexes, genders, and sexualities as well as in the register of international relations. I then consider Neuwirth/Wurst's figuration as *either* one thing *or* another—as *either* the 'normal homosexual' *or* the 'perverse homosexual' in both of these registers. I conclude by considering how Neuwirth/Wurst makes possible a thorough rethinking of what the process of 'European integration' might mean and what a sovereign 'integrated Europe' might become. But this possibility, I argue, can only be realized if we read Neuwirth/Wurst through the lens of queer logics of statecraft.

To be clear, I employ queer logics of statecraft neither to celebrate nor to condemn the vast spectrum of 'differences' across which Neuwirth/Wurst is figured, as making either move would reduce Neuwirth/Wurst to one or another variety of the 'simple sovereign subject' (Soto 2010, 3–4) who would necessarily be read as *either* a dangerous 'impurity' *or* as a transgressive, liberating 'pure impurity' (Maya, quoted in Soto 2010, 3–4). Instead, I employ queer logics of statecraft to explore how Neuwirth/Wurst is figured as *either* dangerous *or* liberating as well as both dangerous *and* liberating at the same time, to analyze what these (im)possible figurations of Neuwirth/Wurst (might) do and (might) mean.

Before I launch into this reading, I set the scene by offering a few historical details about the Eurovision Song Contest—the platform for 'European' integration that propelled Neuwirth/Wurst to fame—and a few theoretical details about integration theory and its practice in 'Europe'.

THE EUROVISION SONG CONTEST AND
THE INTEGRATION OF 'EUROPE'

The modern project of 'European' integration grew out of a post–World War II desire by 'European' states 'to create, by establishing an economic community, the basis for a broader and deeper community among peoples long divided by bloody conflicts and to lay the foundations of institutions which will give direction to a destiny henceforward shared' (European Economic Union 1957, 2). Over the years, an increasing number of first Western-bloc and then former Eastern-bloc 'European' countries have signed up to this pan-'European' aim, forming a variety of formal institutions from the European Coal and Steel Community (established in 1950) to the Western European Union (est. 1954) to the European Economic Community (est. 1957) to the present-day European Union (est. 1993).

The variability of these formal institutions notwithstanding, 'European' integration has always been imagined as a process productive of 'an emerging state, a bigger version of the states being incorporated into it, a higher version of the states being incorporated below it' (Walker 2000, summarizing Haas 1970). As R. B. J. Walker explains, this vision of 'European' integration is built upon a modern understanding of state sovereignty that functions across two spatial axes—a horizontal territorial axis and a vertical legal and ethical axis (Walker 2000, 15). Because the practice of sovereignty—the practice of investing legitimate political authority in an agent in whose name a political community governs—enables this agent (this 'sovereign man', for example) to draw a line between who can legitimately be included and excluded from the political community 'he' grounds (Walker 2000, 22), Walker claims that sovereignty is an inherently spatial practice.

On Walker's reading, modern 'European' integration aspires to expand horizontally, to increase its territorial scale. In the language of 'European' integration, greater territorial scale is equated with progressing the project of 'European' integration. Temporally, this increased scale is also classified by pan-'Europeans' as attesting to the greater maturity of 'Europe', because it marks the progress of 'Europe' from distinctive, warring nation-states to one integrated, more peaceful state-like political community (Walker 2000, 16).

At the same time, 'European' integration aspires to create a top-down hierarchical chain of authority around legal and ethical issues, with pan-'European' legal institutions (e.g., European Court of Human Rights) exercising sovereign authority and ethical leadership over individual national 'European' legal institutions. For Walker, this pan-'European' desire to replace 'the horizontal universality of modern nation-states' with a hierarchical universe of 'European' legal institutions 'expresses a profound nostalgia for an imminent return of the Great Chain of Being' found in medieval Christendom (Walker 2000, 17), in which it was God's sovereign authority that bestowed upon medieval rulers their divine right to rule over their subjects. This was before 'modern man' displaced God as the (popular) sovereign foundation of the modern nation-state. Taken together, claims Walker, 'The history of debates about European integration [is] largely a story of claims about the relative priority of horizontal space and vertical space, of territorial space and a spatially conceived hierarchy of higher and lower' (2000, 18).

Walker's reading of 'European' integration does not end quite as pan-'Europeans' would have it—either in the successful establishment of pan-'European' sovereignty or in its failure thanks to entrenched individual nation-based 'European' sovereignties. Rather, it ends in puzzlement over how these two understandings persist in defining the horizon of what modern 'Europe' is or might become. This is because for Walker, following Ernst Haas, 'The imaginaries of both a states-system [of 'European' nations-states] and a hierarchy of levels [with some 'European' community over these 'European' nation-states] seem just too simple' to describe modern 'Europe' (Walker 2000, 19). For it fails to express the character of sovereignty itself, which Walker defines as 'a complex practice of authorization' that makes the horizontal and vertical spatial arrangements he describes meaningful and authoritative (2000, 22). Explains Walker, 'State sovereignty is not a permanent or unchanging principle or institution but a practice with history, or better, a genealogy, and a practice with characteristic modes of performance. State sovereignty is historically constituted and historically variable' (2000, 23), regardless of whether or not it aspires to designate a distinct national space or a pan-'European' space.

This does not stop 'European' political communities from attempting to solve complex problems of the authorization of an authority and its proper relationships among citizens, states and a 'European' superstate 'by obscuring/reifying a multiplicity of potential identities and interests under the (paradoxically) universalizing banner of a single sovereign identity/interest [e.g., a state or the 'European Community'] (Walker 2000, 24). This is done, as we learned from Ashley (1989), by crafting a particular authority—God in classical times, sovereign man in modern times—as the presumably ahistorical, authoritative sovereign foundation of 'Europe' who both springs from and guarantees the legitimacy of the horizontal and vertical spatial arrangements of a sovereign 'Europe' in a way that affirms 'the impossibility of reopening the questions [about 'European' sovereignty'] to which it responds' (Walker 2000, 25). Put in Richard Ashley's terms, modern 'European' statecraft is modern 'European' mancraft.

It is out of this imaginary of 'European' integration that the Eurovision Song Contest grew. The Eurovision Song Contest was the brainchild of the European Broadcasting Union (EBU), a collective of individual 'European' national broadcasters. Described as 'the first "Europeans" who thought of a European cultural policy' (Bourdon 2007, 264), the EBU was charged with regenerating the dream of 'European' cultural integration once it became clear that post–World War II 'European' cultural integration did not automatically follow from economic integration. Combining communicative theories of nation building with theories of television, EBU members developed a 'communicative view of the nation' (in IR, for example, see Deutsch 1966; Anderson 1983; Kegley 1993) that positioned television as the key medium to 'address the problem of European culture as if Europe should be modelled on the large European nation' (Bourdon 2007, 276, 275). Seizing on television as a form of visual communication that could overcome obstacles to cultural integration posed by a multilingual and multinational 'Europe', 'Many of the EBU members were convinced that television was the medium that could forge a new collective conscience and help the new Europe supersede the old nations' (Bourdon 2007, 264–265). This led them to launch a series of live broadcast format TV shows simulcast throughout 'Europe', in hopes of creating a 'broader and deeper community' of 'Europeans' and to publicize the EBU itself. The Eurovision Song Contest was their first such broadcast.

The Eurovision Song Contest is the largest song contest in the world and one of the most popular televisual events in contemporary 'Europe'. Begun in 1956, it pits nationally selected acts from each participating, eligible 'European' country against one another in a song contest.[2] Performed songs range from catchy pop tunes to melodramatic ballads and generally reference the nation they represent—through costumes, musical styles and lyrics, dance moves, set designs, and language (although the majority of acts are now performed in English). The competition's finale has been broadcast on live television and radio throughout 'Europe' since the competition's inception and helped to launch the careers of the Spanish singer Julio Iglesias and the Swedish pop group ABBA (who won for their performance of 'Waterloo').

As Jérôme Bourdon notes, the success of the Eurovision Song Contest overshadowed the larger aims of the EBU. He puts it like this: 'The operation was successful but the patient died: the Song Contest fast became highly popular, to the point that in many countries the word "Eurovision" refers not to a brave effort to broadcast in a truly European way, but to a specific event, the Song Contest itself' (2007, 265). Some fifty years later, the Eurovision Song Contest (hereafter 'Eurovision') is one of the longest running TV shows in the world, with an estimated annual viewing audience of 180 million (Eurovision.com). Today, it is broadcast on live television not only throughout 'Europe' but also in Australia, Canada, Egypt, Hong Kong, India, Jordan, Korea, New Zealand, and the United States, and it is streamed live on the web at Eurovision.tv (Eurovision.com).

Eurovision has not—as EBU 'cultural Europeans' had hoped—'engineered the European soul' into existence (Bourdon 2007, 277). Rather, like many transnational institutions and events that embrace some ideal of transnational community—from the United Nations to the Olympics—Eurovision often accentuates nationalist sentiments rather than cultivates pan-'European' ones. For example, national broadcasters generally hype their nation's entry, national viewing populations generally rally around their nation's act, and national feelings of pride or shame can follow from voting results (especially as the triumphant national act wins not just the Song Contest itself but the right for the nation from which the act comes to host the following year's Eurovision).

One of the most striking aspects of Eurovision is the nationalist voting trends of its participating states. While nations cannot vote for their own entries (thus promoting pan-'Europeanism'), they regularly vote for those states with whom they are somehow closely aligned. For example, the UK and Ireland regularly give one another top votes, as do Germany and Turkey, Spain and Portugal, and Russia and Ukraine. These voting patterns closely map onto the histories of changing 'European' borders and onto historical migration trends that enable (quasi-)nationalist voting to appear to be transnational (e.g., when Spanish ex-pats or their descendants who live in Portugal vote for the Spanish entry). What alters these highly predictable outcomes are generally two phenomena—any given year's regional/global political context and how acts appeal to both traditional fans (heteronormative, cisidentified fans, whose allegiance to the contest is based in its pan-'European' roots) and nontraditional fans (homonormative, queer, or trans* fans, who watch the contest for its camp appeal) who constitute Eurovision's national telephone voters *and* to the recently introduced national judging panels composed of music professionals who award 50% of their nation's votes.

At Eurovision 2014, Russia's annexation of the Crimea two months before the Song Contest provided the immediate regional/global context that year. The general anti-Russian sentiment the annexation generated at least in the West and in the Western-facing regions of the remaining Ukraine ensured that the Russian act performing in Copenhagen—twin sisters whose song was by Eurovision standards not bad at all—was booed and awarded only four out of a potential twelve points from Ukraine. In turn, the Ukrainian act was booed by a small contingent of pro-Russian audience members and received only seven out of a possible twelve points from Russia. Sentiments around Russia's federal antigay 'propaganda' law also fed into Eurovision 2014. While in the news since its passage in 2013, this Russian law became a focal point of European and international contention during the Russian-hosted Sochi Winter Olympics three months before the Song Contest, further mobilizing support for or opposition against its figuration of the 'homosexual' as perverse (for general debates, see Wilkinson 2013; 2014). It was against this geopolitical background that the 'bearded drag queen' Tom Neuwirth and/as Conchita Wurst performed at and won Eurovision 2014.

That a self-identified 'homosexual' drag queen would win Eurovision 2014 comes as little surprise, particularly to 'LGBT/queer/trans*' Eurovision fans who have watched the event year on year. This is both because the self-identified trans* Israeli singer Dana International who Neuwirth/Wurst cites as an inspiration won Eurovision in 1998 (Halutz 2014)[3] and because the 'LGBT/queer/trans*' Eurovision fan base has grown so large over the years that some commentators describe Eurovision as 'the Gay World Cup', 'gay Christmas', or 'Passover for homos' (for discussion, see Baker 2014a). And in 2015, Australia was invited to be a guest entry in the contest, a move some attributed to the vast 'LGBT/queer/trans*' Australian viewing audience. Yet that a '*bearded* drag queen' (and, as I will go on to elaborate, *this specific figuration of* the 'bearded drag queen') was even competing in the event seemed to shock and appall many 'European' political and religious leaders on the one hand and to galvanize support for a homonormative agenda of tolerance around sexual diversity on the other. What divided these two factions was how they interpreted the figuration of Neuwirth/Wurst—as *either* a 'perverse homosexual' *or* as a 'normal homosexual'—and how they connected that figuration to 'Europe'.

For example, Neuwirth/Wurst was publically reviled by some Eastern 'European' political and religious leaders in the run-up to the Eurovision finals. Russia's deputy prime minister, Dmitry Rogozin, claimed that Neuwirth/Wurst 'showed supporters of European integration their European future: a bearded girl' (quoted in Davies 2014). Russian nationalist politician Vladimir Zhirinovsky claimed Neuwirth/Wurst signified 'the end of Europe' because 'they don't have men and women any more. They have "it"'' (Davies 2014). After Neuwirth/Wurst's victory, several church leaders in the Balkans declared that the floods that devastated the region in the aftermath of Eurovision were 'divine punishment' for Neuwirth/Wurst's victory. As Patriarch Amfilohije of Montenegro put it, 'This [flood] is not a coincidence, but a warning. God sent the rains as a reminder that people should not join the wild side' (Telegraph Foreign Staff 2014). In contrast, Austrian Green MEP Ulrike Lunacek—the first openly lesbian politician in the European Parliament—led a group of MEPs from different political parties who invited Neuwirth/Wurst as Conchita Wurst to give a concert and a speech at the European Parliament after Neuwirth/Wurst's victory. At the event, Lunacek commented, 'Conchita Wurst has a very important political message, that doesn't have anything to do with parties or regular work in the party. It has to do with what the EU stands for: Equal rights, fundamental rights, the right to live your life without fear, for LGBT and other minorities' (EurActiv 2014).

What makes these incitements of Neuwirth/Wurst as a 'European' issue so interesting are two things. First, given the strong nationalist and weak pan-European' tendencies of Eurovision, it seems odd that the figuration of Neuwirth/Wurst should rise to the level of 'European' political commentary. Religious commentaries for or against Neuwirth/Wurst might be less unexpected, in light of ongoing debates in religious circles about 'homosexuality' and the 'homosexual'. But taking Neuwirth/Wurst seriously as a figuration of 'integrated Europe itself' because of her/his/their Eurovision participation and victory suggests that Eurovision is sometimes a space in which what stands for if not 'the European soul' then 'an integrated Europe' is seriously contested, if not resolved. How these contestations take place and are (momentarily) stabilized matters deeply to those nations that are identified (by themselves or by others) as 'European'.

Neuwirth/Wurst's Eurovision victory mattered for 'Europe itself', then, because—in Catherine Baker's terms—Neuwirth/Wurst's victory made her/him/them 'available as a symbol for denoting . . . ideological and geopolitical clashes' (Baker 2014b)[4] as well as agreements around what it means to be a unified and/or fractured 'Europe' and what it means to be identified as/with this 'Europe'. Neuwirth/Wurst as 'integrated Europe itself', then, was not some purely cultural symbol of 'the gay world cup' (as if a culture vs. politics dichotomy were sustainable; for critiques, see, e.g., Weber 2013). Neuwirth/Wurst was a battleground in national and 'European' political disputes over which specific, singular understanding of Neuwirth/Wurst—as the 'perverse homosexual' or as the 'normal homosexual'—might function as the logos in the logocentric procedure of 'statecraft as mancraft' (Ashley 1989) to ground 'European' statecraft and 'Europe itself'.

What else makes these incitements around Neuwirth/Wurst as a 'European' issue so interesting is how individual national and collective pan-'European' attempts to stabilize Neuwirth/Wurst as either the singular 'perverse homosexual' who marked 'the end of Europe' or as the singular 'normal homosexual' who marked a new age of the tolerance of diversity for 'Europe' seemed to fail. For as Neuwirth/Wurst was put into national and pan-'European' discourses of power/knowledge/pleasure, he/she/they always seemed to convey more than *either* the 'normal homosexual' *or* the 'perverse homosexual'. What else Neuwirth/Wurst seemed to convey was the 'normal *and/or* perverse homosexual'—the plural logoi of a queer logic of statecraft that abides by a pluralized Barthesian logic of the *and/or*. In so doing, Neuwirth/Wurst calls into question the very spatial arrangements of sovereignty—both horizontally and vertically—that an *either/or* logic of statecraft as mancraft is called upon to place beyond question.

In their figurations of Neuwirth/Wurst, 'European' leaders failed to consider Neuwirth/Wurst through the lens of queer logics of statecraft, mobilizing Neuwirth/Wurst through traditional logics of statecraft as mancraft, as if Neuwirth/Wurst and/as 'an integrated Europe' were knowable and placeable within the *either/or* dichotomous terms of 'European' horizontal or vertical space. This is why their debate was about the value or lack thereof of 'European' integration as imagined in the same terms 'European' integration had been imagined since the end of World War II. As a result, these European leaders generally failed to consider (much less appreciate) what plural constituted Neuwirth/Wurst and how the plural *and/or* logic he/she/they embodies is what made 'European' attempts to claim or disown—to normalize or to pervert—this normal *and/or* perverse figure both possible and impossible. This in part explains why national and pan-'European' attempts to regiment Neuwirth/Wurst as a singular vision of 'integrated Europe itself' seemed to be anything but ahistorical and natural.

The remainder of this chapter unpacks Neuwirth/Wurst's figuration as/ of the 'Eurovisioned bearded drag queen'. It does this by making three moves. First, it reads Neuwirth/Wurst's figuration of the 'Eurovisioned bearded drag queen' as both a Barthesian plural figure in general and as what Gloria Anzaldúa calls 'a border figure' more specifically. This reading establishes Neuwirth/Wurst as an *and/or* figure in relation to sexes, genders, and sexualities, which is how Neuwirth/Wurst is commonly read. Yet, second, this reading also explores Neuwirth/Wurst as a pluralized 'border figure' in the registers of race, geopolitics, and traditional understandings of religious and secular authority as well. All of this arguably situates Neuwirth/Wurst as a figure who could be called upon to serve as a queer logoi in a queer logics of statecraft as mancraft but who seems to defy traditional *either/or* logics of statecraft, which raises the question this chapter addresses in its third reading of Neuwirth/Wurst. That question is—how is it possible for 'European' leaders to figure Neuwirth/Wurst through an *either/or* logic as if Neuwirth/Wurst were a singular, ahistorical logos of statecraft as mancraft, when so much evidence suggests this is not the case? My answer in part lies in an exploration of how 'European' leaders mobilized many of the earlier figurations discussed in this book—of the 'perverse homosexual' (as the 'underdeveloped', the 'undevelopable', the 'unwanted im/migrant', and the 'terrorist) versus the 'normal homosexual (as 'LGBT rights holder')—to figure Neuwirth/Wurst as the 'Eurovisioned bearded drag queen' as *either* a new normalized figure to be celebrated *or* as a long-standing perverse figure who threatens 'Europe itself'.

THE 'EUROVISIONED BEARDED DRAG QUEEN'

Neuwirth/Wurst in the Borderlands of the Normal *and/or* Perverse

A borderland is a vague and undetermined place created by the emotional residue of an unnatural boundary. It is in a constant state of transition. The prohibited and forbidden are its inhabitants. *Los atravesados* [the crossers] live here: the squint-eyed, the perverse, the queer, the troublesome, the mongrel, the mulato, the half-breed, the half dead; in short, those who cross over, pass over, or go through the confines of the "normal". (Anzaldúa 1987, 3)

Tom Neuwirth and/as Conchita Wurst is a figure found in the borderlands of sex, gender, sexuality, race, geopolitics, and secular and religious authority who may be said to continuously 'cross over, pass over, or go through the confines of the "normal"' (Anzaldúa 1987, 3). This sometimes makes Neuwirth/Wurst appear to be perverse, as in Anzaldúa's depiction of the border figure. Yet, as I will argue here, it also makes Neuwirth/Wurst appear to be both normal *and/or* perverse in general and in particular in debates about 'European integration'.

In 'European' discourses around Eurovision, it is sexes, genders, and sexualities that are the most commented-upon axis of Neuwirth/Wurst's borderland figuration. This seems to be because both in name (Conchita/shell/vagina + Wurst/sausage/penis) and in appearance, Neuwirth/Wurst crosses a number of sexed, gendered, and sexualized binary borders—male versus female, masculine versus feminine, heterosexual versus homosexual. As Tom Neuwirth, Neuwirth/Wurst appears to be (more compatible with normalized understandings of the) male, masculine, and 'homosexual' than Neuwirth/Wurst appears as Conchita Wurst, who is figured as (more compatible with normalized understandings of the) female, feminine, and heterosexual than is Tom.

This understanding of Tom Neuwirth as opposed to Conchita Wurst is found not only in how 'European' leaders and the press more generally discuss Neuwirth/Wurst in relation to Eurovision but also on Neuwirth/Wurst's conchitawurst.com website. On the biography page of the website, Tom is described as a 'private person' who suffered discrimination during his teenage years, which Neuwirth/Wurst has talked about elsewhere as being because of Tom's 'homosexuality' (Bromwich 2014; Wurst 2015). Throughout Tom's bio, Tom is sexed and gendered through the male and masculine pronoun 'he'. In contrast, Conchita Wurst is described as 'the art figure' Tom created. Conchita is sexed and gendered through the female and feminine pronoun 'she' throughout. No mention is made of Conchita's sexuality on the web page, although elsewhere Neuwirth/Wurst has spoken of Conchita Wurst as in a relationship with 'my handsome husband [the performance artist] Jacque in Paris', who Neuwirth/Wurst refers to using male and masculine pronouns (Adams 2012). Conchita's relationship with Jacque makes her otherwise ambiguous sexuality recoverable within a straight, heterosexual logic that pairs female figures with male partners.

What we have here, then, is Tom as the male, 'perverse homosexual' who performatively expresses his 'homosexuality' by creating 'the art figure' Conchita Wurst as an impersonation of (a more normalizable, if exaggerated) female heterosexuality. In so doing, then, the 'drag queen' Neuwirth/Wurst appears to cross over and pass over sexed, gendered, and sexualized binaries of male versus female, masculine versus feminine, and heterosexual versus homosexual.

On some readings, this is enough to make Neuwirth/Wurst a queer figure, a figure who—in Anzaldúa's terms—'go[es] through the confines of the "normal"' (1987, 3), just like the other 'perverse' and 'troublesome' border figures Anzaldúa describes. Yet reading Anzaldúa more closely, we notice that she complicates her understanding of the 'border figure' through her account of its locations, movements, and temporalities. This is made clear in Anzaldúa's account of the U.S.-Mexico border as '*una herida abierta* [an open wound] where the Third World grates against the first and bleeds' (1987, 3) and of how the 'border figure' (specifically the 'lesbian Chicana' for Anzaldúa) is positioned in relation to this border. Anzaldúa writes:

I press my hand to the steel curtain – —
chainlink fence crowned with rolled barbed wire . . .

1,950 mile-long open wound
   dividing a *pueblo* [town/community], a culture
   running down the length of my body
     staking fence rods in my flesh,
     splits me splits me
       me raja me raja

   This is my home
   this thin edge of
     barbwire (Anzaldúa 1987, 2–3).

In this poetic passage, Anzaldúa positions the 'border figure' as someone who does not just 'cross over, pass over or go through' a border (1987, 3); she positions this figure as one who is so impaled by a border that they both live on and *as* 'a dividing line' in that 'vague and undetermined place created by the emotional residue of an unnatural boundary' (1987, 3). This 'dividing line' can be found in the intimate spaces of the body and the home, the local or national spaces of *el pueblo* and the international spaces between and among sovereign nation-states. And it can refer to any 'dividing line' found in these spaces—from those attempting to divide sexes, genders, and sexualities to those attempting to divide races, civilizations, and geopolitical territories, for example.

Because the 'border figure' both crosses and lives on/as the border, the 'border figure' suggests both mobility and immobility. For wherever the 'border figure' moves, it carries within itself its border(s), its home—'this thin edge of barbed wire' that maintains it as 'an open wound'. In so doing, the 'border figure' suggests that when *los atravesados* are on the move, their borders are on the move with/in them. This is how the 'border figure' puts the border on the move. At the same time, the 'border figure' disrupts progressive spatial and temporal narratives of forward mobility. For the border lives in the 'border figure' as a *persistent* presence—as a moment of static, a constant crack[le], a nonprogressive, out-of-sync pause—that distorts progressive narratives of spatial and temporal movement across/ at the border. It does this by appearing as a *here and now*, even as it presumably moves to and between a *there and then*. This is not to say that the border itself is static immobility. To the contrary, the border is 'in a constant state of transition' (Anzaldúa 1987, 3). Rather, then, it is to suggest that it is this very state of *constant* transition—a transition that is in a sustained state of transitioning without ever arriving at a state of having fully transitioned—that confronts and possibly provokes those who encounter the 'border subject'.

As a mobile figure who carries its variously implanted borders with/in it, the 'border figure' is reminiscent of many of the figurations discussed in chapter 4—from the 'unwanted im/migrant' to the 'queer diasporic subject'. For as each of these figurations moves, their borders (e.g., North vs. South, developed vs. underdeveloped, homeless vs. feeling at home) move with them. Yet there is something else that is distinctive about the particular 'border figure' that emerges from Anzaldúa's work and that I want to suggest is akin to how Neuwirth/Wurst functions as a 'border figure'. That distinctiveness is what I think of—following Sedgwick—as a queer distinctiveness. It is a distinctiveness that makes it impossible for this 'border figure' to signify monolithically on one side or the other of a border, a dividing line, a binary opposition in relation to sexes, genders, and sexualities. This might be because the 'border subject'—as a carrier of the border within—cannot signify as one thing or another. Or—as I want to suggest it functions in Anzaldúa's work and in Neuwirth/Wurst's performative embodiment of the 'drag queen'—it might be because this 'border figure' (also) *will not* signify as one thing or another.

What is distinctive about both Anzaldúa's figuration of the 'queer Chicana' and Neuwirth/Wurst's mobilization of the 'drag queen' is that in both cases, these 'border figures' deliberately *refuse* to keep to one side or the other of the various binaries that attempt to hold them and their desires in place and in time. They deliberately *refuse* to signify monolithically. And their refusals are arguably rooted in a specific (personal and/or political) project that—while differently articulated—is something they have in common. In this shared project, their aim seems to be to make the border itself a point of contestation by drawing attention to the various borderlands their particular 'border figure' inhabits as/in 'the emotional residue of . . . unnatural boundar[ies]' (Anzaldúa 1987, 3). This is arguably what Anzaldúa's specific figuration of the 'queer Chicana' does and what Tom Neuwirth and/as Conchita Wurst's specific figuration of the 'drag queen' does.

For Anzaldúa, this refusal comes in the form of living on/as the border as the 'queer Chicana'. For Neuwirth/Wurst, it comes in the form of inhabiting the figuration of the 'male homosexual as drag queen'. For Neuwirth/Wurst, this inhabiting is not (as it so often is in relation to this figuration) as a figure who can pass as (hyper)female, (hyper)feminine and/or (hyper)heterosexual. Instead, it is as a figure who cannot *and will not pass* as *either* traditionally male *or* female, masculine *or* feminine, heterosexual *or* homosexual. This figure is, of course, the 'bearded drag queen' or the 'bearded lady' (as Neuwirth/Wurst refers to this figure). For Neuwirth/Wurst, Conchita's highly manicured beard functions as a masculinity disruptive to her otherwise female/feminine/heterosexual figurations. Unlike the beards of the 'white hipster' or the 'racialized-as-nonwhite Muslim', Conchita's closely cropped beard is worn at Eurovision as more of a five o'clock shadow that poses questions about her sex, her gender, and her sexuality and (as I will argue later) her nationality, her civilization, and her race without resolving any of these questions. This makes Neuwirth/Wurst a figure who provokes questions about borders and bordering practices by living on/as rather than just moving through those borders[5] that attempt to define him/her/them and confine him/her/them to *either* the normal *or* the perverse.

The figures of the 'bearded drag queen' and the 'bearded lady' both have long histories that precede Neuwirth/Wurst's mobilization of them. As it has been mobilized in queer histories of theater and performance, the 'bearded drag queen' dates back to at least its use by the Cockettes, a 1960s/1970s 'genderfuck' performance collective formed in San Francisco (Stryker and Van Buskirk 1996, 63) that included 'an eclectic mix of gay and straight, black and white, men and women' (Scott 2002), including bearded drag queens.

The figure of the 'bearded lady' has a much longer—and strikingly different—history. Most accounts of the 'bearded lady' figure her as a female Christian saint who refuses 'to get married and enter the patriarchal order (Guenther 2015). This is what the stories associated with Saint Galla (who grew a beard after being widowed), Saint Paula (who told a virgin who grew a beard that this would deter rapists), and the variously named Saint Wilgefortis / Saint Starosta / Saint Uncumber (who grew a beard to prevent her marriage, only to be crucified by her affronted father) all suggest (Guenther 2015; also see Johnson 2007; Krappe 1945; Wallace 2014). In each of these cases, the 'bearded lady' is 'a border figure' who is out of sync—is a deliberate static (Barthes 1976, 9)—with respect to patriarchy, heterosexual marriage, and (reproductive) heterosexual sex. Because she looks to a Christian God as her sanctuary, she is further positioned as embracing eschatological time as a way to refuse progressive reproductive temporality.

As a figure who is fearful of what will happen to her in the home or in the name of the patriarchal authority who rules the home (heterosexual sex, rape, marriage), the 'bearded lady' embodies the unorthodox reinterpretation of 'homophobia' that one of Anzaldúa's lesbian students articulated. On this student's account, 'homophobia' does not refer to the fear of the 'homosexual' or of 'homosexuality'. Rather, it refers to the 'fear of going home. And of not being taken in' (1987, 20). It is also fear of the 'reigning order of heterosexual males', marked by their 'sexual lust and lust for power and destruction' that figure '*los atravesados*'/'the crossers' as 'unacceptable, faulty, damaged' (1987, 20).

The 'bearded lady' is arguably that figure who—confronted with this phobia in/of the patriarchal home—defies expectations, wearing her beard 'to oppose openly and resolutely, with daring or with effrontery'[6] the unnatural borders of sexed, gendered, and sexualized authority as they are anchored in and as they attempt to anchor her into the traditional patriarchal home. Indeed, in the story of the variously named Saint Wilgefortis / Saint Starosta / Saint Uncumber, this 'bearded lady' does not just grow a beard to escape her marriage, she actively prays to God to help her maintain her vow of chastity, and God replies by giving her a beard to repel her future husband (Rabadi 2002). This explains why the 'bearded lady' is commonly referred to as the 'bearded virgin' or the 'bearded madonna', and it demonstrates the connection between the 'bearded lady' and the Christian God. This, then, is one way in which Neuwirth/Wurst's figuration of the 'bearded drag queen' as the 'bearded lady' engages with Christian theology.

In addition to figuring himself/herself/themselves as the 'bearded lady', there is yet another way that Neuwirth/Wurst is connected to Christian theology. This is through Neuwirth/Wurst's consumption as 'a Jesus-like figure', 'a gay Jesus', 'an inverted Christ figure'.[7] While Neuwirth/Wurst never verbalizes this connection, he/she/they provoke this reading—both through his/her/their appearance and through how he/she/they performed the song 'Rise Like a Phoenix' at Eurovision. For 'Rise Like a Phoenix' is an anthem celebrating a resurrection, and as Neuwirth/Wurst performs it, Neuwirth/Wurst stretches his/her/their arms out to the side, evoking the image of Christ on the cross.

What we have in Neuwirth/Wurst, then, is a persona who performatively inhabits at least three figurations of the bearded, 'gowned' body at the same time—the 'bearded lady', the '(inverted) Christ', and the 'bearded drag queen'. By crossing without fully combining these figures, Neuwirth/Wurst effectively weaves them and their previously separate and separable histories together. The result is a queer border figure who contains within itself as many barbs as Christ's crown of thorns and as much barbed wire as Anzaldúa's border fence. The effect is to add a queer link in the 'Great Chain of Being' running from a Christian God in heaven to His heavenly Son on earth to a Saintly Bearded Woman to a Bearded Drag Queen.

It is as this complexly crossed (unholy) trinity of the 'bearded lady', the '(inverted) Christ', and the 'Eurovisioned bearded drag queen' that Neuwirth/Wurst rises like a phoenix out of the ashes of death to seek retribution on behalf of those 'troubling', 'unrecognizable' figures who are tormented by earthly familial, national, and religious authorities who attempt to police the boundaries between as well as arrange the unifications of presumably opposed sexes and genders in a heterosexual, patriarchal order. Sounding like a resurrected Saint Wilgefortis / Saint Starosta / Saint Uncumber confronting the father who crucified her, Neuwirth/Wurst sings:

> Rise like a phoenix
> Out of the ashes
> Seeking rather than vengeance
> Retribution
> You were warned
> Once I'm transformed
> Once I'm reborn
> You know I will rise like a phoenix
> But you're my flame (Mason et al. 2014)[8]

Once the votes were counted, Neuwirth/Wurst was declared the winner of Eurovision 2014. With the Eurovision Song Contest and all it suggests about 'European integration' as his/her/their platform, Neuwirth/Wurst offered this as his/her/their victory speech: 'This night is dedicated to everyone who believes in a future of peace and freedom. You know who you are—we are unity and we are unstoppable' (BBC 2014). Upon uttering these words, Neuwirth/Wurst faced the audience with a defiant look on his/her/their face and thrust the Eurovision trophy into the air. Backstage, Neuwirth/Wurst elaborated on his/her/their victory remarking, 'I dream of a world where we don't have to talk about unnecessary things like sexuality, who you love. I felt like tonight Europe showed that we are a community of respect and tolerance' (BBC 2014).

As a figure who uses sexes, genders, and sexualities to cross religious and secular authority as a way to authorize 'Europe' as 'a community of respect and tolerance', Neuwirth/Wurst fuses the 'European community' with 'respect and tolerance' of sexed, gendered, and sexualized variance. In so doing, Neuwirth/Wurst stands as a figure of defiance in relation to the double understanding of homophobia discussed above—as the fear of the 'homosexual' and of 'homosexuality' on the one hand and as the fear in the 'homosexual' of the home, on the other. What is less apparent—and, indeed, what is often actively concealed—is how Neuwirth/Wurst embodies a third meaning of 'homophobia'—what I would call fear in the 'homosexual' of the homeland.

This third understanding of homophobia seems to be the very thing that Neuwirth/Wurst's victory at Eurovision triumphs over. For it is this victory that Neuwirth/Wurst mobilizes to christen a newly figured respectful and tolerant 'European community'. This 'European community', Neuwirth/Wurst is suggesting, is not a place that the 'homosexual' has to fear. But by temporalizing this 'European community' as having emerged 'tonight', Neuwirth/Wurst does two things. First, Neuwirth/Wurst suggests this respectful and tolerant 'European community' is the culmination of a progressive 'European' journey to 'a world where we don't have to talk about unnecessary things like sexuality, who you love' (BBC 2014). At the same time, Neuwirth/Wurst simultaneously concedes that the 'European Community' did not exist with this respect and tolerance for 'homosexuality' and the 'homosexual' before 'tonight'. In other words, before the Eurovision 2014 final, 'homosexual' figures like Neuwirth/Wurst may well have lived in fear of their homelands. And, quite specifically, it seems that Tom Neuwirth *before* Conchita Wurst was one of those 'homosexuals' who explicitly *did* fear his homeland because of how he as a 'homosexual' was treated there.

This understanding of homophobia as the fear in the 'homosexual' of the homeland and Neuwirth/Wurst's complicated relationship to this understanding of homophobia finds expression in the official biographical details about Neuwirth/Wurst, Tom Neuwirth, and Conchita Wurst that were circulated before, during, and in the immediate aftermath of

Eurovision 2014. To make this case, let's begin by considering the version of Neuwirth/Wurst's conchitawurst.com biography page that was available at the time of Eurovision in May 2014. Titled 'CONCHITA WURST biography', this page begins with a quote for which there is no attribution—'Two hearts beating in my chest'. Underneath this quote is the following paragraph:

> They are a team just working in sync. Although they have never met before—they are constantly missing each other in the mirror. The private person Tom Neuwirth and the art figure Conchita Wurst respect each other from the bottom of their hearts. They are two individual characters with their own individual stories, but with one essential message for tolerance and against discrimination.[9]

After offering separate biographies for Tom and Conchita, the page concludes with an explanation of how Conchita came into being, noting:

> Because of the discrimination against Tom in his teenage-years, he created Conchita, The Bearded Lady, as a statement. A statement for tolerance and acceptance—as it's not about appearances: it's about the human being. 'Everybody should live their lives the way they want, as long as nobody else gets hurt or is restricted in their own way of life'.

In a later version of the biography page, Conchita's genealogy with respect to Tom is further clarified.

> Conchita owes her existence to the fact that Tom had been dealing with discrimination all his life. Therefore he created a woman with a beard—a striking statement and catalyst for discussions about terms like "different" and "normal", as well as a vehicle to bring his message to the entire world in a clear and unmistakable way.[10]

On the surface, this story of how Conchita Wurst came to embody Tom Neuwirth's 'striking statement' against discrimination seems to be a rejection of only the first two understandings of homophobia discussed above (as well as of a wide range of phobias of sex-/gender-/sexuality-variant people). Yet if we read Neuwirth/Wurst though the specific details about Tom and Conchita provided on the biography page of conchitawurst.com and elsewhere around the time of Eurovision 2014, we can trace how the additional understanding of homophobia as the fear in the 'homosexual' of the homeland is embedded in these figures. On conchitawurst.com, Tom's and Conchita's bios read like this:

Tom
- born on 6.11.1988 in Gmunden.
- raised in the Styrian countryside.
- Tom appeared in 2007 on the Austrian casting show 'Starmania'.
- He graduated from the Graz School of Fashion in 2011.
- and since then he has lived in various locations in Vienna.

Conchita
- born in the mountains of Colombia.
- and raised in Germany.
- She appeared in 2011 on the Austrian casting show 'Die große Chance'.
- and was one of the national contestants for the ESC [Eurovision Song Contest] in 2012.
- and is the Austrian representative for ESC in 2014.[11]

Here, Tom is figured as an Austrian birthright citizen, making him 'European'. While not mentioned on the bio page, Tom's apparent whiteness allows him to be read as not just 'European' but as 'properly European'. In contrast, Conchita is figured as a Colombian citizen who—because she was raised in Germany—might also be a German citizen. A biography of Conchita that was widely circulated after Neuwirth/Wurst's selection in September 2013 as Austria's representative to Eurovision 2014 offers further details about Conchita.

Conchita Wurst grew up in the Colombian highlands surrounded by the sound of swinging powder puffs and the rustling of layers made out of delicate tulle. One day her mother, a popular actress, met by fate her father, Alfred of Knack and Wurst, an even more successful theater director—and fell in love with him. Within that same year she gave birth to her first daughter Conchita, named after the great-grandmother BarbadaConchita (the Bearded). It soon became obvious that the small "Knackwurst" was determined to become someone great and successful (Konstantopoulos 2013).

Because this September 2013 biography was most widely circulated in Austria, it is important to tease out the play on words in Conchita's father's name—Alfred of Knack and Wurst. Wurst, as noted above, refers literally to 'sausage' and figuratively to 'penis' or the colloquial expression 'It doesn't matter', which Neuwirth/Wurst says refers to how it doesn't and shouldn't matter what one's gender presentation is or who one loves. Knack is also a loaded term in German. It literally means "attractive, juicy, voluptuous' and generally refers to a bursting sound, as in the sound of the knack-wurst (German sausage) busting out of its skin. Together, these meanings of knack combine in another popular German expression—knackarsch, which refers to a voluptuous ass bursting attractively out of one's tight jeans. This is what is suggested by Conchita 'the small "Knackwurst", who goes on to find fame in 'Europe'. Combined with Neuwirth/Wurst's figuration as the 'homosexual', what is also suggested by Conchita's linage to Knack and Wurst is the entire scene of sodomy (the nice ass and the bursting penis).[12]

Read together, what these biographical details about Tom and Conchita tell us is that it was the third understanding of homophobia—homophobia as fear in the 'homosexual' of the homeland—that seems to have led Tom Neuwirth to create Conchita Wurst.[13] This is because Tom invented Conchita not just as a strikingly sexed, gendered, and sexualized statement about 'difference' and defiance but also as a strikingly transnational and transracial refuge from the homophobia he experienced in his Austrian homeland. For Conchita is not merely Austrian or 'European', as Tom is; she is a figure who was 'born in the mountains of Colombia'—a place romanticized in Western coffee bean advertisements that would play well in Viennese coffee culture[14]—to a Colombian mother and German father before being raised in Germany. She is the product of a transnational family, and it is her maternal Colombian linage that accounts for her appearance as the 'bearded lady'. What might be implied here is that it is only in the imagined idyllic space of Colombia—like the imagined idyllic space of the city—where the nonheteronormative bearded Conchitas can find acceptance.[15]

Conchita's pedigree also potentially marks her as transracial, an aspect of the 'border figure' that is foreshadowed in Anzaldúa's poetic claim that the border fence, 'me raja' (it splits me). For the Spanish word *raja* can be used to signify sex (*raja* means vagina) and race (*tener raja* means to have black blood). From a dominant Western perspective, then, this puts the 'purity' of Conchita's race and 'Europeanness' into doubt, further figuring Conchita through the trope of racial degeneration as racial mixing (Bhabha 1994; Stoler 1995; Hoad 2000). For Conchita might be 'indigenous' and/or 'white' and/or some other type of 'mestiza' or 'black-blooded' figure, just as she might be Colombian like her mother and/or German like her father and/or Austrian like Tom who performs her.

These additional biographical details about Tom and Conchita, then, multiply the axes upon which Conchita functions in Neuwirth/Wurst's triangulated *and/or* logics. For while Neuwirth/Wurst relies upon Conchita's (and Tom's) *and/or* sexes, genders, and sexualities to compose a fundamental part of his/her/their (unholy) trinity of religious and secular authority, Neuwirth/Wurst also relies upon these very same *and/or* logics to compose two additional trinities in which Conchita, Tom, and Neuwirth/Wurst are embedded—one around nationality (Colombian, German, Austrian) and another around race (indigenous, white, mestiza). At the same time, in the register of 'civilization' Neuwirth/Wurst also resembles 'the half and half' figure Anzaldúa describes as 'the coming together of [presumed] opposite qualities within' (1987, 19). For while Neuwirth/Wurst remains (because both Tom and Conchita remain) within what Samuel Huntington calls the civilization of Western Christendom, Neuwirth/Wurst is impaled with the very barbed wire border that Anzaldúa critiques and that Huntington reifies—between what Anzaldúa calls the 'First World' and the 'Third World' (1987, 3) and between what Huntington calls 'the American Creed' and 'the Hispanic Challenge' (2009).

By creating Colombian Conchita as Austrian Tom's refuge from his fear of the homeland, then, Neuwirth/Wurst stands as a defiant reversal of dominant Western discourses that inscribe 'border figures' and 'trans-type figures'—as they are variously sexed, gendered, sexualized, racialized, nationalized, and civilizationalized—as anarchical dangers in/ to all manner of binary logics. These binary logics include the primary logic of traditional statecraft—order versus anarchy. Furthermore, by fashioning Conchita as a 'transborder figure' who travels from the 'savage Hispanic-mestizo civilization' that is the legacy of imperial Spain to 'civilized Europe', Tom puts Conchita's (and Tom's and Neuwirth/Wurst's) sexes, genders, sexualities, races, nationalities, and civilizations on the move from the global South to the 'European' homeland. In so doing, this '*Eurovisioned* bearded drag queen' not only grates against the unnatural border between 'proper Europeanness' and 'less proper Europeanness', he/ she/they also threaten to bring 'the violence of the world we live in *at the heart of the home* [and, I would add, at the heart of the homeland], at the heart of the national self' (Fortier 2008, 60; also see Ahmed 2000; Salecl 2004, 24; Žižek 1998; and see chapter 4 on the unwanted im/migrant), even as it makes Conchita's 'rise like a phoenix' as 'European' at Eurovision possible.

Overall, then, Neuwirth/Wurst as a pluralized *and/or* figure combats homophobia, but not just by replacing traditional homophobic fears of 'homosexuality' and the 'homosexual' with tolerance and an appreciation of difference. For Neuwirth/Wurst's strategy to combat traditional homophobia is rooted in his/her/their demand for an acknowledgment of another type of homophobia—fear in the 'homosexual' of the homeland. It is because of this demand that Neuwirth/Wurst puts sexes, genders, and sexualities *as well as* nationality, race, and civilization on the move in order to create Conchita as a transnational, transracial, transcivilizational refuge from homophobia for Tom and other victims of all manner of phobias, including homophobia, over variances in sexes, genders, and sexualities. This appears to be why Neuwirth/Wurst crosses spatial and temporal binaries as well as religious and secular boundaries to constitute himself/herself/themselves as a phoenix rising from the ashes of

'European' homophobia with the authority to seek vengeance on behalf of a wide array of 'transborder figures'.

It is as a triple trinity around authority, nationality, and race that necessarily expresses itself through sexes, genders, and sexualities that Neuwirth/Wurst becomes available to 'Europe' as a potential plural logoi of a queer 'European' statecraft as mancraft, upon whom a queerly imagined 'integrated Europe' might be grounded. For Neuwirth/Wurst both embraces and pushes beyond traditional understandings of sovereignty in the vertical and horizontal terms 'European' integrationists have long desired (Walker 2000). As a 'transborder figure' embodying both the possibilities and the impossibilities of integration, Neuwirth/Wurst is the queer guarantor of the vertical 'Great Chain of Being' between Christian godly and earthly authority and is the 'transnational/racial/civilizational' figure who queerly extends the horizontal reach(es) of 'the European homeland itself'. In so doing, Neuwirth/Wurst becomes a figure through whom a thorough rethinking of what the process of 'European integration' might mean and what a sovereign 'integrated Europe' might be becomes possible.

This is not to say that Neuwirth/Wurst's figuration of the 'Eurovisioned bearded drag queen' is unproblematic. A critical reading of Neuwirth/Wurst's figuration might point to Neuwirth/Wurst as (yet another) colonialist appropriation and/or 'tropicalist' appropriation (Aparicio and Chávez-Silverman 1997; also see Amar 2011)[16] of race through the performance of brownface,[17] culture through the performance of Colombianness, and exotic femininity through the performance of the hyperfeminized and disruptively masculinized 'bearded lady'.[18] It would also note that trans* people bear the burden of the backlash against 'the artistic character' Conchita Wurst, whereas 'the private person' Tom Neuwirth who does not identify as trans* can escape much this trans*phobia in his everyday life (Baker 2014a; also see Northup 2014). My point here, then, is neither to celebrate nor condemn Neuwirth/Wurst's complex figuration. Instead, my point is to underscore how Neuwirth/Wurst as a 'transborder figure' offers a queer (while still problematic and certainly not feminist) challenge to traditional understandings of 'European integration' and of a 'simple sovereign man' (Soto 2010, 3–4) as the foundation of a (simply) sovereign 'integrated Europe'.

It is my argument that this queer challenge to rethink integration and 'an integrated Europe itself' is only possible by utilizing the lens of a queer logic of statecraft, which appreciates the multiple pluralities Neuwirth/Wurst's queer *and/or* figuration crafts and mobilizes. Yet this is not how 'European' leaders engaged with Neuwirth/Wurst. Whether to embrace Neuwirth/Wurst or to oppose him/her/them, 'European' leaders instead uniformly insisted upon inserting Neuwirth/Wurst into familiar *either/or* logics of statecraft as mancraft, in which Neuwirth/Wurst had to stand for *either* one thing *or* another in all of his/her/their many registers. It is to these readings of Neuwirth/Wurst through the binary logics of traditional statecraft as mancraft that I now turn.

Neuwirth/Wurst as *Either* the 'Normal Homosexual' *or* the 'Perverse Homosexual'

Who is the 'homosexual' Tom Neuwirth and/as the bearded drag queen Conchita Wurst? What type of '(homo)sexuality' and what type of relationship to '(homo)sexuality' does Neuwirth/Wurst figure for 'an integrated Europe'?

These questions framed 'European' debates about Neuwirth/Wurst before, during and after the 2014 Eurovision Song Contest. How they framed 'European' debates was by engaging with Neuwirth/Wurst as a figure who was knowable and placeable in relation to dichotomous understandings of space, time, and desire along axes of sex, gender, sexuality, race, geopolitics, and religious and secular narratives of authority. It was by mobilizing the *either/or* logic through which these terms were made to operate that some 'European' leaders attempted to impose and stabilize their account of Neuwirth/Wurst as a proposed sovereign logos of 'European' statecraft as mancraft.

While 'European' leaders explicitly disagreed over the 'true nature' of Neuwirth/Wurst, they implicitly agreed that Neuwirth/Wurst had a true, singular, ahistorical nature. They agreed, in other words, that Neuwirth/ Wurst was *either* normal *or* perverse. And because Neuwirth/Wurst's true nature was performed at Eurovision, they further agreed that Neuwirth/ Wurst's true nature was connected to (or possibly stood for) 'integrated Europe itself'. For these 'European' leaders, deciding the proper course for 'European' integration seemed to be as simple as deciding upon the true character of Neuwirth/Wurst as a proposed logos of an 'integrated Europe'. And the true character of Neuwirth/Wurst, it seemed, could be revealed by simply deciding if this 'homosexual' and the forms of sex, gender, and '(homo)sexuality' he/she/they championed were normal or perverse.

In the remainder of this section, I detail how this *either/or* logic of a 'European' statecraft as mancraft attempted to stabilize Neuwirth/Wurst as *either* a normal *or* a perverse potential logos of an 'integrated Europe' by addressing the question: How did dichotomous understandings of space, time, and desire function to make Neuwirth/Wurst knowable and placeable, as/in relation to 'an integrated Europe'? To answer this question, I begin by tracing how some 'European' leaders figured Neuwirth/Wurst as the 'perverse homosexual' before I examine how other 'European' leaders figured Neuwirth/Wurst as the 'normal homosexual'.

Neuwirth/Wurst as the 'Perverse Homosexual'

Before, during, and after Eurovision 2014, Neuwirth/Wurst divided 'European' opinion. Some widely circulated comments by mostly Eastern European leaders (especially from Russia[19] and the Balkans) figured Neuwirth/Wurst as 'perverse', while some widely circulated comments by mostly Western European leaders figured Neuwirth/Wurst as 'normal'. Some people took this as evidence of an East versus West divide over Neuwirth/Wurst as a figure who stood for unorthodox types of integration, including 'European integration itself'. Yet an East versus West dichotomy is insufficient to explain how coalitions formed around Neuwirth/Wurst and his/her/their meaning in relation to 'Europe itself'. This is for two primary reasons.

First, some 'Western European' leaders embraced denunciations of Neuwirth/Wurst as perverse (integration). For these 'Western European' leaders, this opposition was rooted in their political, social, and religious conservatism, as the most vocally opposed to Neuwirth/Wurst were all located on the far right of the 'Western European' political spectrum. For 'Eastern European' leaders, this opposition was rooted in this same conservatism. Yet it was also rooted in how 'Eastern Europeans' had historically experienced post–Cold War 'European integration' as a Western bloc political project to contain Eastern bloc territorial expansion in 'Europe' and as a Western bloc economic strategy to foster capitalism in a postwar 'Europe' presented with a communist alternative. At the time of Eurovision 2014, 'European integration' was perceived by especially far-right Russian leaders as an attempt to (further) isolate Russia in (relation to) 'Europe' by wooing an increasing number of (former) Eastern bloc states into the EU, including Ukraine.

For an array of complicated reasons, then, Neuwirth/Wurst united many far-right 'European' leaders in the new 'culture wars' in 'Europe'. As Alina Polyakova explains,

> In the renewed culture war between Western social liberalism and Eastern traditional conservatism for which Conchita Wurst has become a symbol, Europe's far-right parties have stood with the Russians. In its party program, Austria's FPÖ defines family as "a partnership between a man and woman with common children." UKIP's Nigel Farage has said that gay marriage in France was unnecessary. (Polyakova 2014)

What further united many of these 'European' conservatives is their embrace of Vladimir Putin's mobilization of 'culture' to argue in favor of national sovereignty as opposed to European integration, especially around issues of monetary policy and immigration. For example, the de facto spokesperson for the 'European' far-right French ultranationalist leader Marine Le Pen 'hailed Russia's president as a true patriot and defender of European values', describing him as 'a defender of "the Christian heritage of European civilization"' (Polyakova 2014). Yet, importantly, even the 'European' Far Right was split over Neuwirth/Wurst. As Polyakova notes,

'Geert Wilders, leader of the Dutch Party for Freedom, styles himself as a promoter of gay rights, which he sees as in line with traditional Dutch values' (Polyakova 2014).

Second, just as Neuwirth/Wurst divided opinion among 'European' leaders, so too did Neuwirth/Wurst divide populations within 'European' states. This was evident in Eastern Europe, where the Russian Eurovision voting public favored Neuwirth/Wurst and the state-appointed Russian Eurovision jury opposed Neuwirth/Wurst (Rosenberg 2014; Renwick 2014). It was also evident in Western Europe, where the United Kingdom's previous long-standing Eurovision presenter Terry Wogan claimed Neuwirth/Wurst's bearded lady transformed Eurovision into a 'freak show' (Wogan 2014) while the UK Eurovision voting public placed Neuwirth/Wurst high in their rankings.

For these reasons, it is incorrect to reify some 'Eastern Europe' opposed to some 'Western Europe', some 'right-wing Europe' opposed to some 'liberal Europe' or any specific 'European' nation-state and its presumed attitudes about Neuwirth/Wurst, wherever it is located in (relations to) 'Europe'. In this section, then, I am less interested in which kind of 'European' spoke for or against Neuwirth/Wurst than I am in how comments made by variously figured 'European' leaders specifically figured Neuwirth/Wurst as *either* normal *or* perverse. While these terms—like any others—are wholly inadequate, I use the terms 'mostly Eastern European leaders' and 'mostly Western European leaders' when describing those who the press identified as primarily responsible for the statements I will go on to analyze.

The question mostly Eastern European leaders publically posed about Neuwirth/Wurst was this: *Is* this Eurovisioned figure properly integrated, *can* this Eurovisioned figure be properly integrated, and *should* this Eurovisioned figured be properly integrated socially, politically, and religiously in/as 'Europe itself'? As leaders who identified as anti-'European' integrationist politicians and as traditional Christian religious leaders, their answers were unsurprisingly no, no, and definitely not. This was because the kind of *and/or* unity Neuwirth/Wurst stood for did not accord with what they considered to be proper binary understandings of sex, gender, sexuality, race, nationality, civilization, and authority. These leaders did not try to 'appreciate the plural' logics (Barthes 1974, 5) that made Neuwirth/Wurst meaningful in/to 'Europe'. Rather—and quite importantly—they reduced Neuwirth/Wurst's pluralities to some presumably unified understanding of 'the perverse', opposed it to their presumably unified understanding of 'the normal', and set themselves up as the champions of the 'traditional', 'normal' values that Neuwirth/Wurst threatened in/as 'Europe itself'.

They did this by casting Neuwirth/Wurst as a new 'alien strain' of the 'perverse homosexual' that threatened the purity of humanity. For example, Bulgarian MEP candidate Angel Dzhambazki remarked, 'This bearded creature, called with the European name Conchita Wurst is like genetically modified organism and won the Eurovision. And I wonder, if the vice of our time is that we tolerate the perversity. I don't want such a song contest for my children' (Kosharevska 2014). As a 'bearded creature' beyond nature and natural reproduction, Neuwirth/Wurst as Conchita Wurst was also spoken of as beyond sex, as in Russian nationalist politician Vladimir Zhirinovsky's observation, 'They don't have men and women any more. They have "it" ' (Davies 2014). Neuwirth/Wurst is also figured as a perversion of the sacred connection between the Christian God and the saintly bearded lady. For example, the Russian Orthodox Church referred to Conchita Wurst as 'an abomination', claiming that her victory was 'one more step in the rejection of Christian identity of European culture' (quoted in Edgar 2014). Holding Conchita Wurst responsible for the post-Eurovision floods in the Balkans, Patriarch Amfilohije of Montenegro claimed, 'God sent the rains as a reminder that people should not join the wild side' (Telegraph Foreign Staff 2014). And Bulgarian ultranationalist VMRO (Internal Macedonian Revolutionary Organization) member Krasimir Karakachanov declared that 'the symbol of Europe must be Joan of Arc, and not Conchita Wurst' (Pitt 2014).[20] As a perversion of the 'Great Chain of Being' between God and man, then, Neuwirth/Wurst on these readings is neither a route to Christian redemption nor a figure with any redemptive qualities himself/herself/themselves.

Russian president Vladimir Putin combined these ideas in his post-Eurovision comments about Neuwirth/Wurst, stating:

> The Bible talks about the two genders, man and woman, and the main purpose of union between them is to produce children. . . . For us it is important to reaffirm traditional values. . . . I personally am very liberal (on matters of personal morality). People have the right to live their lives the way they want. But they should not be aggressive, or put it up for show. (Edgar 2014)

These statements suggest that what offend these 'European' leaders is how Neuwirth/Wurst threatens to replace the traditional family—understood as white, heterosexual, bourgeois, cisgendered, and Christian—as the proper engine of (non)biological and social reproduction. Neuwirth/Wurst does this by 'aggressively' putting on a show of his/her/their genetically modified alien perverse desires as if they expressed legitimate ways to be and to live in the world. In so doing, these leaders infer, Neuwirth/Wurst can be understood as recruiting vulnerable children into 'perverse homosexuality' through a kind of mimetic reproduction (i.e., a form of asexual reproduction that births new 'deviants' by enticing 'the innocent' to imitate 'the perverse').

If this form of asexual reproduction sounds familiar, it is because it is akin to the type of reproduction Western discourses suggest the 'al-Qaeda terrorist' uses to reproduce terrorist cells (as discussed in chapter 4). By symbolizing this sort of 'deviant' mimetic reproduction, then, Neuwirth/Wurst functions in the rhetoric of these 'European' leaders as a kind of civilizational barbarian who can never—and indeed is not meant to—sustain the traditional Christian family. Temporally, this figures Neuwirth/Wurst as beyond the bounds of Christian eschatological time (which these traditionalists claim to respect) and beyond the bounds of proper modern developmental time (which these traditionalists tie to a respect for Christian traditions). By perverting both God's time and man's time, Neuwirth/Wurst strays from two temporal trajectories at once—the Christian path to redemption and the earthly path to development. Because of his/her/

their simultaneous religious and secular failures, then, Neuwirth/Wurst is figured as the 'irredeemable undevelopable'. This makes Neuwirth/Wurst a threat to the (Christian) Malthusian couple and to the Parsonian family. This may explain why Angel Dzhambazki in an interview about Conchita Wurst commented, 'The resolution for the human rights of the third gender is absolutely an unacceptable targeting of humanity against nature' (Kosharevska 2014).

This also makes Neuwirth/Wurst a threat to the nation, to 'European civilization', and to 'Europe itself'. For as we saw in chapter 3, traditional Western discourses on the family ground the future of the nation, the civilization, and the region upon the future of the family. For it is the traditional family that ensures biological *as well as social and political reproduction* by birthing, rearing, and educating children. Neuwirth/Wurst is not only denied any legitimate roles in these processes, but understood as perverting these processes as an 'abomination' of both nature and culture. This may explain why Vladimir Zhirinovsky proclaimed about Neuwirth/Wurst, 'It's the end of Europe. It has turned wild. . . . Fifty years ago the Soviet army occupied Austria. We made a mistake in freeing Austria. We should have stayed' (Davies 2014).

Zhirinovsky's comment suggests another figuration of the 'perverse homosexual' lurking in these commentaries about Neuwirth/Wurst—the figure of the 'unwanted im/migrant'. For what Zhirinovsky seems to be objecting to is not just how the 'underdeveloped' or even 'undevelopable' Austria has presumably succumbed to perversion since being liberated from Soviet occupation but also how the (now cultural) conquest of 'Europe' has been moving from West to East, carrying perversion with it. This sentiment comes through in a petition that the All-Russian Parent Meeting organized prior to Eurovision 2014 in its attempt to prevent 'the transvestite contestant Conchita Wurst, who leads the lifestyle inapplicable for Russians' from being broadcast on Russian television. In its petition (which collected fifteen thousand signatures), it requested 'that the state broadcaster remove Eurovision from its TV schedule, accusing "European liberals" of subjecting their children to a "hotbed of sodomy"' (Edgar 2014). Through this petition, Neuwirth/Wurst as Conchita Wurst is cast as the 'unwanted im/migrant' who televisually and morally puts the 'European liberal' condoning of sodomy on the move from perverse Austria into normal Russia. This is how Neuwirth/Wurst as undevelopable sexes, genders, and sexualities on the move threatens to bring televisual dangers into the heart of the Russian/'European' homeland. Upon winning Eurovision, Neuwirth/Wurst declared, 'I would like to spend a week with Putin, so that I could better understand him' (Molloy 2014). This statement both reverses who the incomprehensive creature lurking about 'Europe' is (from Neuwirth/Wurst to Putin) and threatens to put Neuwirth/Wurst himself/herself/themselves on the move materially from perverse Austria into normal Russia.

In all of these ways, Neuwirth/Wurst is figured by some mostly Eastern European leaders as an alien strain of the 'perverse homosexual' who takes specific form as versions of the 'irredeemable undevelopable', the 'civilizational barbarian', and the 'unwanted im/migrant' in order to corrupt children, the family, the home, the homeland, and Christian theology by putting 'perverse' sexes, genders, and sexualities on the move both horizontally and vertically. Horizontally, Neuwirth/Wurst moves televisually, morally, and potentially even physically from 'Western Europe' into 'Eastern Europe'. Vertically, Neuwirth/Wurst interjects himself/herself/themselves as a mobile queer link in the 'Great Chain of Being' between God and man. In light of this figuration of Neuwirth/Wurst as perverse, it is not surprising that far-right anti-integration 'Europeans' like Russian deputy prime minister Dmitry Rogozin claimed that Conchita Wurst and her Eurovision victory 'showed supporters of European integration their European future: a bearded girl' (Davies 2014).

As a sinner against the laws of God and man—nature and culture—it is this particular figuration of the 'perverse homosexual' as this specific 'bearded girl' who presents himself/herself/themselves as a potential singular logos of 'European' statecraft as mancraft. It is this 'bearded girl' who is available to underwrite the sovereign authority of individual and integrated 'European' nation-states horizontally and vertically as unstoppable unity. It is this 'bearded girl' whom these 'European' leaders reject.

To avoid the perverse fate this figuration of Neuwirth/Wurst offers to 'Europe itself', these 'European' leaders and their followers strenuously reaffirm the binaries between male and female, masculine and feminine, heterosexual and 'homosexual', religious authority and secular authority, traditional 'Europe' and liberal 'Europe', and family-friendly television and 'the hotbed of sodomy' that is Eurovision. We see this not only in the statements analyzed above, but in Russian legislator Vitaly Milonov's proposal to boycott Eurovision in the future and replace it with a Russian-hosted alternative Eurasian song contest (Kozlov 2015). We also see it in the 'prove you are not Conchita' beard-shaving Twitter campaign that swept through Russia after Neuwirth/Wurst's Eurovision victory.[21] This is a gesture that echoes particularly Western Islamophobic fears of the beard globally after 9/11 and Russian fears of the beard nationally in the context of Russia's wars with Chechnya. What it suggests is that for a Russian to 'prove you are not Conchita', he must paradoxically demasculinize himself by exposing his facial skin in order to reaffirm his whiteness, his Christianity, and his civilizational 'Europeanness', all of which support his 'European' gender identity on *either* one side *or* the other of a traditional binary.[22] This is how racialization, nationalization, and civilization creep into these figurations of Neuwirth/Wurst as perverse, which are generally read only through the lens of sexes, genders, and sexualities.

By reducing Neuwirth/Wurst's *and/or* plurality around sexes, genders, sexualities, and authority to a specific, singular figuration of the 'perverse homosexual' and opposing it to some presumably 'traditional, normal European', these 'European' leaders figured Neuwirth/Wurst as the border between their vision of some 'normal Europe' and some 'perverse Europe' that accorded with Neuwirth/Wurst's perverse (non)biological, social, and political understanding of unstoppable unity. In so doing, they participated in what Anzaldúa calls a bordering practice. As she puts it, 'Borders are set up to define the places that are safe and unsafe, to distinguish *us* from *them*. A border is a dividing line, a narrow strip along a steep edge' (1987, 3). Neuwirth/Wurst functioned in this discourse to separate us from them, the safe from the unsafe, the normal from the perverse. And what made that possible was Neuwirth/Wurst's figuration as the 'perverse homosexual'.

Neuwirth/Wurst as the 'Normal Homosexual'

What I want to suggest in the remainder of this section is that border-ing practices are also very much at play in crafting Neuwirth/Wurst as the 'normal homosexual' and that these bordering practices are—albeit very differently—just as objectionable. These bordering practices func-tion by celebrating Neuwirth/Wurst's *and/or* plurality in the registers of sexes, genders, and sexualities so long as it can be recuperated within a whitened, Europeanized homonormativity. In other words, Neuwirth/Wurst is figured here as a variation of Hilary Clinton's 'LGBT', as dis-cussed in chapter 5. It is Neuwirth/Wurst as this particular 'normal homosexual' who was championed by mostly Western European lead-ers, placed on a 'normal' versus 'perverse' binary, and opposed to those mostly Eastern European understandings of Neuwirth/Wurst as the 'perverse homosexual' analyzed earlier. My argument is that Western European (and later world leaders) were able to celebrate Neuwirth/Wurst's 'unstoppable unity' as a potential logos of statecraft as mancraft for 'Europe itself' and later for a particular globalized 'human commu-nity' only because they occluded specific aspects of Neuwirth/Wurst's complex figuration from that unity. Those aspects are race, nationality, and civilization.

This is evident in both Neuwirth/Wurst's ever-changing biographi-cal profile that Neuwirth/Wurst or his/her/their publicists circulated on Neuwirth/Wurst's behalf and in the statements 'European' and then United Nations leaders made about Neuwirth/Wurst. My analysis focuses on Neuwirth/Wurst's biographies by examining the implications of three key biographies in particular—the September 2013 biography, the May 2014 biography, and the November 2014 biography.

After his/her/their selection in September 2013 as Austria's representa-tive to Eurovision 2014, this official biography of Conchita Wurst appeared (hereafter referred to as the 2013 bio).

Conchita Wurst grew up in the Colombian highlands surrounded by the sound of swinging powder puffs and the rustling of layers made out of delicate tulle. One day her mother, a popular actress, met by fate her father, Alfred of Knack and Wurst, an even more successful theatre director—and fell in love with him. Within that same year she gave birth to her first daughter Conchita, named after the great-grandmother BarbadaConchita (the Bearded). It soon became obvious that the small "Knackwurst" was determined to become someone great and successful. (Konstantopoulos 2013)

Sometime in the run-up to Eurovision 2014, conchitawurst.com offered the two separate biographies of Tom and Conchita (hereafter the May 2014 bio), which are reproduced above. These biographies—which describe Tom as Austrian and Conchita as 'born in the mountains of Colombia' and 'raised in Germany'—appeared on conchitawurst.com until at least mid-November 2014, shortly after Neuwirth/Wurst's appearances as Conchita Wurst at the European Parliament in Brussels (October 2014) and at the United Nations (November 2014).

By December 2014, the bios had been modified to read as follows (hereafter the December 2014 bio):

Tom was born on November 6, 1988 in Gmunden, Austria and grew up in the small Styrian village of Mitterndorf. In 2007 he participates in the ORF casting show "Starmania" and takes the second place. In 2011 he completes his studies at the Fashion School in Graz, Austria and has been living in Vienna since then.

Conchita made her first public appearance on the ORF casting show "Die große Chance" in 2011. In 2012 she participates in the Austrian qualifying round for the Eurovision Song Contest and takes the second place again. 2014 is about to become her most successful year to date: Conchita wins the Eurovision Song Contest in Copenhagen and captivates European and worldwide audiences. She is finally at the top—all over Europe![23]

Accompanying all of these bios is a strong statement in support of tolerance, especially the tolerance of sex/gender/sexual variance, as suggested by the colloquial translation of Wurst—'It's all the same.'

I'm fighting for tolerance every day.[24]

Conchita, The Bearded Lady, [is] as a statement. A statement for
tolerance and acceptance—as it's not about appearances; it's about
the human being (May 2014 bio).

[Tom and Conchita] . . . both take a strong stance for tolerance and
against discrimination (December 2014 bio).

Read closely, these official biographies reveal several things. First, the
biographies circulated by Neuwirth/Wurst's team become less flamboyant
as Neuwirth/Wurst becomes more famous. Well before Eurovision 2014,
Conchita Wurst is described as being raised 'surrounded by the sound
of swinging powder puffs and the rustling of layers made out of delicate
tulle'. Once Neuwirth/Wurst was firmly on the way to fulfilling Conchita's
ambition 'to become someone great and successful', her May 2014 biography drops its flowery prose, in favor of presenting 'just the facts' about
Tom and Conchita as bullet points. This same 'just the facts' presentation
of Tom's and Conchita's bios is also evident in the December 2014 bio,
although it has reverted to prose.

Second, 'the facts' about Conchita change from her 2013 bio to her May
2014 bio. The 2013 bio claims Conchita 'grew up in the Colombian highlands'. But the May 2014 bio claims Conchita was 'born in the mountains of
Colombia and raised in Germany'. As the bios relocate Conchita's rearing
from Colombia to Germany—the powerhouse of contemporary 'Europe'—
they sharply shift tone from flamboyant to factual. Together, these revisions invite a reading of Colombia as an exotic global Southern locale that
produces fully foreign fantastical creatures. This is opposed to matter-of-
fact global Northern 'European' Germany, which seems to be a place in
which 'the exotic' is tamed. In Conchita's case, this taming is evidenced
by the instrumentalizing of her exotic origins into a formal bullet-pointed
CV. This move maintains Conchita as 'the exotic global Southerner'. But it
figures her as not so exotic that 'Europeans' cannot identify with her. For
she shares with them not just their documentary form of exchanging professional details; she also shares their 'European' upbringing. Indeed, she
shares Tom's 'European' upbringing—a fact that is missing from the 2013

bio. It is this 'European' upbringing that might explain Conchita's success in 'Europe', as evidenced by her May 2014 bio, which notes her appearances on Austria's *Die große Chance* and her participation in Eurovision. It is also this fact that makes Conchita eligible to compete in Eurovision.

Third, the 'fact' that Tom and Conchita share a common 'European' upbringing is missing from Conchita's 2013 bio because Tom is missing from Neuwirth/Wurst's bios until 2014. On the version of the biography page of conchitawurst.com that was available in May 2014, Tom is described as 'a private person' who has never met his creation, the 'art figure' Conchita Wurst, even though they share the same body. Tom's biography changes little once it is introduced. No facts change—Tom is figured from May 2014 onward as Austrian, 'European', presumptively white, male, cisgendered, and homosexual. However, Tom's bios do change in style, matching the stylistic changes of Conchita's bios. And a few additional details about Tom appear in his bios as they are revised between May 2014 and December 2014.

This, fourth, is in stark contrast to Conchita's bios. For each subsequent biography of Neuwirth/Wurst is increasingly economical with 'the facts' about Conchita. In addition to how 'the facts' about Conchita's upbringing change in the September 2013 and May 2014 bios, details about Conchita herself are erased with every rewriting of the bios. In the September 2013 bio, for example, readers are told that Conchita was 'named after the great-grandmother BarbadaConchita (the Bearded)'. This information establishes Conchita's gender variance as a biological attribute of her matriarchal Colombian linage. The May 2014 bio of Conchita deletes this genealogical information. In this bio, Conchita is merely figured as 'born in the mountains of Colombia and raised in Germany'. But by the time the November 2014 bio is released, even this information is missing. For this bio is simply a CV of Conchita's professional accomplishments presented in prose form. It gestures toward the September 2013 bio's foreshadowing of Conchita's success when it writes of Conchita's Eurovision victory, 'She is finally at the top—all over Europe!' But any explicit connection between Conchita and Colombia—through family genealogy, place of birth, or place of rearing—has disappeared.

What should we make of these changes to Neuwirth/Wurst's biographies?

On the one hand, the accumulating omissions from Conchita's backstory might make Neuwirth/Wurst's figuration of Conchita less contestable. For they obscure how Neuwirth/Wurst appropriates stereotypical global Northern understandings of race, place, sexes, genders, and sexualities to create his/her/their exotic (for some), monstrous (for others) global Southern hyperfeminized and disruptively masculinized 'art figure'. In so doing, Neuwirth/Wurst's bios appear to be less neocolonialist and tropicalist in global terms. Indeed, by the final bio Conchita's Spanish name can be read as figuring her as a global Northern Spaniard rather than a global Southern Colombian. Yet while this bio invites a reading of Conchita as fully 'European', it merely substitutes global Northern stereotypes about the global Southern 'Hispanic' with equally contestable 'Northern European' stereotypes about the racialized, sexed, gendered, and sexualized 'Southern European'. In so doing, it preserves 'Europe' as a signifier of 'Enlightened development' as opposed to Latin and South America as a space of 'un-Enlightened un(der)development'. And it still does nothing to address concerns about how Neuwirth/Wurst's transfiguration might negatively affect those people who live their everyday lives as 'mixed race' and/or as trans* in relation to the often violent visual regimes of normative 'Europeanness'.[25] While these omissions, then, might make Conchita Wurst more palatable as a symbol of tolerance to some 'Europeans', they hardly make her a 'politically correct' figure.

On the other hand, the accumulating omissions from Conchita's backstory effect the kind of tolerance Conchita and Tom symbolize. This is because as Conchita's backstory is edited out of existence, so too is some of Tom's backstory. Tom remains a figure who was discriminated against because of his 'homosexuality' as a teenager, and Conchita remains his artistic expression for tolerance and against discrimination. Yet the types of tolerance and antidiscrimination Tom and Conchita stand for narrow as Conchita's bio narrows. This is because the editing out of Conchita's Colombian backstory edits out both Neuwirth/Wurst's complex crossing of race, nation, and civilization and Tom's motivation for creating this *particular* sex-/gender-/sexuality-variant character as his refuge from one of his *specific experiences* of homophobia—the fear in the 'homosexual' of the 'European' homeland. This means that Neuwirth/Wurst as Tom *and/or* Conchita stands against discrimination and for tolerance only as whitened, Europeanized subjects and only in the first two registers of homophobia discussed above—as fear of the 'homosexual' and as fear in the 'homosexual' of the home—but not in the third register, as fear in the 'homosexual' of the homeland.

This could not be more significant for several reasons. First, by spatially renationalizing Neuwirth/Wurst within the 'Western European home-land', Neuwirth/Wurst's victory at Eurovision 2014 becomes a temporal tale that evidences increasing tolerance in the 'white Western European' of sexed, gendered, and sexualized variance at the expense of its tolerance for racial, national, and civilizational differences.

Second, only two kinds of homophobia that Tom was exposed to as a teenager appear in this tale, and they are firmly located in Tom's past. What Neuwirth/Wurst's victory at Eurovision 2014 demonstrates is that in contemporary 'white Western Europe', these forms of homophobia have largely given way to tolerance. Taken together, these first two points allows 'white Western Europeans' to embrace Neuwirth/Wurst as a cel-ebration of their own progress in expanding the range of 'the normal' to include a figure who they would have previously read as 'the perverse', while preserving all manner of (crossed) racialized, nationalized, and civilizationalized figures as perverse. If these moves sound familiar, it is because they are the very same moves Secretary of State Hilary Clinton made in her 'Gay rights are human rights' speech to figure the 'LGBT' as normal.

Third, these moves further allow 'Western Europeans' to criticize those predominately 'Eastern European' leaders who insist upon con-demning Neuwirth/Wurst and other 'homosexuals' as perverse. What this means, then, is that—like those 'Eastern European' leaders discussed above—many 'Western Europeans' embraced Neuwirth/Wurst not as the 'normal *and/or* perverse homosexual' but as the 'new normal homosex-ual', whom they valued over and opposed to readings of Neuwirth/Wurst as the 'perverse homosexual'. This figures those 'Western Europeans' who embrace Neuwirth/Wurst as the 'developed' and those 'Eastern Europeans' who revile Neuwirth/Wurst as the 'undevelopable'.

Fourth, the *either/or* logics that produce this particularly white Western 'normal homosexual' make it available as a potential logos of 'the newly tolerant (white Western) Europe' in a 'European' statecraft as mancraft. But, just as with every 'homosexual' in an *either/or* logic of statecraft as mancraft, the plurality of Neuwirth/Wurst's *and/or* figurations had to be reduced to *either* one thing *or* another for Neuwirth/Wurst to function in this logic. As noted above, to craft Neuwirth/Wurst as the 'perverse homosexual', mostly Eastern European leaders had to reduce all of Neuwirth/ Wurst's plurality to 'the perverse'. To craft Neuwirth/Wurst as the 'normal homosexual', mostly Western Europeans had to contain how Neuwirth/ Wurst performed 'transness'. 'Transness' could not be performed in the register of transnationality outside of a 'European' context. As a result, it could not be performed in the register of transraciality outside of a 'European' context. And it could not be performed in the register of biological genealogy outside of a 'European' context.

Once all of these aspects of Neuwirth/Wurst's transperformativity are stripped away, so too is the fictitious explanation for Neuwirth/ Wurst's sex/gender/sexuality variance—Conchita's resemblance to her Colombian great-grandmother BarbadaConchita. Uprooted from Colombia, Conchita is unrooted from her beard. Conchita's beard—like Neuwirth/Wurst's beard—is but a detachable accessory in the drag queen's kit. This, I want to suggest, makes Neuwirth/Wurst as Conchita Wurst all the more powerful, particularly in this mostly Western European tale of his/her/their normalization. For as a detachable accessory,[26] Conchita's beard is less like a unique gift from God to the sainted 'bearded lady' to protect her from patriarchal culture than it is an object that can be shared by all of those who 'oppose openly and resolutely, with daring or with effrontery' (OED) the two types of homophobia Neuwirth/Wurst stands against. Indeed, around Eurovision 2014, fans of Neuwirth/Wurst donned Conchita-like beards, just as her detractors shaved off their beards to prove they were not Conchita.

The significance of the unrootedness of Conchita's beard goes far beyond its appropriation or rejection in the world of fandom. For as a man-made object available to all rather than a biological attribute gifted from God to someone exceptional, Conchita's beard does not situate Neuwirth/Wurst in the 'Great Chain of Being' between God and man. Rather, Conchita's beard smashes this hierarchical understanding of sovereign authority to the ground. It is out of the ashes of this traditional, conservatively Christian vertical configuration of old Europe that Neuwirth/Wurst as Conchita Wurst rises like a phoenix as a secular symbol of a newly tolerant Europe that answers to no higher legal or moral authority than 'modern man'. The classical understanding of 'sovereign man' as the logos of the old Europe is the intolerant flame that spurs on Neuwirth/Wurst to seek retribution. Neuwirth/Wurst does so in the name not only of the 'homosexual' and 'the sex/gender/sexuality variant' but also of humanity itself. The horizontal inclusion of all people in the human community is the fundamental axis of integration that matters in this account of Neuwirth/Wurst. This is the 'unstoppable unity'—of the majoritized and the minoritized—this secularly regrounded figuration of Neuwirth/Wurst symbolizes.[27]

This figuration of Neuwirth/Wurst as unstoppable unity accords perfectly with Enlightenment accounts of modern sovereignty, whether on behalf of an integrated 'European community' or on behalf of a global community. For once Neuwirth/Wurst was extracted out of Christian eschatological time and fully inserted in the progressive temporality of modernity, Neuwirth/Wurst became available to signify man's progress on earth, including in terms of integration. This explains why Neuwirth/Wurst was invited to the EU to perform as Conchita Wurst and was celebrated as having 'a very important political message that . . . has to do with what the EU stands for: Equal rights, fundamental rights, the right to live your life without fear, for LGBT and other minorities' (Austrian Green MEP Ulrike Lunacek, quoted in EurActiv 2014). This also explains why the same invitation was made to Neuwirth/Wurst as Conchita Wurst by the United Nations, where Neuwirth/Wurst met with UN secretary general Ban Ki-Moon. Speaking of Neuwirth/Wurst's meeting with Ban Ki-Moon, Ban's spokesperson commented,

> Everyone is entitled to enjoy the same basic rights and live a life of worth and dignity without discrimination. This fundamental principle is embedded in the UN Charter and the Universal Declaration of Human Rights. Conchita is a symbol in that sense and I think it's good for them to meet. [The meeting allows us] to reassert his [Ban Ki-Moon's] support for LGBT people and for them to ensure that they enjoy the same human rights and protection that we all do. (Duffy 2014)

But, of course, Neuwirth/Wurst does not stand for all humanity in these *either/or* logics of collective statecraft as mancraft. Neuwirth/Wurst, like the liberally crafted tolerated 'LGBT', stands for a specific national, racial, and civilizational figuration of the human.

Had Neuwirth/Wurst as Conchita Wurst not been constrained within the specific national, racial, and civilizational limits of what it means to be 'European' and what it means to be human, the modernist progressive normalizing narrative especially 'Western Europeans' tell themselves about Neuwirth/Wurst could not have been sustained. For the story a Colombian Conchita tells us about the 'European homosexual' Tom is that what it takes for the 'homosexual' to be at home in 'Europe' is to take refuge in an alter ego who lives somewhere else. For Tom, that 'somewhere else' is the fantasy space of Colombia that acts as the stage upon which his art creation Conchita—as a figure detached from Tom's everyday life and 'European' everyday life—can perform.[28] This Neuwirth/Wurst does not fully belong to/in 'Europe', which means this Neuwirth/Wurst would become an even less likely candidate to become a sovereign foundation for 'a new Europe' or a progressively 'integrating Europe'. Instead, this Neuwirth/Wurst's 'unity' is 'unstoppable' because his/her/their sexes, genders, and sexualities—like his/her/their races, nationalities, and civilizations—do not stop at the

borders of 'Europe'. This makes Neuwirth/Wurst a figure who threatened to expand 'Europe' horizontally beyond the continental and
therefore racial, national, and civilizational terms in which 'European'
integrationists imagine 'Europe'. What this means is that—for all his/
her/their problematic appropriations of 'trans' phenomena—this
Neuwirth/Wurst poses the question of 'European integration' in far
more registers than contemporary Eastern, Western, or indeed integrated 'Europeans' can contend with.

In light of this, it should come as no surprise that Neuwirth/Wurst's
profile on the official Eurovision website has never included any reference
to Conchita Wurst as Colombian and never mentioned BarbadaConchita.
Rather, it states, 'Tom Neuwirth was born on November 6th, 1988, and he
for the first time performed as his alter ego Conchita Wurst in 2011', and
'Conchita Wurst was born as Tom Neuwirth on November 6th, 1988 in
Gmunden, Austria'.[29] The official Eurovision line, then, is that Neuwirth/
Wurst is nothing more than a drag act. After winning Eurovision 2014,
Neuwirth/Wurst expressed his/her/their agreement with this impression,
commenting, 'When politicians, like really famous ones, say that I'm a reason Europe will crush into pieces, I have to say I've never received a bigger
honor. You know they think I'm that powerful—thank you. I'm sorry to
disappoint you, but I'm just a drag queen' (Neuwirth/Wurst quoted on
Newsnight 2014).

CONCLUSION

By way of conclusion, I want to unpack Neuwirth/Wurst's self-deprecating
claim to be 'just a drag queen' because this comment performs three
important elisions. First, like Neuwirth/Wurst's biographies, it omits
the complexity in Neuwirth/Wurst's figuration of his/her/their specific 'Eurovisioned bearded drag queen' that my multiple readings of
Neuwirth/Wurst draw out. In so doing, it erases Neuwirth/Wurst's
demand for a particular transbordered 'Europe', a demand that in part
explains why Neuwirth/Wurst's drag queen mattered deeply to far more

Eastern European, Western European, and global leaders than one might have reasonably expected.

Second, it wrongly assumes that 'Europe' was not and is not always already in pieces.[30] Indeed, questions about which pieces—of the globe, of 'culture', of 'civilization'—belong to 'Europe' when, where, how, and why are as old as 'Europe itself'. In R. B. J. Walker's terms, this explains why 'Europe' is never where it is supposed to be or what it is supposed to be (2000, 14)—with respect to the 'Europe' of Eurovision or any other 'Europe'. Indeed, as Jacques Derrida argues, to think of 'Europe' is to experience the aporia—'the conditions of possibility as conditions of impossibility' (1993, 15). This 'Europe' that presents itself as a never fully formed promise (Derrida 1992) 'recurrently duplicates itself interminably, fissures itself, and contradicts itself' (Derrida 1993, 16). Reflecting on 'today's Europe', Derrida writes,

> *What is proper to a culture is to not be identical to itself.* Not to not have an identity, but not to be able to identify itself, to be able to say 'me' or 'we'; to be able to take the form of a subject only in the non-identity to itself, or if you prefer, only in the difference *with itself.* There is no culture or cultural identity without this difference *with itself* (1992, 9–10).

This leads us to the third elision in Neuwirth/Wurst's claim to be 'just a drag queen'. It deflects attention away from the aporiatic aspects of 'Europe' and Neuwirth/Wurst alone and together. It leads us away from thinking about 'the critical difference' (Johnson 1980) they each embodies and the promise they each hold in and beyond 'Europe itself'. Taken alone, each of these figures can be described as Derrida describes 'Europe', as a promised identity that is not identical to itself because it duplicates, fissures, and contradicts itself. In so doing, each of these figures escapes the grasp of an *either/or* logic. In fact, Derrida pointedly makes this claim about 'Europe' (1993, 15),[31] Barthes pointedly makes this claim about sexes, genders, and sexualities (1974), and I pointedly make this claim about the 'Eurovisioned bearded drag queen'. What this suggests is that to encounter either 'Europe' or Neuwirth/Wurst is to experience aporia. To encounter both together, I want to suggest, is to experience how the possibly 'impossible desires' (Gopinath 2005) of the 'normal *and/or* perverse homosexual' are figured by—and in turn figure—an impossibly possible 'Europe'.

It should come as no surprise that my readings of 'Europe' and of the 'Eurovisioned bearded drag queen' do not match those of 'European' leaders or even that of Neuwirth/Wurst's account of himself/herself/themselves. For Neuwirth/Wurst was taken up as a question before 'Europe' through traditional debates about horizontal reach (integrated community vs. individual sovereign nation-states) and vertical authority (how to figure the 'Great Chain of Being') that have long dominated a traditional 'European' integrationist imaginary. Inhabiting this imaginary, 'European' leaders expressed their will to know Neuwirth/Wurst through a traditional *either/or* logic of statecraft as mancraft—as singular, as stable, as an ahistorical sovereign man to be embraced or opposed. This allowed them to 'weaponize' Neuwirth/Wurst (Black 2014) as a foundation for their strategic organization and regulation of an 'integrated Europe itself'. Their execution of this 'European' procedure of statecraft as mancraft became all the more coherent as, over time, Neuwirth/Wurst's official biographies acquiesced to this logic by editing Neuwirth/Wurst into a more knowable and placeable 'European' subject. All of this reduced the questions Neuwirth/Wurst raised before 'Europe' to one: Are we 'Europeans' for liberal tolerance or against it, and does or should our liberal tolerance of the 'homosexual' stand for 'an integrated Europe'?

What is curious about this rendering of sovereign subjectivities in this traditional logic of statecraft as mancraft is that neither Neuwirth/Wurst nor 'Europe' presents himself/herself/themselves/itself as—or indeed passes as—singular, ahistorical complete projects or subjectivities, especially around questions of integration and unstoppable unity. What this suggests is that Neuwirth/Wurst as a sovereign foundation for 'Europe' makes more sense as a plurally *and/or* foundation for an always already plurally *and/or* 'Europe', even as 'European' leaders busily disavow *and/or* logics altogether.[32]

If we were to allow what 'European' leaders disallow—if we were to appreciate the plural logics that make both Neuwirth/Wurst and 'Europe' possible *and/or* impossible—more salient and politically powerful questions emerge. These include the following:

- How might Neuwirth/Wurst function as a queerly plural foundation for a pluralized 'European' statecraft as mancraft?
- How might this challenge traditional vertical and horizontal imaginaries of 'European' integration?
- What might 'the future of peace and freedom' that this pluralized Neuwirth/Wurst claims to stand for look like?
- How might the impossibly possible future Neuwirth/Wurst imagines order, reorder, and disorder not just 'Europe itself' but the regimes of knowledge about *sovereignty itself* that have prevailed at least since the Treaty of Westphalia, which demand that IR scholars understand and practice sovereignty as if it were exclusively singular?

To entertain these questions is to begin to appreciate the plural *and/or* logics that Neuwirth/Wurst injects into IR. It is to begin to appreciate why figurations of the 'homosexual' and the understandings of sovereignty that they generate and upon which they depend are not *wurst*, because they are not all the same in the practices of state sovereignty, the processes of regional integration, and the global imaginaries of what it means to be human.

Sovereignty, Sexuality, and the 'End of Man'

What I mean by 'the end of man' is . . . the end of all these forms of individuality, of subjectivity, of consciousness, of the ego on which we build and from which we have tried to build and to constitute knowledge. . . . The West has tried to build the figure of man in this way, and this image is in the process of disappearing.

—MICHEL FOUCAULT (1971)

The figure of man[1]—as capturable and containable within a singular subjectivity—is the fulcrum of modern Western knowledge production (also see Sedgwick 1993). My argument in this book is that Western states-people and scholars have 'tried to build the figure of man in this way' (Foucault 1971), so he may function as a singular, sexualized 'sovereign man' who grounds a political community, on the one hand, and a community of scholarly knowledge producers who typically render him as if he were sexualized *or* sovereign on the other.

By reading two broad and overlapping bodies of scholarship together—(transnational/global) queer studies and (queer) international relations—I have attempted to trace some of the dominant figurations of 'modern man' as 'sovereign man' that are produced through attempts to answer the questions: What is 'homosexuality'? and Who is 'the homosexual'? This will to knowledge about the 'homosexual' who is understood as that figure who somehow embodies 'homosexuality', I argue here, is a feature of modern statecraft as modern mancraft. Statecraft as mancraft expresses those attempts by a modern state (or other political community) to present its sovereign foundation—its 'sovereign man'—as if it were the singular, preexisting, ahistorical ground that authorizes all sovereign decisions in its political community. Rooted in Victorian understandings of the 'perverse homosexual', this will to knowledge about the 'homosexual' produced some surprising figurations of 'primitive man' who was opposed to 'modern sovereign man'. These include the 'underdeveloped' and the 'undevelopable'. Reading IR literatures with queer studies literatures, I argue that these specific figurations of the 'homosexual' appear in IR theories of modernization and development and are reworked in contemporary immigration and security debates as the 'unwanted im/migrant' and the 'terrorist'. In making these arguments, I point to the specific (neo)colonial/(neo)imperial *sexualized* heteronormative orders of international relations these various figurations help to make possible.

While these figurations of the 'perverse homosexual' persist to this day, they are now accompanied by increasingly dominant homonormative figurations of the 'normal homosexual'. As noted by many transnational/global queer and queer IR theorists, while the 'normal homosexual'—especially as the 'gay rights holder'—is a figure who rightly has the right to claim rights, this figure also makes possible (neo)colonialist/(neo)imperial sexualized orders of international relations that divide the world into 'normal states' and 'pathological states' depending upon how well these states are deemed to be treating their 'homosexuals'.

Read together, the story these chapters tell is one in which figurations of the 'homosexual' emerge, stabilize, and restabilize international theory and practice. In so doing, figurations of the 'homosexual' seem to be constantly proliferating. For example, contemporary figurations of the 'perverse homosexual' as the 'unwanted im/migrant' and the 'al-Qaeda terrorist' now sit alongside ever-proliferating figurations of the 'normal homosexual' as the 'LGBT', as the 'gay patriot', and as that domesticated figure who forms half of the 'gay married couple'. This proliferation of figurations of the 'homosexual' is occurring in spite of Foucault's claim made more than forty years ago that the Western image of 'modern man' upon whom these specific figurations of the 'homosexual' are varia- tions 'of individuality, of subjectivity, of consciousness, of the ego on which we build and from which we have tried to build and to constitute knowledge . . . is in the process of disappearing' (1971).

This proliferation of figurations of the 'homosexual' might suggest that Foucault was wrong—that a Western will to knowledge about the 'homo- sexual' is not leading to the end of this 'homosexual man'. Yet this conclu- sion depends upon making two problematic moves. One is to disregard Foucault's genealogical accounts of 'modern man', which demonstrate that 'man' was never a singular subjectivity. 'Man' was never singularly 'sane' or 'insane' (Foucault 1965) or 'law-abiding' or 'criminal' (Foucault 1975) or 'heterosexual' or 'homosexual' (Foucault 1980). Rather, 'man' had to be produced as if he were singular so that—in Richard Ashley's terms—he could function in modern statecraft as modern mancraft as the subject who supports or opposes 'sovereign man'. The second problematic move required to accept this conclusion is to consider the production of the 'homosexual' *independently* from the specific logics that produce him. My argument in this book is that the figure of the 'homosexual' who appears in statecraft as mancraft is produced through two logics—a traditional logic of the *either/or* and a queer logic of the *and/or*. The former logic attempts to impose subjectivities as if they were singular to establish sin- gular sexualized orders of international relations; the latter attempts to understand and critique this imposition, while appreciating the logics by which subjectivities and orders are (produced as) plural in relation to sexes, to genders, and to sexualities.

The logic of the *either/or* is not blind to the fact that 'man' takes plural forms. This is why figurations of 'man' proliferate. Yet these plural forms of 'man' are always reducible to one singular, generalizable 'man'. My discus- sions of the 'perverse homosexual' and the 'normal homosexual' evidence this. What these discussions demonstrate is that like any *either/or* figure, the 'homosexual' in modernist discourse is understood as a singular 'man' who takes plural forms. Generally, the 'homosexual' is that figure who is somehow associated with 'homosexuality'. But that association depends upon the specific historical and geopolitical arrangements of space, time, and desire that constitute specific regimes of knowledge about specific 'homosexuals'. And those regimes of knowledge in *either/or* logics create a specific 'homosexual' by containing every register of his potential plurality within a binary logic that is constructive (but never deconstructive) of the 'homosexual' by adding together his *either/or* attributes to create him as a specific kind of 'homosexual'. Let me unpack this procedure.

For example, sex, gender, sexuality, reproduction, race, class, ability, authority, civilization, and so on are recast in binary terms as male versus female, masculine versus feminine, heterosexuality versus homosexuality, progressively reproductive versus dangerously (non)reproductive, white versus black, bourgeois versus proletariat, abled versus disabled, ruler versus ruled or unruly, modern versus primitive, civilized versus uncivilized or uncivilizable, territorialized versus on the move. A specific figuration of the 'homosexual' is produced by adding up his unique binary qualities. The 'underdeveloped', on this logic, equals the perversely homosexualized + the feminized + the racially darkened + the primitivized + the ruled + the dangerously reproductive + the civilizable + the territorialized. The 'al Qaeda terrorist' equals the perversely homosexualized + the feminized + the racially darkened + the primitivized + the unruly + the dangerously nonreproductive + the socially, politically, and religiously uncivilizable + the on the move. The 'LGBT' equals the normalized homosexual + the masculinized + the racially whitened + the bourgeois + the progressively productive + the modern + the ruler + the civilized + the territorialized. And on and on. As more categories of 'difference' become (produced as if they were) 'known', regimes of knowledge about the 'homosexual' proliferate, creating new possibilities to craft additional figurations of the 'homosexual' as or against 'sovereign man'. This is how traditional statecraft as mancraft inserts the singular 'homosexual' in his plural forms into its intimate, national, regional, and international games of power that effect sexualized orders of international relations. And this is how 'modern man' as 'sovereign man' proliferates and persists.

Reconsidered through the lens of queer logics of statecraft—a lens that contests those exclusively binary expressions of 'difference' that demand that all subjectivities can *be* and can be *known* as singularly signifying subjectivities across every potentially plural register they occupy or engage—the persistence of 'modern man' as 'sovereign man' is put into doubt. This is for two reasons. First, queer logics of statecraft direct us to an appreciation of those queer figures who cannot or will not signify monolithically around sex, around gender and/or around sexuality. This is a point queer theorists like Eve Sedgwick make (1993). More than this, though, queer logics of statecraft enable us to appreciate how queerly plural figures might order, reorder, or disorder national, regional, and international politics and the singular understanding of sovereignty upon which these orders have depended at least since the Treaty of Westphalia. This is the story Tom Neuwirth and/as Conchita Wurst tells in relation to contemporary 'Europe', as recounted in chapter 6. Neuwirth/Wurst's story is the same story many other figurations of or opposed to 'sovereign man' have been telling for a very long time—be they 'the revolutionary state and citizen' (Lind and Keating 2013) or 'the hegemonic state' (Weber 1999). For none of these figures can be captured or contained by an *either/or* logic of traditional statecraft as mancraft. This is because their subjectivities are formed through and expressed by a pluralized logic of the *and/or*—a logic that understands these figures as both *either* one thing *or* another *or* possibly another while it simultaneously understands them as one thing *and* another *and* possibly another.

As these queerly plural figurations of the 'homosexual' of/in relation to 'sovereign man' come into focus, what also often comes into focus with them is the concerted effort required to attempt to present not just these figurations but *any figurations* of 'sovereign man' as if he were singular, as if he preexisted attempts to constitute him as such, as if he had no history. This is the second way in which queer logics of statecraft put the persistence of the 'singular modern man' Foucault describes in doubt. For rather than evidencing the existence much less persistence of this 'modern man', what they evidence is the endless reworkings—the desperate, constant refigurations of, in this case, the 'homosexual' as/in relation to 'sovereign man' that underscore the fragility of both 'modern man' and 'modern sovereignty'. These endless reworkings of 'modern man' as 'sovereign man' expose the endless games of power these refigurations require, hinting that these particular modern games of sovereign statecraft as sovereign mancraft are unlikely to work forever. Put in Foucault's terms, what comes into relief through queer logics of statecraft is how the attempted figuration of the 'homosexual' as singular 'sovereign man' and the singular understanding of sovereignty upon which it depends are 'in the process of disappearing' (1971).

By neglecting to take queer logics of statecraft as mancraft into account, opportunities are lost to better understand how a variety of political games of power function in relation to the 'homosexual'. On the one hand, because the vast majority of IR scholarship insists that any incorporation of sexuality into IR (if it is to be incorporated at all) must be (presumably) knowable and always codable in *either/or* terms, consideration of how queer *and/or* modalities of queerly pluralized *and/or* subjectivities and their effects on the organization, regulation, and conduct of intimate, national, regional, and international relations threaten to fall out of IR theory and practice. On the other hand, consideration of how singular figurations of the 'homosexual' in traditional *either/or* logics of statecraft as mancraft are confronted and confused by *and/or* figurations of these same 'homosexuals' threatens to fall out of transnational/global queer studies. For example, Puar's and Puar and Rai's accounts of the 'al-Qaeda terrorist' allow for multiple incarnations of this figure (as the monster, the terrorist, and the fag who is also the dangerous Muslim or the dangerous Arab or the dangerous Sikh, for example; see Puar and Rai 2002; Puar 2007). Yet because Puar and Rai only read this figure through the *either/or* logics of statecraft as mancraft that Western governments employed to incite, stabilize, and regiment this figure in their domestic and foreign policies, Puar and Rai overlook how the 'al-Qaeda terrorist' functions through queer logics of statecraft, which employ *and/or* logics to confuse and confound Western domestic and foreign policies (Weber 2002). Similarly, transnational/queer studies literatures that read the formations and resistances of the 'gay rights holder' through monolithic constructions of 'homonormativity' (Duggan 2003), 'homonationalism' (Puar

2007), or 'the human rights industrial complex' (Puar 2013) tend to reify *either/or* logics of power versus resistance.[2] Queer logics of statecraft, in contrast, are attentive to the resistive possibilities within these normativities because of their attention to how *and/or* logics function in sovereignty discourses, for example, through Foucauldian notions of counterconduct as applied to human rights (see Odysseos 2016). All of this has the effect of limiting the opportunities for both (queer) IR and (transnational/global) queer studies scholars to reconsider sovereignty itself.

My argument is *not* that (queer) IR scholars offer better explanations of international relations than do (transnational/global) queer studies scholars or vice versa. My argument is that—read separately—neither scholarly tradition lives up to its intellectual or political promise, especially in how they read sovereignty and sexuality in international contexts. Yet read in combination, these overlapping bodies of scholarship can and do further enrich understandings of how 'sovereign man' as 'sexualized sovereign man' functions in existing and emerging sexualized understandings of intimate, national, regional, and international relations that *both sustain and threaten to suspend* traditional understandings of sovereignty.

My focus on sovereignty and sexuality, then, has not been intended to designate some new field of 'queer IR' as a new sovereign subject of study that knows who the 'homosexual' in international relations really is or what sovereignty always was, always is, or always will be or should be. My aim instead has been to contest the 'political delusion of sovereignty' (Cocks 2014) and its corresponding personal and political delusions of sexuality that sustain and contain 'all these forms of individuality, of subjectivity, of consciousness, of the ego [as a singular subjectivity or as discrete scholarly communities] on which we build and from which we have tried to build and to constitute knowledge' (Foucault 1971) about 'sovereign man', about 'sexualized man', and about 'sexualized sovereign man'. In doing this, my aim is the same as Foucault's. Foucault's reflections on his own preoccupation with 'the end of man'—with my embellishments—express what I mean:

> And so I don't say the things I say [about discourses of sovereignty, about the singular 'sexualized sovereign man' they strive to produce

or about the all-too-often disconnected scholarly traditions of (queer) IR as opposed to (transnational/global) queer studies] because they are what I think, but rather I say them . . . precisely to make sure they are no longer what I think. To be really certain that, from now on, outside of me, they are going to live a life or die in such a way that I will not have to recognize myself in them. (1971)

NOTES

ACKNOWLEDGMENTS

1. This special issue was the outcome of the Gender and International Relations Tenth Anniversary Conference, organized by Louiza Odysseos and Linda Etchart in 1998, where I presented my still unpublished paper 'What's So Queer about International Relations?'
2. Also see Smith and Lee (2015).

CHAPTER 1

1. For a fuller discussion of Diderot's fable, see Rees 2013.
2. JanMohamed is among the first to explicitly think sexuality as 'racialized sexuality' in his critique of Foucault's reading of the repressive hypothesis (1992; see discussion in Soto 2010, 7–8; and chapter 3 in this volume), while Stoler highlights Foucault's occlusion of race in his appropriation of this specific fable. Writes Stoler, 'The truth is spoken by that loquacious jewel of sex, but it is not any sex that speaks—only a gendered exoticized version. The will to know the truth of ourselves is in sex, but not in it alone. The discourses of sexuality are racialized ways of knowing that relate somatic signs to hidden truths' (1995, 204).
3. See, for example, Cynthia Enloe 2000 on 'the woman question', Kathy Ferguson 1993 on 'the man question', Michel Foucault 1980 on 'the homosexual question', and Jasbir Puar 2010 and Rahul Rao 2014 on 'the queer question'. All of these and all IR literatures address themselves to the games of power in one form or another.
4. This does not mean there is no discussion of sexuality in IR. Rather, it is to suggest that many of these discussions would benefit from further engagement with (transnational/global) queer studies scholarship. For (queer) IR that explicitly engages with sexuality from a queer perspective, see, e.g., Weber 1994a; 1994b; 1998; 1999; 2002; 2014a; 2014c; Peterson 1999; 2013; 2014; R. K. M. Smith 2003; Altman 2006; Kelly 2007; Pratt 2007; Rao 2010; Agathangelou 2013; Marjaana 2010; Owens 2010; Sjoberg 2012; Sjoberg and Shepherd 2013; Sabsay 2013; Richter-Montpetit 2014a; 2014b; and 2014c.

5. As Foucault notes, there are many kinds of sovereignty, including classical, disciplinary, and biopolitical sovereignty. IR scholars who critically engage with Foucault point to additional sovereignties, like agonal sovereignty (Debrix and Barder 2012). By taking a sovereign figure like the sultan Mangogul as my point of departure to introduce sovereignty into studies of sexuality, like Foucault I do not mean to imply that a classical form of sovereignty is the only type of sovereignty at play in the games of power/knowledge/pleasure that Foucault and others investigate.

6. This does not mean there is no discussion of sovereignty in (transnational/global) queer studies or by (transnational/global) queer studies scholars. But it is to say that these discussions of sovereignty could benefit from further engagement with (queer) IR scholarship on sovereignty.

   For scholarship by (transnational/global) queer studies scholars that explicitly engages with sovereignty, see, for example, Povinell and Chaunce 1999; Puar 2007; Ritchie 2011; Rifkin 2012; Smith 2010; and Berlant 2007, whose work I discuss in more detail later.

7. My aim is not to review all of the (transnational/global) queer studies literature on sexuality nor all of the (queer) IR literature on sovereignty. Instead, my aim is to offer one partial account—among the vast array of accounts—of how sovereignty and sexuality are entwined with one another in order to encourage and enrich academic and public policy conversations about sovereignty and sexuality.

8. While debates about the meaning of the term 'queer', whether queer can be or ought to be defined (Butler 1994; Warner 2012; Wilcox 2014), and how 'queer' is or should be connected to normativities and antinormativities (Wiegman and Wilson 2015) rage on, many self-identified queer scholars cite Eve Kosofsky Sedwick's description of queer as their point of departure. Sedgwick's fuller elaboration of queer is that it designates 'the open mesh of possibilities, gaps, overlaps, dissonances and resonances, lapses and excesses of meaning when the constituent elements of anyone's gender, of anyone's sexuality aren't made (or *can't be* made) to signify monolithically' (1993, 8).

   Sedwick's exposition of queer makes clear the affinities queer studies has with feminist studies and gender studies—with their analyses of the political work that gender, sex, and (sometimes) sexuality do—and to poststructuralist studies—with its analyses of the political work that multiple significations do (for classical statements of such work in feminist IR see, for example, Tickner 1992; Peterson 1992, Enloe 2000; and in poststructuralist IR see, for example, Ashley and Walker 1990; Campbell 1992; Doty 1996a; and Weber 1995). Yet queer studies is not reducible to feminist studies, gender studies, or poststructuralist studies. Nor is it the sum total of these theoretical dispositions. As an academic practice, queer studies has been and remains, as Teresa de Lauretis described it, an attempt 'to rethink the sexual in new ways, elsewhere and other-wise' in relation to but also beyond traditional gay and lesbian studies, feminist and gender studies, and poststructuralist studies (de Lauretis 1991, xvi; Rubin 1992; Butler 1990).

9. Sedgwick's critique of 'paranoid critical theory' also expresses (among other things) her concerns with binary logics, whether these logics are meant to be 'oppressive' or 'resistive'. See Sedgwick 2003, 123–152. Thanks to Darcy Leigh for discussions on this point.

10. Foucault claimed the confessional as a modern form of the genie's ring, through which subjects were compelled to speak the truth of their sex and sexuality. These confessional spaces take many forms today, including the doctor's office, the television interview, and the personal web page. On how to read personal web pages see Hansen 2005.

11. As Sam Killermann explains, 'Trans* is an umbrella term that refers to all of the identities within the gender identity spectrum. There's a ton of diversity there, but we often group them all together (e.g., when we say "trans* issues). Trans (without the asterisk) is best applied to trans men and trans women, while the asterisk makes special note in an effort to include all non-cisgender gender identities, including transgender, transsexual, transvestite, genderqueer, genderfluid, non-binary, genderfuck, genderless, agender, non-gendered, third gender, two-spirit, bigender, and trans man and trans woman'. See http://itspronouncedmetrosexual.com/2012/05/what-does-the-asterisk-in-trans-stand-for/. In contrast, a cisgender person is someone who identifies with the gender/sex he or she was socially assigned at birth. For more definitions, see http://queerdictionary.tumblr.com/terms. Also see Stryker, Currah, and Moore 2008; Stryker and Currah 2014; and Tompkins 2014. In IR, see Shepherd and Sjoberg 2012.

12. See, for example, Ashley 1988; 1989; Biersteker and Weber 1996; Walker 1993; Weber 1995; 1998; 1999; 2011; Tagma 2009; Soguk 1997; 1999; Berman 2003; Campbell 1992; Doty 1996a; 1996b; 2007; 2011; Bartelson 1995; Nelson 2004; 2009; Shapiro 1991; 1994, Inayatullah 1998; Constantinou 2013; Shinko 2012; Ó'Tuathail and Dalby 1998; Ruback 2011; Bigo and Walker 2007; Lisle and Pepper 2005; Edkins 2000; Huysmans, Dobson, and Prokhovnik 2006; Closs Stephens 2013.

13. Ashley's use of the term 'mancraft' is intentionally sexed and gendered, to convey how sovereign power is (often) male and masculinized. For a critical feminist engagement with Ashley's notion of statecraft as mancraft, see Runyan and Peterson, who write, 'Although Richard Ashley speaks to the will to power of "statecraft as man-craft" to control all that it defines as outside of its control—anarchy, war, crisis, and so on—he does not root this analysis in the patriarchal relations of "man-state" seeking to control "women", which it construes as an unreasonable (mad), anarchical, "outsider" or "other"' (1991, 68). For another engagement with the gendered aspects of 'statecraft as mancraft', see Tagma and Durgun (in progress).

14. Ashley makes this point, but not in the register of 'queer'. He argues that while states and other political communities attempt to craft a particular version of 'modern man' as 'sovereign man', his critique of 'statecraft as mancraft' allows us to appreciate how 'sovereign man becomes, not an authentic voice to be spoken by theory and in the justification of theory, but an effect whose inscription, transformations, and effectiveness in the disciplining of modern discourse is in need of a theoretical accounting' (1989, 312). My argument in chapter 2 extends this 'theoretical accounting' in the register of 'queer' and empirically puts it to work in this queer register in chapter 6. For a wider discussion of Ashley's work, see Weber 2010.

15. The genie's ring here is often something like the 'gender variable' or the 'sexuality' variable in a regression analysis that informs scholarship and foreign policy research. For critiques, see Weber 1998a; 2014a.

16. What I am calling transnational/global queer studies is my merging of what has been called transnational feminist and queer scholarship (e.g., Grewal and Kaplan 1994; Povinelli and Chaunce 1999; Eng, Halberstam, and Muñoz 2005) with what I elsewhere have referred to as queer global studies (Weber 2014a; 2014c). I employ the term transnational/global queer studies here because the terms 'transnational' and 'global' spark different associations for queer studies scholars and IR scholars. For example, while 'transnational' conveys to both sets of scholars a consideration of processes beyond national boundaries, to IR scholars 'transnational' can be understood to exclude consideration of important 'global' processes and organizations. These may include but are certainly not reducible to 'globalization', for example, which is how 'global' is sometimes understood by transnational feminist and queer scholars. My use of the term transnational/global queer studies is offered as a way to avoid reductive understandings of either 'transnational' or 'global'. Thanks to Miranda Joseph for pushing me to clarify this point.

17. See, for example Weber 1994a; 1994b; 1998; 1999; 2002; Peterson 1999; Puar and Rai 2002; Puar 2007; Kuntsman 2008; 2009).

18. These regimes of 'normality' and 'perversion' around sexes, genders, and sexualities are intertwined with regimes of 'normality' and 'perversion' around race, religion, ability, class, and many other regimes of knowledge, as (transnational/global) queer studies and (queer) IR scholars have long noted.

19. My focus on Western and global Northern discourses is not to suggest that sexuality and sovereignty do not converge in the global South, in a variety of forms. For example, in his analysis of the 'security archipelago', Paul Amar traces how 'the Global South is not merely a source of resistant forms of localism; it is also a factory for globalizing forms of moralization, militarization, and control' (2013, 244) that arise out of global circuits of 'human-security states' (236). As he explains, 'In the universe of human security, sexuality is implicated in modes of governance that blend parahumanization . . ., hypervisibilization . . ., and securitization' (2013, 17).

20. There are numerable other available theoretical trajectories through poststructuralist and queer theory upon which to figure queer subjectivities and queer logics. My focus on Barthes's work is not meant to exclude these other trajectories; rather, it is meant as one illustration of them. For other pathbreaking examples of such work, see, for example, Halberstam and Livingston (1995), who build upon Irigaray's work, or Braidotti (1994), who builds upon the work of Deleuze and Guattari. More recently see, for example, the special issue of *Social Text* titled 'What's Queer about Queer Studies Now' coedited by Eng, Halberstam, and Muñoz (2005) and the special issue of *differences* titled 'Queer Theory without Anti-normativity' coedited by Wiegman and Wilson (2015). Thanks to Jackie Stacey for bringing the Wiegman and Wilson special issue to my attention.

21. There are innumerable figurations of the 'terrorist', many of which share the general genealogy of the 'al-Qaeda terrorist' that I outline in chapter 4, while others that do not (e.g., white men in the US militia movements like Timothy McVeigh who drove a car bomb into an Oklahoma federal building in 1995 or white men embracing US white supremacist ideologies like Dylann Roof, who shot and killed unarmed, mainly female, black worshipers in a historic black church in South

Carolina in 2015). This is why I sometimes write about the 'terrorist' in general terms (who in IR discourses is generally known to be 'undevelopable' or 'barbaric' or 'uncivilizable', which is why those racialized as white are so rarely marked as the 'terrorist') and other times write about a very specific figuration of the 'terrorist' as the 'al-Qaeda terrorist', who is a figure arising out of the histories I sketch out in chapter 4 as well as additional historical and contemporary constructions of race and religion, for example. It is also important to note that the 'al-Qaeda terrorist' is not the only contemporary figuration of the 'Islamic terrorist', as emerging figurations of the 'Islamic State (ISIS) terrorist' demonstrate. These figurations need to be distinguished analytically because distinct Western discursive mobilizations of space, time, and desire give rise to them. For example, in the register of space, the 'ISIS terrorist' is connected to geopolitical territory and the 'Islamic family' differently than is the 'al-Qaeda terrorist'. This has consequences for how home and homeland are cast in relation to the 'ISIS terrorist', geopolitically and in terms of how sexuality and 'sexuality on the move' function in relation to this figure.

22. My application of homonormativity and homonationalism is not uncritical. See my discussion in chapter 5 on the advantages but also the limitations these concepts offer in intellectual and political practice.

23. This refers to Neuwirth/Wurst's announcement upon winning Eurovision, 'We are unity. And we are unstoppable'. See chapter 6.

24. Crucially, I am *not* arguing that 'queer' or 'queer logics of statecraft' or plurally queer figurations of the 'homosexual' are in and of themselves transgressive. I make this argument at length in chapter 6, in my discussion of the 'Eurovisioned bearded drag queen'. This argument, I will suggest, underscores a point made by queer Chican@ and Latin@ theorist Sandra Soto, who, drawing upon the work of independent scholar Dana Maya, argues against 'the celebration of hybridity', in the registers of race and of queer. Soto writes, 'What the key terms used to mark racialized difference as inherently transgressive have in common is their indelible dependence on what can only be a fantasy of a normative center inhabited by homogeneous, static, racially pure, stagnant, uninteresting, and simple sovereign subjects. The celebration of hybridity not only helps reify the fantasy of a sovereign subject but also threatens to transmute marginality itself into a form of authenticity, only here rendered by the notion of "pure impurities," to borrow a term from the independent scholar Dana Maya' (Soto 2010, 3–4).

In making these arguments about queer logics of statecraft, I am also rejecting an understanding of 'queer' as (just) a 'critique of normativity', which Robyn Wiegman and Elizabeth Wilson (2015) argue is among 'the prevailing supposition' about queer in queer studies literatures. See my discussion below.

25. On postsovereignty, see, for example, Shapiro 1994; Keating 2004; and Cocks 2014.

26. Berlant is interested in thinking about 'a kind of interruptive agency that aspires to detach from a condition or to diminish being meaningful' (2007, 759) in terms of something called 'sovereignty'. Ashley is interested in describing the logics that make possible the construction of a fictive 'sovereign man' who is said to be the agent on whose behalf some phantasmical 'sovereign state' can claim to make meaningful, rational decisions (1989). Ashley, then, gives an account of the logics that

make possible the very agents Berlant complicates with her analysis of interruptive agency, albeit it in the register of national and international sovereignties rather than in the register of everyday practical sovereignties in which Berlant works. Read together with Berlant's, Ashley's work offers an analysis of how subjectivities are composed and captured by the very formations of sovereignty that Berlant's interruptive agency aspired to detach from. In this sense, Ashley's analysis is integral to—rather than competitive with—Berlant's analysis. This is evident in how Ashley and Berlant reject individual and collective understandings of 'sovereignty' as such and painstakingly work to interrupt such expressions of sovereignty. For a discussion of how Ashley's work functions to interrupt IR more broadly, see Weber 2010.

27. These include Berlant and Warner's attempt to create 'queer publics' within and beyond the academy (1998) and to ensure that the then-emerging work going by the name of 'queer' did not understand itself to be captured by or in a quest to capture either an academic discipline or the very types of state practices it set out to critique.

28. For a critique of Campbell's move, see Weber 1998b, n. 7.

29. Audre Lorde coined the term 'mythical norm'. She writes, 'In america, this norm is usually defined as white, thin, male, young, heterosexual, christian, and financially secure. It is with this mythical norm that the trappings of power reside within this society' (1984, 116). Thanks to Melanie Richter-Montpetit for directing me to Lorde on this point.

30. This is not to say that I agree completely with Enloe's approach. While her question 'Where are the women?' is a powerful one that, for her, sparks the feminist curiosity she espouses, it does tend to occlude other important questions about the formation of sexed, gendered, and sexualized subjectivities, like 'Who is a "woman"?' Formulating the question this way moves us away from feminist standpoint analysis toward feminist poststructuralist analysis. This is why I do not ask, 'Where is "the homosexual"?' but trace how answers to the question 'Who is "the homosexual"?' powerfully produce the who and the where around the 'homosexual' in ways that require analytical attention and political contestation.

31. An example is when a famous feminist IR scholar, when she was asked at a public talk to comment on queer international theories a good decade after queer IR took root in IR, replied, 'No one in IR does queer theory'.

CHAPTER 2

1. Separating the drag artist Neuwirth from his creation Wurst is difficult if not impossible. My construction of "Neuwirth and/as Wurst" marks this tension, which I explore later in the chapter and in chapter 6.

2. Thanks to Maureen McNeil for this formulation.

3. For a selection of further statements against queer assimilation, also see Stanley and Smith 2011; Halberstam 2012; Bornstein 1995; Sycamore 2006; 2008; and Conrad 2014.

4. These figurations date back much further than the Victorians, appearing, for example, in European gendered, sexed, and racialized figurations of indigenous peoples in the Americas, figured as 'the Indian' who was sometimes barbaric and other

times noble, sometimes as 'the princess' and other times 'the squaw', but invariably 'the savage'. Rooted in the political theories of such figures as Thomas Hobbes (1996), John Locke (1980), and Jean-Jacques Rousseau (1978), they made their way into IR theories more generally. In IR see Alker 1992; Shaw 2008; and Beier 2005. More generally, see Francis 1992; Klein and Ackerman 1995; A. Smith 2005; and Leigh 2009. Thanks to Darcy Leigh for discussions of this point.

5. See Stoler 1995 on how sexualized figures in the colonies informed the invention of the 'European' figures discussed by Foucault.

6. Or, in the case of "the hysterical woman", desired no (heterosexual) sex.

7. This is Berlant and Warner's definition of heteronormativity (1995). The idea that sexuality must be seen as coherent is something that Butler discusses in *Undoing Gender* (2004, 136) and that appears in debates about 'monosexuality' vs. 'bisexuality', for example. In the latter respect, see, for example, Hemmings 2002 and Eisner 2013. For a critique of Berlant and Warner's notion of heteronormativity—especially how it arguably replies upon antinormativity in how it embraces rather than eschews the repressive hypothesis—see Wiegman and Wilson 2015, 16–17.

8. Haraway employs figuration to capture ideas about embodiment and materiality in the context of feminist technoscience studies.

9. In his application of Ashley's notion of statecraft as mancraft, Nevzat Soguk explicitly addresses these issues. He does so by returning us again to Foucault, particularly to Foucault's ideas about the formation of subjectivities through incitement, stabilization, and regimentation (Soguk 1999). What Soguk explicitly details are how states become involved in these three moments of subject formation in their practices of statecraft as mancraft.

In the context of statecraft as mancraft, Soguk suggests that incitement describes how popular and institutional discourses bring into being both a figure of sovereign man who is seen as reasonable and those figures who are constituted as threats to sovereign man. In this respect, incitement draws upon both the moves Haraway identifies as part of the process of figuration and the moves that Derrida identifies as part of the process of hierarchicalization. These maneuvers are entrenched in the next two moments of statecraft as mancraft—stabilization and regimentation. Stabilization further inscribes these figures of man by locating them in relation to 'a specific problem of and before the sovereign state' (e.g., how global terrorism penetrates the US state). Finally, regimentation 'formulate[s] and channel[s] imaginable statist solutions to the problem' (Soguk 1999, 17 and 22–23).

These moments and maneuvers of statecraft as mancraft are found around innumerable international figurations (Berman 2003; Soguk 1999; Tagma 2009; Weber 2011; 2013), including the 'homosexual'. What makes the 'homosexual' such an interesting figure in the logocentric procedure of modern statecraft as modern mancraft is how—particularly in different historical eras and in different geopolitical locations—the 'homosexual' has been figured variously as sovereign man, as the antithesis of sovereign man, and as potentially both sovereign man and his antithesis as the same time and place.

10. Kenneth Waltz is not the only IR theorist who relies upon some of the inscriptions of order verses anarchy and their relationships to history that Ashley critiques. Another classic example is Martin Wight (1960). For a critical reading of Wight's formulation, see Weber 1998c.

11. Because traditional IR theories inscribe the domestic realm as peaceful and the international realm as anarchical, Ashley describes 'man as an effect of war' (1989, 298). This makes man an effect not just of the international space of anarchy but also of the warring interpretations of man put forward by individual sovereign nation-states that circulate and are contested in international relations. As Halit Mustafa Tagma notes, analyzing 'statecraft as mancraft' involves tracing how hegemonic interpretations of man always temporarily arrest and displace alternative interpretations of man, giving the appearance that there exists some 'authentic sovereign man' who appears to be spatially and temporally universal, when in fact he is always spatially and temporally particular. In performing this genealogical accounting of 'statecraft as mancraft', Tagma suggests that Ashley carries on in the spirit of Foucault's critique of Kant, which investigates how 'modern reasoning man' is produced as universal *in relation to specific and necessary limits*. Tagma argues that—as these figures appear in Ashley's 'statecraft as mancraft'— 'modern man' as 'sovereign man' is 'the man who must be perpetually preoccupied with trying to find and establish the limits that he cannot transgress' (Tagma, in progress).

12. This is what queer studies scholar Dean Spade calls the 'LGB-fake-T' movement, which refers to lesbian, gay, bisexual, and only supposedly transgender (Spade 2004). One can go further, arguing that because Clinton collapses the 'LGBT' with the 'gay', the terms 'lesbian' and 'bisexual' also fall out of this presumptively inclusive movement. Thanks to Melanie Richter-Montpetit for alerting me to Spade's work here.

13. In his later work, Derrida arguably relaxes his account of the logocentric procedure. See Derrida on aporia (1993), in relation to his reading of Europe (1992), which I discuss at length in chapter 6. For one illustration of how aporia has been taken up in IR conversations to critique early constructivist IR, see Doty 1997.

14. Ashley describes sovereign man as occupying *both* the position of being in history and aspiring to a place at the end of history—being particular while aspiring to be universal—all of which Ashley mobilizes to explain how any distinction between the domestic and the international cannot be guaranteed. In its place, there is merely the endless deferral of 'the historicization and politicization of sovereign man as the center and foundation of modern narratives of history' (1989, 308–309). Argues Ashley, it is 'the problem of the inscription of man as a sovereign figure, a paradigmatic center of history's truth and meaning' (1989, 309) that both enables and disables the coding of the domestic as ordered and peaceful and of the international as anarchy and war. In making these claims, then, Ashley's account of statecraft as mancraft recognizes (while not naming as such) *and/or* logics—as they produce modern man and as they produce domestic and international orders—to make arguments that deconstruct the figure of sovereign man and the orders he

makes possible as absolute, durable, or indeed actual. Where Ashley stops short in his analysis is in considering that *and/or* logics might not always be eschewed by those wielding sovereign logics in the logocentric procedure but embraced by them to make the logocentric procedure possible.

15. See chapter 6 for examples.

CHAPTER 3

1. For discussions of ableism and (dis)ability in relation to the figuration of the 'homosexual' and to queer theory more broadly, see McRuer 2003; 2006; 2010; McRuer and Wilkerson 2003; McRuer and Mollow 2012; and Puar 2009; 2012.

2. I use masculine pronouns to refer to these and the majority of the figures I analyze in this book because this is how they are engendered in the discourses I am analyzing here. My intention is to draw attention to the erasures these terms perform, before I critically analyze these erasures in chapters 6.

3. As I go on to explain later in this chapter, both Freud and Almond use both of these temporal tropes. Yet it is degeneracy that is the dominant trope in Freud and decadence that is the dominant temporal trope in Almond. I am overemphasizing the dominant temporal trope and its use by Freud and Almond because, in so doing, I can more clearly demonstrate how the 'underdeveloped' and the 'undevelopable' are figured.

4. I have rewritten Hoad's quote here so I do not get ahead of my story. Hoad actually writes, 'What the decadent/degenerate shares with the primitive is a position on the fringes of the normative evolutionary narrative. Neither can exist in the present' (2000, 137). I have replaced 'decadent/degenerate' with 'degenerate' here to remain focused on the point Freud is making. I restore Hoad's sentence to his original formulation with 'decadent/degenerate' later, where I read these two figures together.

5. Although tensions in Freud's depathologization of the 'homosexual' complicate these figurations.

6. In addition to Peterson's work in international relation, also see, for example, some of the classical feminist sociological accounts of nationalism, heterosexual reproduction, and state-building, including Yuval-Davis, Anthias, and Campling 1989 and Ranchod-Nilsson and Tétreault 2000. For additional queer readings of heterosexuality and the family, see, for example, Butler 1997 and Duggan 2003. In relation to the neoliberal economic links to crisis in an international relation context, see N. Smith 2015.

7. The implications of Parsons's work on gender roles for understandings of trans* people is explicit in Janice Raymond's essentialist feminist critique of transsexualism. Raymond writes, 'My main conclusion is that transsexualism is basically a social problem whose cause cannot be explained except in relation to the sex roles and identities that a patriarchal society generates' (1980, 79). Sadly, Raymond's position is still championed by trans exclusionary radical feminists (TERFs) like Sheila Jeffreys (2014, 39). In contrast, Sandy Stone's critical response to Raymond (1991) is a classic piece that opened up a queer, antiessentialist reading of trans*. To follow contemporary trans* scholarship, see the journal *Trans*gender Studies Quarterly*, published by Duke University Press.

While I note that the 'trans*' (which itself contains a plurality of figurations) shares some of the same figurations as the 'homosexual' in Parsons's work (e.g., as socially dysfunctional), it would be wrong to equate these two figurations across the many registers in which I discuss the 'homosexual' here. For their specific figurations in sociology, psychology, and medicine, for example, are not identical. This means that the ways in which the 'homosexual' is figured in relation to space, time, and desire sometimes corresponds to and at other times departs from how the 'trans*' is figured in relation to these same understandings. It is beyond the scope of this investigation to trace the complexities of the historical formations of the 'trans*' in relation to those of the 'homosexual'. For some indications of these histories, see, for example, Meyerowitz 2002; Stryker 2008; Stryker and Whittle 2006; Stryker and Currah 2014.

8. Michael Rogin's concept of political amnesia refers to 'a cultural structure of motivated disavowal'. As he puts it, 'Since amnesia means motivated forgetting, it implies a cultural impulse both to have the experience and not to retain it in memory. . . . Amnesia signals forbidden pleasure or memory joined with pain' (quoted in Summerville 2000, 70; also see Rogin 1990).

9. As Wiarda notes, Almond's 'intellectual shame' runs very deep, including his 'admission that prior to his writing of *The Politics of Developing Areas*, he had never visited any of the developing nations' (Wiarda 1989–1990, 68; also see Almond 1970b). In one of his revisions of his modernization and development theory, Almond still clung to the merits of his Parsonian approach, which he described as a 'determinacy-equilibrium approach'. Wrote Almond, 'I see no sin in this determinacy-equilibrium approach' (Almond 1970b, 24).

10. In Almond's case, this is because Parsons's theorization of the nuclear family and its relationship to the sexual deviance of the 'homosexual' was so repudiated. See Kingsbury and Scanzoni 1993.

11. Also see, for example, Cornwall, Correa, and Jolly 2008; Gosine 2009; Lind 2009; Lind and Share 2003.

CHAPTER 4

1. This incitement has its roots in the post–World War II popular and institutional discourse that figured the 'underdeveloped' and the 'undevelopable' as potential threats emerging out of crumbling Western colonial empires. These discourses, as we saw in chapter 3, were stabilized as a specific problem for the Western bloc of sovereign nation-states through 'the Great Dichotomy between more primitive and more advanced societies' (Huntington 1971, 285), which linked civilizational development to sexual development through numerous nineteenth- and twentieth-century evolutionary theories, including modernization and development theory (Hoad 2000; Almond and Powell 1966). These discourses then regimented statist solutions to this civilizational/sexual/political developmental problem through a range of public policies that employed development as an intimate, social, and biopolitical as well as necropolitical (neo)liberal governmentalizing and securitizing strategy (Foucault 2004; Doty 1995; Duffield 2007; Mbembe 2003), often through the explicit or implicit application of modernization and

development theory (Almond and Powell 1966). In this way, the 'underdeveloped' and the 'undevelopable' were cast as perverse, irrational, anarchic civilizational and sexual threats to the normal, rational, orderly, civilizational, and sexual logos of Western developmental statecraft—'the reproductive heterosexual nuclear family' (Parsons 1966; also see Peterson 1999; 2010; 2013; 2014a; 2014b). I discuss some of this later in this chapter, but also see chapter 3.

2. For an excellent genealogy of Huntington's ideas and their implications for the 'War on Terror' and on US responses to multiculturalism, see Palumbo-Liu 2002.

3. For a brief summary of Huntington's ideas and their relationship to modernization and development theory, see Weber 2013. And for an excellent critique, see Debrix 2003; 2007.

4. Much of this 'unease' Westerns feel about the 'unwanted im/migrant' and the 'terrorist' arises from how the boundaries of sovereign nation-states and/as the boundaries of 'civilizations' fail to keep these 'underdeveloped' or 'undevelopable' postcolonial figures in the geopolitical spaces assigned to them by Westerners. This is in part because, as Didier Bigo argues, the borders of neoliberal sovereign nation-states less resemble solid markings on a map that can be imposed upon the globe than they do the folds and flows of a Mobiüs ribbon (Bigo 2002). This gives rise to a desire for 'the management of unease' around unwelcome civilizational and developmental others, which takes the form of attempting to translate a desire for ease into a spatial arrangement that will achieve the exclusion of unwanted others. Bigo calls this spatial arrangement a 'ban-opticon'.

   Bigo's conceptualization of the ban-opticon is a play on Foucault's theorization of the panopticon. The panopticon is a mode of governmentality through which populations appear to be watched by the state so they can be corrected by the state for society. Bigo notes that governmentality through the panopticon—the watching of all populations—makes sense in a developmental context, which assumes all those populations being watched can be developed into useful members of society within the state. Yet with the rise of neoliberal risk society, states have given up on the correction of 'potentially dangerous minorities'. Bigo explains, 'The emphasis is no longer on curing or promoting individual development but on playing with fears by designating potentially dangerous minorities' (Bigo 2002, 82). 'The management of unease' is a mode of governmentality that 'transforms misgivings into a form of rule' (Bigo 2002, 82), whereby dangerous populations are watched so they can be spatially excluded or contained but not corrected. This is how 'the management of unease' gives rise to entirely new governmentalizing programs of securitization, which create new organizations of international relations.

5. In this sense, the 'underdeveloped' is forever in what Dipesh Chakrabarty calls 'the waiting room of history'. See Chakrabarty 2000, 8. For a discussion in a queer IR context, see Rao 2014.

6. Here Fortier is referencing McClintock's argument. As Fortier explains, 'The temporal and the spatial merge within a distinction between a "more developed" here and a "less developed" or "developing" there, producing what Anne McClintock refers to as "anarchronistic spaces" where "[g]eographical differences across space is figured as historical differences across time"' (Fortier 2001, 97–98; McClintock 1995, 40).

7. There are rich literatures on these processes, which begin by setting policies that regiment knowledge about who is the 'wanted im/migrant' and who is the 'unwanted im/migrant'. These policies govern, for example, detentions and deportations, heteronormative and increasingly homonormative family reunification policies, and bans on presumably promiscuous bodies (queer migrants, HIV-positive migrants, prostitutes, and others who offend normative moralities). For example, see discussions of these policies in Luibhéid and Cantú 2005; Luibhéid 2013; Frowd 2014; Chávez 2009; 2010; and activist resistances to them in especially Chávez 2013.

8. See note 21 in chapter 1 for a discussion of the 'al-Qaeda terrorist' in relation to the 'Islamic State (ISIS) terrorist' and the 'terrorist' more generally.

9. On how terrorism studies takes 'the psyche as its privileged site of investigation', see Puar and Rai 2002, 122.

10. See note 21 in chapter 1 for a discussion of how whiteness is used to disavow white violences as 'terrorist' violences.

11. These reports circulated in the British press in late October 2001. By late November 2001, they were retracted when the missing fighters were spotted in Afghanistan. Since then, however, numerous such figures have appeared in the press.

12. Although for feminist analyses of violence in the home, see, for example, Sjoberg and Gentry 2007; Gentry and Sjoberg 2015; Sjoberg, forthcoming.

13. For additional ways in which the 'al-Qaeda terrorist' is queerly sexed, gendered, and sexualized, see Weber 2002 and see Puar 2007.

CHAPTER 5

1. The 'gay rights holder' and 'the gay patriot'—like all of the figures I analyze in this book—are variously sexed and gendered. Yet, as I will explain, because these figures owe debts to how the figure of the male homosexual was born in Victorian discourses of sexuality and mobilized in contemporary Western discourses of international relations to figure the 'underdeveloped', the 'undevelopable', the 'unwanted im/migrant' and the 'terrorist', I concentrate my focus in this chapter on how the 'gay rights holder' and the 'gay patriot' are generally figured as male and masculine.

2. Ann Pellegrini goes even further than this, arguing that 'family has shifted from site of production to site of consumption' (2002, 137).

3. Duggan's understanding of 'queer' differs from mine, for it equates queer with what is perverse by opposing it to what is (the new) normal. My understanding of queer, in contrast, refers to the normal *and/or* perverse in relation to sex, gender, and/or sexuality. I go on to explain the implications of this understanding of queer, in relation to *either/or* logics and in relation to antinormativities.

4. Thanks to Neil Washbourne for this point.

5. In Puar's words, homonationalism is 'an analytic to apprehend state formation and a structure of modernity: as an assemblage of geopolitical and historical forces, neoliberal interests in capitalist accumulation both cultural and material, biopolitical state practices of population control, and affective investments in discourses of freedom, liberation, and rights' that are 'marked by the entrance of (some) homosexual bodies as worthy of state protection by nation-states' as homosexual

bodies with the right to have rights (Puar 2013, 337). On affective investments, see Agathangelou, Bassichis, and Spira 2008 and Lamble 2013.

6. This set of arguments about 'docile patriots' and 'gay patriots' is fundamental to Puar and Rai's (2002) and Puar's (2006; 2007) analyses of the 'terrorist'. The analysis offered in chapter 4 on the 'terrorist' can be reread through this set of claims.

7. The term 'pinkwashing', like the term 'greenwashing' environmental activists use, was used by activists protesting how corporations cynically embraced the pink ribbon campaign for breast cancer awareness as a strategy to promote their corporate images. Puar's use of the term, then, is very specific. Also see the debate on pinkwashing between Jasbir Puar and Maya Mikdashi (2012a; 2012b) and Heike Shotten and Haneen Maikey (2012).

8. As such, pinkwashing is part of a broader trend in US exceptionalism with respect to international law and human rights regimes and their application domestically and internationally. See, for example, Pease 2009 for a general discussion leading up to an analysis of the United States in relation to the War on Terror. On the War on Terror, also see Ignatieff 2005 and Foot 2008.

9. See, for example, Bosia 2014; O'Dwyer 2013; Momin 2014; Picq and Thiel 2015; Wilkinson and Langlois 2014.

10. Anna Agathangelou offers an alternative reading of Clinton's call for 'gay rights as human rights' through a racialized and sexualized necropolitical lens. Agathangelou argues that in Clinton's speech, 'slavery becomes collapsed as sexuality into the neoliberal imperium within which blacks and black life serve as the literal raw materials to guarantee long-term growth.' In so doing, she suggest that Clinton's speech constitutes 'not only the "straightjacketing" of sexuality, but also racial terror—where "gay rights" becomes a discourse and a practice of (perceived) racial economic superiority and (actual) racial subordination' (2013, 455).

11. In the introduction to their special issue of *differences* entitled 'Queer Theory without Anti-normativity', Robyn Wiegman and Elizabeth Wilson make compatible arguments, as they trace 'the centrality of antinormativity to the political imaginary and analytic vocabulary of queer theory' (2015, 2). They and their contributors go on to consider the question, 'What might queer theory do if its allegiance to antinormativity was rendered less secure?' (2015, 1). To me, insecuring an equation of antinormativity with 'queer' requires queer theorists to think through *and/or* logics and not only *either/or* logics. What additional possibilities and/or understandings of queer open up in theory and in political practice is something I consider in my reading of the 'Eurovisioned drag queen' in chapter 6 and something I return to in my concluding remarks in chapter 7.

12. Odysseos's insights are as applicable to broad concepts like 'homonormativity', 'homonationalism', and 'the human rights industrial complex' as they are to specific figurations of the 'gay rights holder' that appear, for example, as Clinton's figure of the 'LGBT in the shadows' that I discuss later in this chapter.

13. Thanks to Kate Nash for this point.

14. Illustratively, Langlois's performative reading of the ASEAN (Association of Southeast Asian Nations) case makes this point (2014), as does Zivi's reading of same-sex marriage rights in the United States (2014). Also see Lind and Keating

2013. To be clear, I am not arguing that claiming the right to have rights is the *only or the best way* to combat global injustices. See Brown 2004, 161–162, on this point. Rather, I am arguing that it is one tactic among a wider array of tactics that global activists should not give up on.

15. The version of Clinton's speech I consulted did not have page numbers. To make it easier for others to find the quotes I reference, I inserted page numbers on the version of the speech I consulted. See Clinton 2011.

16. At the time of her speech, Clinton's figuration of the 'LGBT' in relation to the 'soldier' can be more accurately described as 'the LGB-Fake-T' that Dean Spade writes about (Spade 2004; also see Richter-Montpetit 2014a; 2014b). Yet at the time of this writing, the female-to-male trans* soldier is beginning to be normativized in the US military, as the case of Airman Logan Ireland suggests. As Fiona Dawson explains, 'Remarkably, after telling his leaders and some peers that his sex was assigned female at birth, he [Ireland] received their support—despite military policy that prevents transgender people from serving openly. Meanwhile, his fiancée, Laila Villanueva, who was assigned male at birth, has a similar scenario, but works without the support of her command' (2015).

17. Albeit from presumably progressive, active Western agents to presumably regressive, passive Third World recipient subjects.

18. In US political speak, Clinton's saying her position has 'evolved' on same-sex marriage is akin to saying she had to wait until it was politically possible to declare her support for same-sex marriage as a US politician who may be aspiring to the presidency.

19. UK prime minister David Cameron when commenting on the passage of same-sex legislation in the UK: 'I am proud that we have made same-sex marriage happen. . . . Making marriage available to everyone says so much about the society we are in and the society we want to live in. . . . If a group is told over and over again that they are less valuable, over time they may start to believe it. In addition to the personal damage this can cause, *it inhibits the potential of the nation*" (Cameron 2013, my italics; discussed more thoroughly in Lind 2014b).

20. For one illustration of the figuration of the 'homosexual' as a carrier of HIV and AIDS in US policy, see Frowd 2014. More recently, the 'LGBT in the shadows' as a carrier of death and disease has morphed into the carrier of Ebola. See Wee 2014.

21. My own position is that while I agree with Spade that Clinton's speech is an instance of pinkwashing, I would argue that Clinton's speech also *exceeds* any categorization as *merely* pinkwashing. For—as I argued earlier—while Clinton's embrace of 'gay rights as human rights' does not 'simply set people free to make the world as they see fit' (Brown 2004, 461), neither is it '*just* a cipher for the totalizing power of the sinister agents behind "the enlightenment project"' (Langlois reading Brown, in Langlois 2012, 561). Rather, it might better be understood as a bundle of sometimes contradictory figurations of 'homosexuality' and the 'homosexual' that may be (compatible with) a US scripting of the world in (neo)imperialist terms *that are also compatible with* an attempt by the United States to see the 'LGBT' (but *not* the 'LGBT in the shadows') accorded status as a full member of 'the universal community of human beings'. This, in my view, makes Clinton's speech irreducible to '*the*

human rights industrial complex' (Puar 2013, 338; my emphasis), to *the* neoliberal imperium' (Agathangelou 2013) on whose behalf *the* human rights industrial complex' is seemingly mobilized or to pinkwashing alone. This further complicates how critiques and celebrations of Clinton's speech may position us in relation to 'the right side of history' and/or 'the wrong side of empire' (Rao 2012).

CHAPTER 6

1. While only a handful of figures are represented, recognized, and read as *and/or* in international relations, it is arguably the case that—as this example of Neuwirth/Wurst will suggest—most if not all figures that are read as *either/or* require an enormous amount of labor to produce them as such, and these *either/or* figurations are difficult if not impossible to sustain.

2. Which countries count as 'European' has changed throughout the competition's history. In the original 1956 Eurovision Song Contest, any state that bordered the Mediterranean was invited to compete, and seven Western European states participated. Since then, the list of eligible participants has expanded as formal and informal understandings of 'Europe' have changed, to include, for example, Eastern European states. Since 2014, fifty-one countries have taken part in the competition, including Western and Eastern European states as well as such Mediterranean states as Israel, Turkey, and Morocco. In 2015, Australia competed in Eurovision as a guest participant, further complicating what 'Europe' means and where 'Europe' is located.

3. While, as Catherine Baker notes, it would be wrong to confuse Dana International with Neuwirth/Wurst for many reasons, including Dana's self-identification as a trans*woman and Neuwirth/Wurst's identification as not trans* (Baker 2014a), these two figures are implicated in some of the same debates over equality and liberty that work themselves out in the registers of the national and the international in relation to Eurovision. While it is beyond the scope of this chapter to read them together, doing so could point to how each of them—in similar and in different ways—contests the reasonable limits of 'Europe itself'. Thanks to Synne L. Dyvik for pushing me on this point.

4. Baker goes on to contest this reductive reading of Neuwirth/Wurst's importance in/to 'Europe', arguing, 'Rather than reading Conchita and her popularity as "one in the eye for Putin", her performance can and should challenge viewers to question their own prejudices rather than the prejudices of others. . . . The ethical imperative that Conchita aims to promote can't be restated often enough: as Judith Butler stated in a recent interview, "[n]o matter whether one feels one's gendered and sexed reality to be firmly fixed or less so, every person should have the right to determine the legal and linguistic terms of their embodied lives"' (Baker 2014a).

5. This idea of living on borders returns us to Ashley's 1989 piece 'Living on Borderlines', in which he developed his notion of 'statecraft as mancraft' and to Derrida's 1977 piece 'Living On: Border Lines', which Ashley's title references.

6. This is one definition of the beard in the Oxford English Dictionary, cited in Guenther, (2015).

7. See Ring 2014, http://countdowntozerotime.com/2014/05/11/eurovision-song-contest-won-by-christ-like-transvestite-who-looks-like-a-gay-jesus-sings-illuminate-theme-song-rise-like-a-phoenix/, and https://thecontemplativeobserver.wordpress.com/category/conchita-wurst/ respectively.

8. 'Rise Like a Phoenix 'was not written specifically for Neuwirth/Wurst. As its composer explains, 'I had "Rise Like A Phoenix" originally composed for another project', but the Austrian record label Unison would not publish it. When the Austrian Eurovision committee approached him for a contribution for Eurovision 2014, Harris thought of and offered them 'Rise Like a Phoenix', which was ultimately selected (Maier 2014).

9. Conchitawurst.com/about/biography; downloaded May 30, 2014.

10. Downloaded March 11, 2015.

11. Conchitawurst.com/about/biography; downloaded May 30, 2014.

12. Melanie Richter-Montpetit produced the reading of Knack and Wurst in this paragraph.

13. Rahul Rao also explores the transnational production of homophobia, albeit in a very different context. See Rahul 2014.

14. Thanks to Melanie Richter-Montpetit for this point. The specific coffee bean advertisement Conchita's Colombia conjures up for me is the 'This is Juan Valdez' advertisement and the Juan Valdez coffee brand. As the Juan Valdez website explains, 'Juan Valdez, our logo character, was born in 1959. Since then he represents more than 500 thousand Colombian coffee growing families. His mission is to communicate to the world, the work and the dedication hidden behind a delicious cup of Colombian coffee'. The website continues, 'The coffee and the stores became the showcase of the best Colombian coffee, being the reflex of a responsible, honest authentic, committed and proud of representing to the thousands of Colombian coffee growers brand'. This constructs Colombia and 'the Colombian' as idyllic places/figures that predate contemporary Western imaginaries that associate them with drugs, criminality, and corruption. See http://www.juanvaldezcafe.com/en/juan-valdez-cafe/our-brand.

15. Thanks to Melanie Richter-Montpetit for this point.

16. Aparicio and Chávez-Silverman (1997) develop the notion of 'tropicalization' as a term that—akin to Edward Said's notion of orientalism—expresses how specifically Latin American and Latinas/os in the United States are othered through traditional colonizing discourses. As they explain the term, to tropicalize 'means to trope, to imbue a particular space, geography, group, or nation with a set of traits, images and values' (1997, 1) that perpetuate 'the imbalance of power in the transcultural relationship, gender-based myths about Latin America and Latina/o sexuality, [and] tensions inherent in contact zones between cultures', for example. They also explore how these 'hegemonic tropicalizations' are resisted. See Aparicio and Chávez-Silverman 1997; and https://books.google.co.uk/books?id=XLS0AAAAIAAJ&source=gbs_book_other_versions.

17. Thanks to Melanie Richter-Montpetit for this point about brownface. See Northup, 2014 for discussion of this point specifically in relation to Neuwirth/Wurst. In making these points, I am not suggesting that race is essential; nor am I denying the

materialities of how technologies of race function. Race—and racial passing—are much more complex than this, as many scholars have pointed out. Public discussions of race, racialization, and racial passing most recently dominated popular US discourse when the case of Rachel Dolezal—a US woman whose parents identify as white but who herself identifies as black and appears to have transformed her outward appearance to conform to her identification as black—broke in 2015. The Dolezal case led numerous scholars and activists to recall and reconsider their understandings of 'passing for black' and what that does. See, for example, Sara Ahmed's June 14, 2015, *Feminist Killjoy* post 'Some Striking Feature: Whiteness and Institutional Passing', especially footnote 1, in which Ahmed discusses her own reflections on the topic of 'passing as black' authored fifteen years earlier (http://feministkilljoys.com/2015/06/14/some-striking-feature-whiteness-and-institutional-passing/; Ahmed 2000) as her point of departure for her then forthcoming reflections on this specific case. Among the texts Ahmed engaged with in her 2000 work were hooks 2000; Griffin 1961; and Sunderland 1997.

18. Such appropriations are not uncommon in either drag performances (see, e.g., Muñoz 1999) or in the Germanophone entertainment industry, especially in the Germanophone 'Schlager' market (Simon 2000). Thanks to Catherine Baker for this second point.

19. As this chapter makes clear, the 'Europeanness' of any sovereign nation-state can never be taken for granted. Yet the case of Russia is particularly interesting. For since the rule of Peter the Great, Russia has been debating and reformulating its identity as 'European', 'Slavic', and/or 'Asian'. These debates and reformulations continue under Putin. In this respect, Russia's historical relationship to 'Europe' is the story of 'Europe itself', a story that is always unfolding but not finally told. Thanks to Zdenek Kavan for an extensive discussion on this point. Thanks to Stefanie Ortman for further discussions. Also see Chepurina and Kaufman (2014).

20. This comment seems to presume that Joan of Arc is not herself a figure who troubles these traditional Christian understandings of both religious devotion and gender conformity. Yet she is a figure who can more easily be folded into traditional religious, racial, national, and civilizational narratives than Conchita Wurst can be. Thanks to Catherine Baker for the discussion on this point.

21. Http://www.bbc.co.uk/news/magazine-27443936.

22. Thanks to Melanie Richter-Montpetit for helping me to articulate this point.

23. Http://conchitawurst.com/about/biography/, downloaded March 20, 2015. This biography page continues to be revised, often appearing under a new URL. The best way to find the latest version is to go to conchitwurst.com and then click on the bio tab.

24. Neuwirth/Wurst as Conchita Wurst in interview accompanying 2013 bio.

25. Thanks to Melanie Richter-Montpetit for drawing out this point on the everyday violences of racialized visual regimes.

26. I make a similar argument about the detachable phallus and its relationship to the US body politic in *Faking It*. See Weber 1999.

27. For a discussion of uprootings and regroundings in the contexts of home and migration, see Ahmed, Castañeda, and Fortier 2000.

28. Thanks to Anne-Marie Fortier for this point.
29. Http://www.eurovision.tv/page/history/year/participant-profile/?song=31403, downloaded March 23, 2015.
30. I make a similar argument about the US body politic as a body in pieces in *Faking It*. See Weber 1999.
31. In a passing comment in *Aporia*, Derrida says that one could do the same sort of analysis of Europe and of death in the register of sexuality, but he neglects to offer such an analysis.
32. Thanks to Synne L. Dyvik for directing me to look not just at Derrida on the aporia but also his earlier reflections on Europe, and for generally pushing me to develop my reading of Neuwirth/Wurst and 'Europe' in this conclusion.

CHAPTER 7

1. This 'man' is grounded in political, religious, and scientific discourses that sex and gender this figure as male and masculine, even though in practice this figure can be female. What this figure as yet cannot be is both male *and/or* female, which is what the story of Neuwirth/Wurst's figuration as the *and/or* tells in chapter 6.
2. Wiegman and Wilson might think of these as reifying longtime queer commitments to antinormativities, to the neglect of asking, 'What might queer theory do if its allegiance to antinormativity was rendered less secure?' (2015, 1).

Adams, William Lee (2012). 'Conchita Wurst Interview: Austria's Drag Queen Talks Celine Dion and Eurovision'. WiWiBlogges. http://wiwibloggs.com/2012/01/10/conchita-wurst-interview-austrias-drag-queen-talks-celine-dione-and-eurovision/13580/, downloaded March 8, 2015.

Adler-Nissen, Rebecca (2014). 'Stigma Management in International Relations'. *IO* 68(1):143–176.

Agathangelou, Anna M. (2013). 'Neoliberal Geopolitical Order and Value: Queerness as a Speculative Economy and Anti-blackness as Terror'. *International Feminist Journal of Politics* 15(4):453–476.

Agathangelou, Anna M., M. Daniel Bassichis, and Tamara L. Spire (2008). 'Intimate Investments: Homonormativity, Global Lockdown, and the Seduction of Empire'. *Radical History Review* 100: 120–143.

Agathangelou, Anna M. and L. H. M. Ling (2004). 'The House of IR'. *ISQ* 6(4):21–49.

Ahmed, Sara (2000). *Strange Encounters: Embodied Others in Post-coloniality.* London: Routledge.

Ahmed, Sara (2006). *Queer Phenomenology: Orientations, Objects, Others.* Durham, NC: Duke University Press.

Ahmed, Sara (2010). *The Promise of Happiness.* Durham, NC: Duke University Press.

Ahmed, Sara, Claudia Castañeda, and Anne-Marie Fortier, eds. (2000). *Uprootings/ Regroundings: Questions of Home and Migration.* Oxford: Berg.

Alker, Hayward, Jr. (1992). 'The Humanistic Moment in International Studies: Reflections on Machiavelli and Las Casas: 1992 Presidential Address'. *International Studies Quarterly* 36(4):347–371.

Alexander, Jacqui (1994). 'Not Just (Any)Body Can Be a Citizen: The Politics of law, Sexuality, and Postcoloniality in Trinidad and Tobago and the Bahamas'. *Feminist Review* 48:5–23.

Almond, Gabriel A. (1970a). 'Determinacy-Choice, Stability-Change: Some Thoughts on a Contemporary Polemic in Political Theory'. *Government and Opposition* 5(1):22–40.

Almond, Gabriel A. (1970b). *The Politics of Developing Areas.* Boston: Little Brown.

Almond, Gabriel A., and Bingham Powell (1966). *Comparative Politics: A Developmental Approach.* Boston: Little, Brown.

Altman, Dennis (2006). 'Taboos and Denial in Government Responses'. *International Affairs* 82(2):257–268.

Amar, Paul (2011). 'Middle East Masculinity Studies: Discourses of "Men in Crisis", Industries of Gender in Revolution'. *Journal of Middle East Women's Studies* 3(7):36–71.

Amar, Paul (2013). *The Security Archipelago: Human-Security States, Sexuality Politics, and the End of Neoliberalism*. Durham, NC: Duke University Press.

Anderson, Benedict (1983). *Imagined Communities: Reflections on the Origins and Spread of Nationalism*. London: Verso.

Anzaldúa, Gloria (1987). *Borderlands / La Frontera: The New Mestiza*. San Francisco: Spinsters / Aunt Lute.

Aparicio, Frances R., and Susana Chávez-Silverman (1997). *Tropicalization*. Lebanon, NH: University Press of New England.

Arendt, Hannah (1994). *The Origins of Totalitarianism*. New York: Harcourt.

Arondekar, Anjali, and Geeta Patel (forthcoming). 'Area Impossible: The Geopolitics of Queer Studies'. Special issue of *GLQ: A Journal of Lesbian and Gay Studies*.

Ashley, Richard K. (1984). 'The Poverty of Neorealism'. *International Organization* 38(2):225–286.

Ashley, Richard K. (1988). 'Untying the Sovereign State: A Double Reading of the Anarchy Problematique'. *Millennium-Journal of International Studies* 17(2): 227–262.

Ashley, Richard K. (1989). 'Living on Borderlines'. In James Der Derian and Michael J Shapiro, eds., *International/Intertextual Relations*, 259–321. Lexington, MA: Lexington.

Ashley, Richard K., and R. B. J. Walker (1990). 'Introduction: Speaking the Language of Exile: Dissident thought in International Studies'. *International Studies Quarterly* 34(3):259–268.

Baker, Catherine (2014a). 'Rising Like a Phoenix: Has Conchita Wurst Opened a New Chapter in the Queer History of Eurovision?' Wordpress blog, May 14, https://bakercatherine.wordpress.com/2014/05/14/rising-like-a-phoenix-has-conchita-wurst-opened-a-new-chapter-in-the-queer-history-of-eurovision/, downloaded January 26, 2015.

Baker, Catherine (2014b). '"The Gay World Cup"? The Eurovision Song Contest, LGBT Equality and Human Rights after the Cold War'. Wordpress blog, April 4. https://bakercatherine.wordpress.com/2014/04/04/the-gay-world-cup-the-eurovision-s ong-contest-lgbt-equality-and-human-rights-after-the-cold-war/, downloaded January 26, 2015.

Banuazizi, Ali (1987). 'Social-Psychological Approaches to Political Development'. In Myron Weiner and Samuel P. Huntington, eds., *Understanding Political Development*, 281–316. Prospect Heights, IL: Waveland.

Barthes, Roland (1974). *S/Z*. Translated by R Miller. New York: Hill and Wang.

Barthes, Roland (1976). *Sade, Fourier, Loyola*. Translated by Richard Miller. New York: Hill and Wang.

BBC (2014). 'Austria Wins Eurovision Song Contest'. May 11. http://www.bbc.co.uk/news/entertainment-arts-27358560, downloaded March 10, 2015.

Bedford, Kate (2005). 'Loving to Straighten Out Development: Sexuality and Ethnodevelopment in the World Bank's Ecuadorian Lending'. *Feminist Legal Studies* 13(3):295–322.

Bedford, Kate (2007). 'The Imperative of Male Inclusion: How Institutional Context Influences World Bank Gender Policy'. *International Feminist Journal of Politics* 9(3): 289–311.

Bedford, Kate (2009). *Developing Partnerships: Gender, Sexuality, and the Reformed World Bank*. Minneapolis: University of Minnesota Press.

Bedford, Kate, and Shirin M. Rai (2010). 'Feminists Theorize International Political Economy'. *Signs* 40(1):1–18.

Beger, Nico J. (2009). *Tensions in the Struggle for Sexual Minority Rights in Europe: Que(e) rying Political Practices*. Manchester: Manchester University Press.

Bergeron, Suzanne (2010). 'Querying Feminist Economics' Straight Path to Development: Household Models Reconsidered'. In Amy Lind, ed., *Development, Sexual Rights, Global Governance*, 54–63. London: Routledge.

Berlant, Lauren (2007). 'Slow Death (Sovereignty, Obesity, Lateral Agency)'. *Critical Inquiry* 35(Summer):754–780.

Berlant, Lauren (2011). *Cruel Optimism*. Durham, NC: Duke University Press.

Berlant, Lauren, and Elizabeth Freeman (1992). 'Queer Nationality'. *boundary 2* 19(1):149–180.

Berlant, Lauren, and Michael Warner (1995). 'What Does Queer Theory Teach us About X?' *PMLA* 110(3):343–349.

Berlant, Lauren, and Michael Warner (1998). 'Sex in Public'. *Critical Inquiry* 24(2):547–566.

Berman, Jacqueline (2003). '(Un)Popular Strangers and Crises (Un)Bounded'. *EJIR* 9:37–86.

Bhabha, Homi (1994). *The Location of Culture*. London: Routledge.

Bially Mattern, Janice, ed. (forthcoming). *Hierarchies*. Cambridge: Cambridge University Press.

Bier, Marshall (2005). *International Relations in Uncommon Places: Indigeneity, Cosmology, and the Limits of International Theory*. Basingstoke: Palgrave Macmillan.

Biersteker, Thomas, and Cynthia Weber, eds. (1996). *State Sovereignty as Social Construct*. Cambridge: Cambridge University Press.

Bigo, Didier (2002). 'Security and Immigration: Toward a Critique of the Governmentality of Unease'. *Alternatives* 27(1):63–92.

Bigo, Didier, and R. B. Walker (2007). 'Political Sociology and the Problem of the International'. *Millennium-Journal of International Studies* 35(3):725–739.

Binnie, J. (2004). *The Globalization of Sexuality*. London: Sage.

Black, Tim (2014). 'Russia-Baiting Reveals Its Wurst Side'. *Spiked*, May 12. http://www.spiked-online.com/newsite/article/russia-baiting-reveals-its-wurst-side/15010#.VRaWXEsVduY, downloaded March 28, 2015.

Bornstein, Kate (1995). *Gender Outlaw: On Men, Women, and the Rest of Us*. New York: Vintage Press.

Bosia, Michael J. (2014). 'Strange Fruit: Homophobia, the State and the Politics of LGBT Rights and Capabilities'. *Journal of Human Rights* 13(3):256–273.

Bourdon, Jérôme (2007). 'Unhappy Engineers of the European Soul: The EBU and the Woes of Pan-European Television'. *International Communication Gazette* 69(3): 263–280.

Brah, Avtar (1996). *Cartographies of Diaspora: Contesting Identities*. London: Routledge.

Braidotti, Rosi (1994). *Nomadic Subject: Embodiment and Sexual Difference in Contemporary Feminist Theory*. New York: Columbia University Press.

Briggs, Laura (2003). *Reproducing Empire*. Berkeley: University of California Press.

Bromwich, Kathryn (2014). 'Conchita Wurst: "Most Artists Are Sensitive and Insecure People. I Am Too"'. *Guardian*, July 6. http://www.theguardian.com/music/2014/jul/06/conchita-interview-sensitive-insecure-eurovision-gay-pin-up-austrian, downloaded July 7, 2015.

Brown, Wendy (2004). ' "The Most We Can Hope For . . .": Human Rights and the Politics of Fatalism'. *South Atlantic Quarterly* 103(2–3):451–463.

Bush, George W. (2001). 'Speech to Congress'. September 20.

Butler, Judith (1993). 'Critically Queer'. *GLQ: A Journal of Lesbian and Gay Studies* 1:17–32.

Butler, Judith (1994). 'Extracts from *Gender as Performance*: An interview with Judith Butler'. Interview by Lynne Segal and Peter Osborne. *Radical Philosophy* 67(Summer):32–39.

Butler, Judith (1997). 'Merely Cultural'. *Social Text* 52–53:265–277.

Butler, Judith (1999). *Gender Trouble*. New York: Routledge.

Butler, Judith (2004). *Undoing Gender*. New York: Routledge.

Butler, Judith (2008). 'Sexual Politics, Torture, and Secular Time'. *British Journal of Sociology* 59(1):1–23.

Butler, Judith (2009). *Frames of War*. London: Verso.

Butler, Judith (2010). 'Critique, Dissent, Disciplinarity'. *Critical Inquiry* 35(Summer): 773–795.

Cage, Feilding, Tara Herman, and Nathan Good (2014). 'Lesbian, Gay, Bisexual and Transgender Rights around the World'. May 16. http://www.theguardian.com/world/ng-interactive/2014/may/-sp-gay-rights-world-lesbian-bisexual-transgender, downloaded May 16, 2014.

Cameron, David (2013). 'David Cameron on Same-Sex Marriage: "I Am Proud We Have Had the Courage to Change"'. *London Evening Standard*, July 18. http://www.standard.co.uk/news/uk/david-cameron-on-samesex-marriage-i-am-proud-we-have-had-the-courage-to-change-8716743.html, downloaded November 9, 2014.

Campbell, David (1992). *Writing Security*. Minneapolis: University of Minnesota Press.

Carroll, James (2004). 'The Bush Crusade'. *Nation*, September 20. http://www.thenation.com/article/bush-crusade, downloaded October 21, 2014.

Castañeda, Claudia (2002). *Figurations: Child, Bodies, Worlds*. Durham, NC: Duke University Press.

Chabram-Dernerseian, Angie (1999). ' "Chicana! Rican? No, Chicana Riqueña!": Refashioning the Transnational Connection'. In Caren Kaplan, Norma Alarcón, and Minoo Moallem, eds., *Between Woman and Nation: Nationalisms, Transnational Feminisms, and the State*, 264–295. Durham, NC: Duke University Press.

Chakrabarty, Dipesh (2000). *Provincializing Europe: Postcolonial Thought and Historical Difference*. Princeton, NJ: Princeton University Press.

Chávez, Karma R. (2009). 'Embodied Translation: Dominant Discourse and Communication with Migrant Bodies-as-Text'. *Howard Journal of Communications* 20(1):18–36.

Chávez, Karma R. (2010). 'Border (In)Securities: Normative and Differential Belonging in LGBTQ and Immigrant Rights Discourse'. *Communication and Critical/Cultural Studies* 7(2):136–155.

Chávez, Karma R. (2013). *Queer Migration Politics: Activist Rhetoric and Coalitional Possibilities*. Urbana-Champaign: University of Illinois Press.

Chepurina, Maria (2011). 'Is Russian Identity European Identity?'. *InFocus*, April 21. http://infocusrevue.com/2011/04/21/is-russian-identity-european-identity, downloaded March 21, 2015.

Clancy, Tom (1994). *Debt of Honor*. New York: HarperCollins.

Clinton, Hillary (2011). 'On Gay Rights Abroad: Secretary of State Delivers Historic LGBT Speech in Geneva'. *Huffington Post*, June 12. http://www.huffingtonpost.com/2011/12/06/hillary-clinton-gay-rights-speech-geneva_n_1132392.html, downloaded August 29, 2014.

Closs Stephens, Angharad (2013). *The Persistence of Nationalism: From Imagined Communities to Urban Encounters*. New York: Routledge.

Cloud, Dana L. (2004). ' "To Veil the Threat of Terror": Afghan Women and the Clash of Civilizations in the Imagery of the US War on Terrorism'. *Quarterly Journal of Speech* 90(3):285–306.

Cocks, Joan (2014). *On Sovereignty and Other Political Delusions*. London: Bloomsbury.

Cohler, Deborah (2010). 'Fireman Fetishes and *Drag King Dreams*: Queer Responses to September 11'. In Laura Sjoberg and Sandra Via, eds., *Gender, War, and Militarism*, 219–230. Oxford: Praeger.

Conrad, Ryan, ed. (2014). *Against Equality: Queer Revolution, Not Mere Inclusion*. Oakland, CA: AK Press.

Constantinou, Costas M. (2013). 'Between Statecraft and Humanism: Diplomacy and Its Forms of Knowledge'. *International Studies Review* 15(2):141–162.

Conway, Jill (1978). 'Stereotypes of Femininity in a Theory of Sexual Evolution'. In Martha Vicinus, ed., *Suffer and Be Still*, 55–72. Bloomington: University of Indiana Press.

Cornwall, Andrea, Sonia Correa, and Susie Jolly (2008). *Development with a Body: Sexuality, Human Rights and Development*. London: Zed Books.

Cowen, Deborah (2009). 'Review of *Terrorist Assemblages: Homonationalism in Queer Times* by Jasbir K. Puar'. *Antipode* 41(3):583–587.

Cox, Robert (1981). 'Social Forces, States and World Orders: Beyond International Relations Theory'. *Millennium* 10(2):126–155.

Crewshaw, Karen (1991). 'Mapping the Margins'. *Stanford Law Review* 43(6):1241–1299.

Darwich, Lynn, and Haneen Maikey (2014). 'The Road from Antipinkwashing Activism to the Decolonization of Palestine'. *WSQ: Women's Studies Quarterly* 42(3):281–285.

Davies, Caroline (2014). 'Conchita Wurst Pledges to Promote Tolerance after Jubilant Welcome Home'. *Guardian*, May 11. http://www.theguardian.com/tv-and-radio/2014/may/11/conchita-wurst-pledges-to-promote-tolerance, downloaded May 30, 2014.

Dawson, Fiona (2015). 'Transgender, at War and in Love'. *New York Times*, June 4. http://www.nytimes.com/video/opinion/100000003720527/transgender-at-war-and-in-love.html, downloaded June 13, 2015.

Debrix, François (2003). 'Tabloid Realism and the Revival of American Security Culture'. *Geopolitics* 8(3):151–190.

Debrix, François (2007). *Tabloid Terror: War, Culture, and Geopolitics*. New York: Routledge.

Debrix, François, and Alexander D. Barder (2012). *Beyond Biopolitics: Theory, Violence, and Horror in World Politics*. New York: Routledge.

de Lauretis, Teresa (1991). 'Queer Theory: Lesbian and Gay Sexualities: An Introduction'. *differences* 3(2):1991.

de Lauretis, Teresa (2011). 'Queer Texts, Bad Habits, and the Issue of a Future'. *GLQ: A Journal of Lesbian and Gay Studies* 17(2–3):243–263.

Derrida, Jacques (1977). 'Living On: Border Lines'. In Harold Bloom et al., eds., *Deconstruction and Criticism*, 75–175. New York: Seabury.

Derrida, Jacques (1981). *Positions*. Translated by Alan Bass. Chicago: University of Chicago Press.

Derrida, Jacques (1992). *The Other Heading: Reflections on Today's Europe*. Pascale-Translated Anne Brault and Michael B. Naas. Bloomington: Indiana University Press.

Derrida, Jacques (1993). *Aporias: Dying—Awaiting (One Another at) the 'Limits of Truth'*. Translated by Thomas Dutoit. Stanford, CA: Stanford University Press.

Deutsch, Karl W. (1966). *Nationalism and Social Communication: An Inquiry into the Foundations of Nationality*. 2nd ed. Cambridge, MA: MIT Press.

Diderot, Denis (1993). *The Indiscreet Jewels*. Translated by Sophie Hawkes. New York: Marsilio.

Doty, Roxanne L. (1996a). *Imperial Encounters*. Minneapolis: University of Minnesota Press.

Doty, Roxanne L. (1996b). 'Sovereignty and the Nation: Constructing the Borders of National Identity'. In Thomas Biersteker and Cynthia Weber, eds., *State Sovereignty as Social Construct*, 121–147. Cambridge: Cambridge University Press.

Doty, Roxanne L. (1996c). 'The Double-Writing of Statecraft: Exploring State Responses to Illegal Immigration'. *Alternatives* 21(2):171–189.

Doty, Roxanne L. (1997). 'Aporia: A Critical Exploration of the Agent-Structure Problematique in International Relations Theory'. *European Journal of International Relations* 3(3):365–392.

Doty, Roxanne L. (2007). 'States of Exception on the Mexico-U.S. Border: Security, "Decisions," and Civilian Border Patrols'. *International Political Sociology* 1:113–137.

Doty, Roxanne L. (2011). 'Bare Life: Border-Crossing Deaths and Spaces of Moral Alibi'. *Environment and Planning-Part D* 29(4):599–612.

Douzinas, Costas, and Conor Gearty, eds. (2014). *The Meanings of Rights*. Cambridge: Cambridge University Press.

Duffield, Mark (2007). *Development, Security and Unending War: Governing the World of Peoples*. Cambridge: Polity.

Duffy, Nick (2014). 'Conchita Wurst to Perform for the United Nations Next Week'. *PinkNews*. http://www.pinknews.co.uk/2014/11/01/conchita-wurst-to-perform-for-the-united-nations-next-week/, downloaded March 23, 2015.

Duggan, Lisa (1995). 'The Discipline Problem'. *GLQ: A Journal of Lesbian and Gay Studies* 2(3):179–191.

Duggan, Lisa (2002). 'The New Homonormativity: The Sexual Politics of Neoliberalism'. In Russ Castronovo and Dana D. Nelson, eds., *Materializing Democracy: Toward a Revitalized Culture*, 175–194. Durham, NC: Duke University Press.

Duggan, Lisa (2003). *The Twilight of Equality? Neoliberalism, Cultural Politics, and the Attack on Democracy.* Boston: Beacon Press.

Duggan, Lisa (2011–2012). 'After Neoliberalism? From Crisis to Organizing for Queer Economic Justice'. Part of the special issue 'A New Queer Agenda', edited by Joseph N. Defilippis, Lisa Duggan, Kenyon Farrow, and Richard Kim, *Scholar and Feminist Online* 10(1–2). http://sfonline.barnard.edu/a-new-queer-agenda/after-neoliberalism-from-crisis-to-organizing-for-queer-economic-justice/#sthash.VZQefQoI.dpuf, downloaded November 14, 2014.

Duggan, Lisa, and Richard Kim (2011–2012). 'Preface: A New Queer Agenda'. *Scholar and Feminist Online* 10(1–2). http://sfonline.barnard.edu/a-new-queer-agenda/preface/, downloaded March 5, 2014.

Easton, David (1957). 'An Approach to the Analysis of Political Systems'. *World Politics* 9(3):383–400.

Easton, David (1967). *A Systems Analysis of Political Life.* New York: Wiley.

Edelman, Lee (2004). *No Future: Queer Theory and the Death Drive.* Durham, NC: Duke University Press.

Edgar, James (2014). 'Putin Attacks Eurovision Drag Artist Conchita for Putting Her Lifestyle 'Up for Show''. *Telegraph*, May 26. http://www.telegraph.co.uk/news/worldnews/europe/russia/10856197/Putin-attacks-Eurovision-drag-artist-Conchita-for-putting-her-lifestyle-up-for-show.html, downloaded March 18, 2015.

Edkins, J. (2000). 'Sovereign Power, Zones of Indistinction, and the Camp'. *Alternatives* 25(1):3–25.

Eisner, Shiri (2013). *Bi: Notes for a Bisexual Revolution.* Berkeley, CA: Seal Press.

Eng, David (1997). 'Out Here and Over There: Queerness and Diaspora in Asian American Studies'. *Social Text* 15(3–4):31–52.

Eng, David (2010). *The Feeling of Kinship: Queer Liberalism and the Racialization of Intimacy.* Durham, NC: Duke University Press.

Eng, David, with Judith Jack Halberstam and José E. Muñoz, eds. (2005). 'What's Queer about Queer Studies Now?' Special issue of *Social Text* 23(3–4):1–17.

Enloe, Cynthia (2000). *Bananas, Beaches and Bases.* Berkeley: University of California Press.

Enloe, Cynthia (2004). *The Curious Feminist.* Berkeley: University of California Press.

Enloe, Cynthia (2013). 'Interview—Cynthia Enloe'. http://www.e-ir.info/2013/03/13/interview-cynthia-enloe/, downloaded August 30, 2014.

EurActiv (2013). 'Conchita Wurst Sings for Equality in the European Parliament'. October 8. http://www.euractiv.com/video/conchita-wurst-sings-equality-european-parliament-309039, downloaded January 26, 2015.

European Economic Union (1957). Treaty of Rome. http://ec.europa.eu/archives/emu_ history/documents/treaties/rometreaty2.pdf, downloaded January 23, 2015.

Eurovisious (2013). 'Eurovicious's Great Big Eurovision Drag Revue!' *Eurovisionist*. http:// www.eurovisionista.com/articles/euroviciouss-great-big-eurovision-drag-revue. aspx, downloaded January 24, 2015.

Fanon, Frantz (1967). *Black Skin / White Masks*. Translated by Richard Philcox. London: Pluto Press.

Fausto-Sterling, Anne (1993). 'The Five Sexes'. *Sciences* 33(2):20–24.

Ferguson, Kathy E. (1993). *The Man Question: Visions of Subjectivity in Feminist Theory*. Berkeley: University of California Press.

Finnemore, Martha, and Kathryn Sikkink (1998). *International Norm Dynamics and Political Change*. Cambridge: Cambridge University Press.

Fitzgerald, James (2014). 'Desire, Dreams, and Differences: Examining the Limits of Queer Necropolitics'. Paper presented at the Millennium Annual Conference, London School of Economics, September 13–14.

Foot, Rosemary (2008). 'Exceptionalism Again: The Bush Administration, the "Global War on Terror" and Human Rights'. *Law and History Review* 26(3):707–725.

Fortier, Anne-Marie (2000). *Migrant Belongings: Memory, Space, Identity*. Oxford: Berg.

Fortier, Anne-Marie (2001). ' "Coming Home": Queer Migrations and Multiple Evocations of home'. *European Journal of Cultural Studies* 4(4):405–424.

Fortier, Anne-Marie (2002). 'Queer Diasporas'. In Diane Richardson and Steven Seidman, eds., *Handbook of Lesbian and Gay Studies*, 183–197. Thousand Oaks, CA: Sage.

Fortier, Anne-Marie (2003). 'Making Home: Queer Migrations and Motions of Attachment'. In Sara Ahmed, Claudia Castañeda, and Anne-Marie Fortier, eds., *Uprootings/Regroundings: Questions of Home and Migration*, 115–135. Oxford: Berg.

Fortier, Anne-Marie (2008). *Multicultural Horizons: Diversity and the Limits of the Civil Nation*. London: Routledge.

Fortier, Anne-Marie (2012). 'The Migration Imaginary and the Politics of Personhood'. In M. Messer, R. Schroeder, and R. Wodak, eds., *Migrations: Interdisciplinary Perspectives*, 31–43. Berlin: Springer Verlag.

Fortier, Anne-Marie (2013a). 'Migration Studies'. In P. Adey, D. Bissell, K. Hannam, P Merriman, and M Sheller, eds., *The Routledge Handbook of Mobilities*, 64–73. London: Routledge.

Fortier, Anne-Marie (2013b). 'What's the Big Deal? Naturalisation and the Politics of Desire'. *Citizenship Studies* 17(6–7):697–711.

Fortier, Anne-Marie (in progress). *Life in the Waiting Room: Citizenship Attribution and Acquisition in Britain*.

Foucault, Michel (1965). *Madness and Civilization: A History of Insanity in the Age of Reason*. Translated by Richard Howard. New York: Pantheon Books.

Foucault, Michel (1971). 'The Lost Interview'. http://www.critical-theory.com/ watch-the-foucault-interview-that-was-lost-for-nearly-30-years/.

Foucault, Michel (1975). *Discipline and Punish: The Birth of the Prison*. Translated by Alan Sheridan. New York: Random House.

Foucault, Michel (1979). *The History of Sexuality.* Vol. 1: *An Introduction.* Translated by Robert Hurley. London: Allen Lane.

Foucault, Michel (1980). *Power/Knowledge: Selected Interviews and Other Writings, 1972–1977.* Edited by Colin Gordon. Translated by Colin Gordon, Leo Marshall, John Mepham, and Kate Soper. New York: Pantheon.

Foucault, Michel (1994). *Dits et écrits IV.* Paris: Gallimard.

Foucault, Michel (1997). 'The Abnormals'. Translated by Robert Hurley. In Paul Rabinow, ed., *Ethics: Subjectivity and Truth,* 51–52. New York: New Press.

Foucault, Michel (2004). *Society Must Be Defended.* Translated by David Macey. London: Penguin.

Foucault, Michel (2009). *Security, Territory, Population: Lectures at the Collège de France, 1977–1978.* Translated by Graham Burchell. New York: St. Martin's.

Francis, Daniel (1992). *The Imaginary Indian.* Vancouver: Arsenal Pulp Press.

Freud, Sigmund (1982). *Three Essays on the Theory of Sexuality.* Edited and translated by James Strachey. New York: Basic Books.

Freud, Sigmund (2005). *The Essentials of Psycho-Analysis.* Translated by James Strachey. New York: Random House.

Frowd, Philippe M. (2014). 'State Personhood, Abjection and the United States' HIV Travel Ban'. *Millennium* 42(3):860–878.

Gallie, W. B. (1955–1956). 'Essentially Contested Concepts'. *Proceedings of the Aristotelian Society* 56:167–98.

Garcia, Jonathan, and Richard Parker (2006). 'From Global Discourse to Local Action: The Makings of a Sexual Rights Movement?' *Horizontes Antropológicos* 12(26):13–41.

Geddes, Patrick, and J. Arthur Thomas (1889). *The Evolution of Sex.* London: W. Scott.

Gentry, Caron, and Laura Sjoberg (2015). *Beyond Mothers, Monsters, Whores.* London: Zed Books.

Gibson-Graham, Julie Katherine (1996). *'The' End of Capitalism (as We Knew It): A Feminist Critique of Political Economy; with a New Introduction.* Minneapolis: University of Minnesota Press.

Gilroy, Paul (1994). 'Diaspora'. *Paragraph* 17(3):207–212.

Gilroy, Paul (2000). *Between Camps: Nations, Cultures and the Allure of Race.* London: Allen Lane.

Gluhovic, Milija (2013). 'Sing for Democracy: Human Rights and Sexuality Discourse in the Eurovision Song Contest'. In Karen Fricker and Milija Gluhovic, eds., *Performing the 'New' Europe: Identities, Feelings and Politics in the Eurovision Song Contest,* 195–217. London: Palgrave Macmillan.

Goldie, Terry (2010). 'Queering the Problem'. *Reviews in Cultural Theory* 1(2), December 26. http://www.reviewsinculture.com/?r=50, downloaded November 11, 2014.

Gopinath, Gayatri (2005). *Impossible Desires: Queer Diasporas and South Asian Public Cultures.* Durham, NC: Duke University Press.

Gosine, Andil (2005). 'Sex for Pleasure, Rights to Participation, and Alternatives to AIDS: Placing Sexual Minorities and/or Dissidents in Development'. IDS Working Paper 228, February ed. Institute for Development Studies, Brighton, England.

Gosine, Andil (2009). 'Monster, Womb, MSM: The Work of Sex in International Development'. *Development* 52(1):25–33.

Gould, Deborah B. (2009). *Moving Politics: Emotion and ACT UP's Fight against AIDS*. Chicago: University of Chicago Press.

Grau, Marion (2004). *Of Divine Economy*. London: A&C Black.

Grewal, Inderpal, and Caren Kaplan, eds. (1994). *Scattered Hegemonies: Postmodernity and Transnational Feminist Practices*. Minneapolis: University of Minnesota Press.

Griffin, Chad (2013). 'Hillary Clinton Joins Fight for Marriage Equality'. Human Rights Watch Blog, March 18. http://www.hrc.org/blog/entry/hillary-clinton-joins-f ight-for-marriage-equality, downloaded November 9, 2014.

Griffin, John Howard (1961). *Black Like Me*. Boston: Houghton Mifflin.

Groth, Alexander J. (1970). 'Structural Functionalism and Political Development: Three Problems'. *Western Political Quarterly* 23(3):485–499.

Guenther, Amy (2015). 'What's in a Name?' *The Bearded Lady Project*. http://thebeard-edladyproject.com/about/whats-in-a-name/, downloaded March 8, 2015.

Gupta, Monisha Das (2006). *Unruly Immigrants: Rights, Activism, and Transnational South Asian Politics in the United States*. Durham, NC: Duke University Press.

Haas, Ernst (1970). 'The Study of Regional Integration: Reflections on the Joy and Anguish of Pretheorizing'. *International Organization* 24(4):607–646.

Halberstam, Judith Jack (2011). *The Queer Art of Failure*. Durham, NC: Duke University Press.

Halberstam, Judith M. (2005). *In a Queer Time and Place: Transgender Bodies, Subcultural Lives*. New York: New York University Press.

Halberstam, Judith M., and Ira Livingston, eds. (1995). *Posthuman Bodies*. Bloomington: Indiana University Press.

Halperin, David M. (2003). 'The Normalization of Queer Theory'. *Journal of Homosexuality* 45(2–4):339–343.

Halutz, Avshalom (2014). 'Eurovision's Bearded Drag Queen Diva Is Set to Take the Stage Tonight Despite Controversy'. *Haaretz*, May 27. http://www.haaretz.com/life/music-theater/1.582344, downloaded April 1, 2015.

Hammonds, Evelynn M. (1999). 'Toward a Genealogy of Black Female Sexuality: The Problematic of Silence'. In Janet Price and Margrit Shildrick, eds., *Feminist Theory and the Body: A Reader*, 93–104. New York: Routledge.

Hansen, Lene (2005). 'The Politics of Digital Autobiography: Understanding www.johnkerry.com.' In Klaus Bruhn Jensen, ed., *Interface://Culture: The World Wide Web as Political Resource and Aesthetic Form*, 151–175. Frederiksberg: Samfundslitteratur Press.

Haraway, Donna (1997). *Modest_Witness@Second_Millennium: FemaleMan_Meets_OncoMouse*. New York: Routledge.

Haritaworn, Jin (2008a). 'Shifting Positionalities: Empirical Reflections on a Queer/Trans of Colour Methodology'. *Sociological Research Online* 13(1):13.

Haritaworn, Jin, Adi Kuntsman, and Silvia Posocco, eds. (2013a). 'Murderous Inclusions: Queer Politics, Citizenship and the "Wars without End"'. Special issue of *International Feminist Journal of Politics* 15(4):445–551.

Haritaworn, Jin, Adi Kuntsman, and Silvia Posocco, eds. (*2013b*). 'Murderous Inclusions'. *International Feminist Journal of Politics* 15(4):445–452.

Haritaworn, Jin, Adi Kuntsman, and Silvia Posocco (2014). *Queer Necropolitics*. New York: Routledge.

Haworth, Abigail (2013). 'Why Have Young People in Japan Stopped Having Sex?' *Guardian*, October 20. http://www.theguardian.com/world/2013/oct/20/young-people-japan-stopped-having-sex, downloaded January 27, 2014.

Hemmings, Clare (2002). *Bisexual Spaces: A Geography of Sexuality and Gender*. London: Routledge.

Hildebrandt T. (2011). 'Same-Sex Marriage in China?' *Review of International Studies* 37(3):1313–1333.

Hoad, Neville (2000). Arrested development or the queerness of savages. *Postcolonial Studies* 3(2):133–158.

Hoad, Neville (2007). *African Intimacies: Race, Homosexuality, and Globalization*. Minneapolis: University of Minnesota Press.

Hobbes, Thomas (1996). *Leviathan*. Oxford: Oxford University Press.

Hopf, Ted (2010). 'The Logic of Habit'. *European Journal of International Relations* 16(4):539–561.

hooks, bell (1982). *Ain't I a Woman: Black Women and Feminism*. Boston: South End Press.

hooks, bell (2000). 'Eating the Other'. In Juliet Schor and Douglas B. Holt, eds., *The Consumer Society Reader*, 345–346. New York: New Press.

Huntington, Samuel P. (1969). *Political Order in Changing Societies*. New Haven: Yale University Press.

Huntington, Samuel P. (1971). 'The Change to Change: Modernization, Development and Politics'. *Comparative Politics* 3(3):283–322.

Huntington, Samuel P. (1975). 'The United States'. In Michel Crozier, Samuel Huntington, and Joji Watanuki, eds., *The Crisis of Democracy: Report on the Governability of Democracies to the Trilateral Commission*, 59–118. New York: New York University Press.

Huntington, Samuel P. (1996). *The Clash of Civilizations and the Remaking of World Order*. New York: Penguin.

Huntington, Samuel P. (2004a). 'The Hispanic Challenge'. *Foreign Policy* 141(2):30–45.

Huntington, Samuel P. (2004b). *Who Are We? The Challenges to America's National Identity*. New York: Simon and Schuster.

Huysmans, Jef, Andrew Dobson, and Raia Prokhovnik, eds. (2006). *The Politics of Protection: Sites of Insecurity and Political Agency*. New York: Routledge.

Ignatieff, Michael (2005). *American Exceptionalism and Human Rights*. Princeton, NJ: Princeton University Press.

Inayatullah, Sohail (1998). 'Imagining an Alternative Politics of Knowledge: Subverting the Hegemony of International Relations Theory in Pakistan'. *Contemporary South Asia* 7(1):27–42.

Jackson, Patrick (2011). *The Conduct of Inquiry in International Relations*. London: Routledge.

Jagose, Annamarie (1996). 'Queer Theory'. *Australian Humanities Review*. http://www. australianhumanitiesreview.org/archive/Issue-Dec-1996/jagose.html, downloaded February 3, 2013.

Jagose, A. (1997). *Queer Theory: An Introduction*. New York: New York University Press.

JanMohamed, Abdul R. (1992). 'Sexuality on/of the Racial Border: Foucault, Wright, and the Articulation of "Racialized Sexuality"'. In Domna Stanton, ed., *Discourses of Sexuality: From Aristotle to AIDS*, 94–116. Ann Arbor: University of Michigan Press.

Jauhola, Marjaana (2010). 'Building Back Better? Negotiating Normative Boundaries of Gender Mainstreaming and Post-tsunami Reconstruction in Nanggroe Aceh Darsussalam, Indonesia'. *Review of International Studies* 36(1):29–50.

Jeffreys, Sheila (2014). *Gender Hurts: A Feminist Analysis of the Politics of Transgenderism*. London: Routledge.

Johnson, Barbara (1980). *The Critical Difference: Essays in the Contemporary Rhetoric of Reading*. Baltimore: Johns Hopkins University Press.

Johnston, Mark Albert (2007). 'Bearded Women in Early Modern England'. *SEL* 47(1):1–28.

Kaufman, Andrew (2014). 'How Dostoevsky and Tolstoy Explain Putin's Politics'. andrewkaufman.com, April 7. http://andrewdkaufman.com/2014/04/ dostoevsky-tolstoy-explain-putins-politics/, downloaded April 26, 2015.

Keating, Michael (2004). *Plurinational Democracy: Stateless Nations in a Post-sovereignty Era*. Oxford: Oxford University Press.

Kegley Jr., Charles W. (1993). 'The Neoidealist Moment in International Studies? Realist Myths and the New International Realities: ISA Presidential Address March 27, 1993 Acapulco, Mexico'. *International Studies Quarterly* 131–146.

Khalil, As'ad Abu (2001). 'Sex and the Suicide Bomber'. *Salon*, November 7. http://www. salon.com/2001/11/07/islam_2/, downloaded October 21, 2014.

khanna, a. (2007). 'Us, sexuality types'. In B. Bose and S. Bhatacharyya, eds., *The Phobic and the Erotic*, 43–51. Calcutta: Seagull Press.

Kingsbury, Nancy, and John Scanzoni. "Structural-functionalism." *Sourcebook of family theories and methods*. New York: Springer US, 1993. 195–221.

Kissinger, Henry (1966). 'Domestic Structure and Foreign Policy'. *Daedalus* 95(2):503–529.

Klein, L., and L. Akerman (1995). *Women and Power in Native North America*. Norman: University of Oklahoma Press.

Kollman, Kelly (2007). 'Same-Sex Unions: The Globalization of an Idea'. *International Studies Quarterly* 51(2):329–257.

Konstantopoulos, Fotis (2013). 'Exclusive: Conchita Wurst Interview'. *Oiko Times*, September 16. http://oikotimes.com/2013/09/16/exclusive-conchita-wurst-interview/, downloaded March 8, 2015.

Kosharevska, Yuliya (2014). 'Interview with Angel Dzhambazki MEP candidate'. *One Europe*, May 23. http://one-europe.info/interview-with-angel-dzhambazki-mep, downloaded March 19, 2014.

Kozlov, Vladimir (2015). 'Russian Legislator Calls for Boycotting Eurovision Song Contest'. *Hollywood Reporter*, March 11. http://www.hollywoodreporter.com/news/ russian-legislator-calls-boycotting-eurovision-780652, downloaded March 21, 2015.

Krappe, Alexander H. (1945). 'The Bearded Venus'. *Folk-Lore* 56(4):325–335.

Kuntsman, Adi (2008). 'The Soldier and the Terrorist: Sexy Nationalism, Queer Violence'. *Sexualities* 11(1–2):142–170.

Kuntsman, Adi (2009). *Figurations of Violence and Belonging: Queerness, Migranthood, and Nationalism in Cyberspace and Beyond*. Bern: Peter Lang.

Lamble, Sarah (2013). 'Queer Necropolitics and the Expanding Carceral State: Interrogating Sexual Investments in Punishment'. *Law and Critique* 24(3):229–253.

Langlois, Anthony J. (2001). *The Politics of Justice and Human Rights: Southeast Asia and Universalist Theory*. Cambridge: Cambridge University Press.

Langlois, Anthony J. (2012). 'Human Rights in Crisis? A Critical Polemic against Polemical Critics'. *Journal of Human Rights* 11(4):558–570.

Langlois, Anthony J. (2014). 'Human Rights, "Orientation," and ASEAN'. *Journal of Human Rights* 13(3):307–321.

Langlois, Anthony J. (2015). 'Human Rights, LGBT Rights and International Theory'. In M. Picq and M. Thiel, eds., *Sexualities in World Politics: How LGBTQ Claims Shape International Relations*, 23–37. New York: Routledge.

Latour, Bruno (1993). *We Have Never Been Modern*. Cambridge: Harvard University Press.

Leigh, Darcy (2009). 'Colonialism, Gender and the Family in North America: For a Gendered Analysis of Indigenous Struggles'. *Studies in Ethnicity and Nationalism* 9:70–88.

Lewis, G. (2006). 'Imaginaries of Europe, Technologies of Gender, Economies of Power'. *European Journal of Women's Studies* 13:87–102.

Lind, Amy (2009). 'Governing Intimacy, Struggling for Sexual Rights: Challenging Heteronormativity in the Global Development Industry'. *Development* 52(1): 34–42.

Lind, Amy, ed. (2010). *Development, Sexual Rights and Global Governance*. London: Routledge.

Lind, Amy (2013). 'Sexual Politics and Constitutional Reform in Ecuador: From Neoliberalism to the *Buen Vivir*'. In Meredith L. Weiss and Michael J. Bosia, eds., *Global Homophobias*, 127–148. Urbana: University of Illinois Press.

Lind, Amy (2014a). 'The Economic Costs of Homophobia: How LGBT Exclusion Impacts Development', World Bank, Washington, DC, March 12.

Lind, Amy (2014b). 'Out in IR: Why Queer Visibility Matters'. *International Studies Review* 16(4), 601–604.

Lind, Amy, and Christine Keating (2013). 'Navigating the Left Turn: Sexual Justice and the Citizen Revolution in Ecuador'. *International Feminist Journal of Politics* 15(4):515–533.

Lind, Amy, and Jessica Share (2003). 'Queering Development: Institutionalized Heterosexuality in Development Theory, Practice and Politics in Latin America'. In Kum-Kum Bhavani, John Foran, and Priya Kurian (eds.). *Feminist Futures: Re-imagining women, Culture and Development*, 55–73. London: Zed Books.

Ling, L. H. M. (2001). *Postcolonial International Relations: Conquest and Desire between Asia and the West*. Basingstoke: Palgrave.

Lisle, Debbie, and Andrew Pepper (2005). 'The New Face of Global Hollywood: *Black Hawk Down* and the Politics of Meta-sovereignty'. *Cultural Politics* 1(2): 165–192.

Locke, John (1980). *Second Treatise of Government*. Indianapolis: Hackett.

Lorde, Audre (1984). 'Age, Race, Class and Sex: Women Redefining Difference'. In *Sister Outsider: Essays and Speeches*, 114–123. Freedom, CA: Crossing Press.

Luibhéid, Eithne (2002). *Entry Denied: Controlling Sexuality at the Border*. Minneapolis: University of Minnesota.

Luibhéid, Eithne, ed. (2008). 'Queer/Migrations: An Unruly Body of Scholarship'. Special issue of *GLQ: A Journal of Lesbian and Gay Studies* 14(2–3).

Luibhéid, Eithne (2013). *Pregnant on Arrival: Making the 'Illegal' Immigrant*. Minneapolis: University of Minnesota Press.

Luibhéid, Eithne, Robert Buffington, and Donna Guy, eds. (2014). *A Global History of Sexuality*. Malden, MA: Wiley-Blackwell.

Luibhéid, Eithne, and Lionel Cantú Jr. (2005). *Queer Migrations: Sexuality, U.S. Citizenship, and Border Crossings*. Minneapolis: University of Minnesota Press.

Maier, Jens (2014). 'Record Companies Refused "Rise Like a Phoenix"'. *Stern*, May 13. https://translate.google.com/translate?sl=auto&tl=en&js=y&prev=_t&hl=en&ie=UTF-8&u=http%3A%2F%2Fwww.stern.de%2Fkultur%2Fmusik%2Fesc-siegerin-conchita-wurst-plattenfirmen-lehnten-rise-like-a-phoenix-ab-2110281.html&edit-text=&act=url, downloaded April 1, 2015.

Mason, Charly, Joey Patulka, Ali Zuckowski, and Julian Maas (2014). 'Rise Like a Phoenix'. lyrics and composition.

Mbembe, Achille (2003). 'Necropolitics'. *Public Culture* 15(1):11–40.

McClintock, Anne (1995). *Imperial Leather: Race, Gender and Sexuality in the Colonial Contest*. New York: Routledge.

McNeil, Maureen (2007). *Feminist Cultural Studies of Science and Technology*. London: Routledge.

McRuer, Robert (2003). 'As Good as It Gets: Queer Theory and Critical Disability'. *GLQ: A Journal of Lesbian and Gay Studies* 9(1):79–105.

McRuer, Robert (2006). *Crip Theory: Cultural Signs of Queerness and Disability*. New York: New York University Press.

McRuer, Robert (2010). 'Disability Nationalism in Crip Times'. *Journal of Literary and Cultural Disability Studies* 4(2):163–178.

McRuer, Robert, and Anna Mollow, eds. (2012). *Sex and Disability*. Durham, NC: Duke University Press.

McRuer, Robert, and A. L. Wilkerson, eds. (2003). *Desiring Disability: Queer Theory Meets Disability Studies*. Durham, NC: Duke University Press.

Mead, Margaret (1928). *Coming of Age in Samoa*. New York: Blue Ribbon Books.

Mead, Margaret (1942). *And Keep Your Powder Dry: An Anthropologist Looks at America*. New York: William Morrow.

Mead, Margaret (1961). 'National Character and the Science of Anthropology'. In Seymour Martin Lipset and Leo Lowenthal, eds., *Culture and Social Character*, 15–26. New York: Free Press of Glencoe.

Merrill, Dennis (2006). 'The Truman Doctrine: Containing Communism and Modernity'. *Presidential Studies Quarterly* 36(1):27–37.

Meyerowitz, Joanne J. (2002). *How Sex Changed: A History of Transsexuality in the United States*. Cambridge: Harvard University Press.

Mikuš, Marek (2011). '"State Pride": Politics of LGBT Rights and Democratization in "European Serbia"'. *Eastern European Politics and Societies* 25(4):834–851.

Mohanty, Chandra Talpaed (1986). 'Under Western Eyes: Feminist Scholarship and Colonial Discourses'. *boundary 2* 12(3):333–358.

Molloy, Antonia (2014). 'Conchita Wurst: 'I would like to spend a week with Vladimir Putin to better understand him'. *Independent*, December 30. http://www.independent.co.uk/news/people/conchita-wurst-i-would-like-to-spend-a-week-with-vladimir-putin-to-better-understand-him-9949822.html, downloaded March 27, 2015.

Morgensen, Scott L. (2010). 'Settler Homonationalism: Theorizing Settler Colonialism within Queer Modernities'. *GLQ: A Journal of Lesbian and Gay Studies* 16:105–131.

Morgensen, Scott L. (2011). *Spaces between Us: Queer Settler Colonialism and Indigenous Decolonization*. Minneapolis: University of Minnesota Press.

Muñoz, José Esteban (1999). *Disidentifications: Queers of Color and the Performance of Politics*. Vol. 2. Minneapolis: University of Minnesota Press.

Muñoz, José (2009). *Cruising Utopia: The Then and There of Queer Futurity*. New York: New York University Press.

Nash, Jennifer (2008). 'Re-thinking Intersectionality'. *Feminist Review* 89:1–15.

Nash, Kate (2015). *The Political Sociology of Human Rights*. Cambridge: Cambridge University Press.

Nath, Dipika (2008). 'Discourses of Liberation or the Master's Tools?' academia.edu, posted January 1. https://www.academia.edu/4439534/Discourses_of_Liberation_or_the_Masters_Tools, downloaded April 25, 2015.

Nayak, Meghana (2014). 'Thinking about Queer IR's Allies'. *International Studies Review* 16(4):615–622.

Nelson, Scott G. (2004). 'Sovereignty, Ethics, Community'. *Philosophy and Social Criticism* 30(7):816–841.

Nelson, Scott G. (2009). *Sovereignty and the Limits of the Liberal Imagination*. New York: Routledge.

Neuwirth, Tom (2014). 'The One Show'. BBC1, May 23. https://www.youtube.com/watch?v=LtLQTAjb5qI, downloaded May 29, 2014.

Newsnight (2014). Interview with Conchita Wurst. BBC, May 23. http://www.bbc.co.uk/news/world-europe-27553400, downloaded May 24, 2014.

Northup, William (2014). 'Conchita Wurst: A Mixed Bag'. *Velociriot*, Mary 14. http://velociriot.org/2014/05/14/conchita-wurst-a-mixed-bag/, downloaded March 20, 2015.

Nyers, Peter (2009). 'The Accidental Citizen: Acts of Sovereignty and (Un)Making Citizenship'. In *Securitizations of Citizenship*, 118–136. Hoboken, NJ: Taylor and Francis.

Nyers, Peter (2010). 'Dueling Designs: The Politics of Rescuing Dual Citizens'. *Citizenship Studies* 14(1):47–60.

O'Dwyer, Conor (2013). 'Gay Rights and Political Homophobia in Postcommunist Europe: Is There an "EU Effect"?' In Meredith L. Weiss and Michael J. Bosia, eds., *Global Homophobia*, 103–126. Urbana: University of Illinois Press.

Odysseos, Louiza (2010). 'Human Rights, Liberal Ontogenesis and Freedom: Producing a Subject for Neoliberalism?' *Millennium* 38(3):747–772.

Odysseos, Louiza (2016). 'Human Rights, Self-Formation and Resistance in Struggles against Disposability: The "Theorising Practice" of Foucault's Counter-conduct'. *Global Society* 30(2), forthcoming.

Odysseos, Louiza, and Hakan Seckinelgin, eds. (1998). 'Gendering "the International"'. Special issue of *Millennium* 27(4).

O'Neill, John (1998). 'Parsons' Freud'. *Cultural Values* 2(4):518–532.

Ó'Tuathail, Gearóid, and Simon Dalby, eds. (1998). *Rethinking Geopolitics*. London: Routledge.

Owens, Patricia (2010). 'Torture, Sex and Military Orientalism'. *Third World Quarterly* 31(7):1041–1056.

Parker, Andrew, Mary Russo, Doris Sommer, and Patricia Yeager, eds. (1992). *Nationalisms and Sexualities*. New York: Routledge.

Parsons, Talcott (1951). *The Social System*. New York: Free Press.

Parsons, Talcott (1964). 'Evolutionary Universals in Society'. *American Sociological Review* 29(June):339–357.

Parsons, Talcott (1966). *Societies: Evolutionary and Comparative Perspectives*. Englewood Cliffs, NJ: Prentice Hall.

Parsons, Talcott, and R. Bales, with J. Olds, M. Zeiditch Jr., and P. Slater (1955). *Family Socialization and International Process*. New York: Free Press.

Patton, Cindy, and Benigno Sánchez-Eppler, eds. (2000). *Queer Diasporas*. Durham, NC: Duke University Press.

Pease, Donald E. (2009). *The New American Exceptionalism*. Minneapolis: University of Minnesota Press.

Pellegrini, Ann (2002). 'Commodity Capitalism and Transformations in Gay Identity'. In Arnaldo Cruz-Malave and Martin Manalansan IV, eds., *Queer Globalizations*, 134–145. New York: New York University Press.

Peters, Jeremy (2014). 'The Decline and Fall of the "H" Word'. *New York Times*, March 21. http://www.nytimes.com/2014/03/23/fashion/gays-lesbians-the-term-homosexual.html?_r=0, downloaded September 8, 2014.

Peterson, V. Spike (1992). *Gendered States*. Boulder, CO: Lynne Rienner.

Peterson, V. Spike (1999). 'Sexing Political Identities/Nationalism as Heterosexism'. *International Feminist Journal of Politics* 1(1):34–65.

Peterson, V. Spike (2010). 'Global Householding amid Global Crises'. *Politics and Gender* 6:271–281.

Peterson, V. Spike (2013). 'The Intended and Unintended Queering of States/Nations'. *Studies in Ethnicity and Nationalism* 13(1):57–68.

Peterson, V. Spike (2014a). 'Sex Matters: A Queer History of Hierarchies'. *International Feminist Journal of Politics* 16(3):389–409.

Peterson, V Spike (2014b). 'Family Matters: How Queering the Intimate Queers the International'. *International Studies Review* 16(4):604–608.

Picq, Manuela, and Markus Thiel (2015). *Sexualities in World Politics: How LGBTQ Claims Shape International Relations*. Abingdon: Routledge.

Palumbo-Liu, David (2002). 'Multiculturalism Now: Civilization, National Identity, and Difference Before and After September 11th'. *Boundary 2* 29(2):87–108.

Pitt, Bob (2014). 'Far-Right Leaders Vow to 'Save Europe' at French Gathering'. Islamophobia Watch, December 1. http://www.islamophobiawatch.co.uk/far-right-leaders-vow-to-save-europe-at-french-gathering/, downloaded March 19, 2015.

Pitt, J. R. (1964). 'The Structural-Functional Approach'. In H. T. Christensen, ed., *Handbook of Marriage and the Family*, 5–124. Chicago: Rand McNally.

Plummer, Ken (2003). 'The Flow of Boundaries'. In David Downes, Paul Rock, Christine, Chinkin, and Conor Gearty, eds., *Crime, Social Control and Human Rights*, 379–393. New York: Routledge.

Polyakova, Alina (2014). 'Strange Bedfellows: Putin and Europe's Far Right'. *World Affairs*, September–October. http://www.worldaffairsjournal.org/article/strange-bedfellows-putin-and-europe's-far-right, downloaded March 28, 2015.

Povinelli, Elizabeth A., and George Chauncey (1999). 'Thinking Sexuality Transnationally: An Introduction. *GLQ: A Journal of Lesbian and Gay Studies* 5(4):439–449.

Pratt, Nicola (2007). 'The Queen Boat Case in Egypt: Sexuality, National Security and State Sovereignty'. *Review of International Studies* 33(1):129–144.

Puar, Jasbir K. (2006). 'Mapping US Homonormativities'. *Gender, Place and Culture* 13(1):67–88.

Puar, Jasbir K. (2007). *Terrorist Assemblages: Homonationalism in Queer Times*. Durham, NC: Duke University Press.

Puar, Jasbir K. (2009). 'Prognosis Time: Towards a Geopolitics of Affect, Debility and Capacity. *Women and Performance* 19(2):161–172.

Puar, Jasbir K. (2010). 'To Be Gay and Racist Is No Anomaly'. *Guardian*, June 2. http://www.theguardian.com/commentisfree/2010/jun/02/gay-lesbian-islamophobia, downloaded November 10, 2014.

Puar, Jasbir K. (2012). 'Coda: The Cost of Getting Better Suicide, Sensation, Switchpoints. *GLQ: A Journal of Lesbian and Gay Studies* 18(1):149–158.

Puar, Jasbir K. (2013). 'Rethinking Homonationalism'. *International Journal of Middle East Studies* 45:336–339.

Puar, Jasbir K., and Maya Mikdashi (2012a). 'Pinkwatching and Pinkwashing: Interpenetration and Its Discontents'. *Jadaliyya*, August 9. http://www.jadaliyya.com/pages/index/6774/pinkwatching-and-pinkwashing_interpenetration-and, downloaded June 14, 2015.

Puar, Jasbir K. and Maya Mikdashi (2012b). 'On Positionality and Not Naming Names: A Rejoinder to the Response by Maikey and Schotten'. *Jadaliyya*, October 10. http://www.jadaliyya.com/pages/index/7792/on-positionality-and-not-naming-names_a-rejoinder-, downloaded June 14, 2015.

Puar, Jasbir K., and Amit S. Rai (2002). 'Monster, Terrorist, Fag'. *Social Text* 20(3):117–148.

Rabadi, Dina (2002). 'Bearded-Lady Saint Offers Comfort to a Generation in Waiting'. *Los Angeles Times*, May 28. http://articles.latimes.com/2002/may/28/opinion/oe-rabadi28, downloaded March 8, 2015.

Rahman, Momin (2014). 'Queer Rights and the Triangulation of Western Exceptionalism'. *Journal of Human Rights* 13(3):274–289.

Ranchod-Nilsson, Sita and Mary Ann Tétreault, eds. (2000). *Women, States and Nations: At Home in the Nation*. Routledge: New York.

Rao, Rahul (2010). *Third World Protest: Between Home and the World*. Oxford: Oxford University Press.

Rao, Rahul (2012). 'On "Gay conditionality", Imperial Power and Queer Liberation'. *Kafilia*, January 1. http://kafila.org/2012/01/01/on-gay-conditionality-imperial-power-and-queer-liberation-rahul-rao/, downloaded August 29, 2014.

Rao, Rahul (2014a). 'Queer Questions'. *International Feminist Journal of Politics* 16(2):199–217.

Rao, Rahul (2014b). 'The Locations of Homophobia'. *London Review of International Law* 2(2):169–199.

Rao, Rahul (2014c). 'Re-membering Mwanga: Same-Sex Intimacy, Memory and Belonging in Postcolonial Uganda'. *Journal of Eastern African Studies*, doi:10.1080/1 7531055.2014.970600.

Raymond, Janice (1980). *The Trans-sexual Empire: The Making of the She-Male*. Boston: Beacon Press.

Razack, S. H. (2004). 'Imperilled Muslim Women, Dangerous Muslim Men and Civilised Europeans: Legal and Social Responses to Forced Marriages'. *Feminist Legal Studies* 12: 29–174.

Rees, Emma L. E. (2013). *The Vagina: A Literary and Cultural History*. London: Bloomsbury.

Remkus Britt, Brett (2015). 'Gay Rights, Colonial Cartographies and Racial Categories in the Pornographic Film *Men of Israel*'. *International Feminist Journal of Politics*, 17(3):398–415.

Renwick, Alan (2014). 'Eurovision: A Continent Divided in Its Sexual Attitudes?' *Politics at Reading* blog, May 11. http://blogs.reading.ac.uk/readingpolitics/2014/05/11/eurovision-a-continent-divided-in-its-sexual-attitudes/, downloaded March 28, 2015.

Richter-Montpetit, Melanie (2014a). 'Beyond the Erotics of Orientalism'. *Security Dialogue* 45(1):43–62.

Richter-Montpetit, Melanie (2014b): 'Beyond the Erotics of Orientalism: Homeland Security, Liberal War and the Pacification of the Global Frontier'. PhD dissertation, York University, Toronto, ON.

Richter-Montpetit, Melanie (2014c). 'Queer Investments in Liberal War'. Paper presented at the Fifty-Fourth Annual International Studies Association Convention, March 26–29, Toronto, ON.

Rifkin, Mark (2012). *The Erotics of Sovereignty: Queer Native Writing in the Era of Self-Determination*. Minneapolis: University of Minnesota Press.

Ring, Trudy (2014). 'Orthodox Church Leaders Blame Conchita Wurst for Balkan Floods'. *Advocate*, May 24. http://www.advocate.com/world/2014/05/24/orthodox-church-leaders-blame-conchita-wurst-balkan-floods, downloaded September 8, 2014.

Ristic, Jelena (2012). 'Female Masculinity: An Interview with Jack Halberstam'. *Hétérographe* 8(Autumn), April 27. http://heterographe.com/?page_id=288, downloaded February 3, 2013.

Ritchie, Jason T. (2011). 'Queer Checkpoints: Sexuality, Survival, and the Paradoxes of Sovereignty in Israel-Palestine'. PhD dissertation, University of Illinois.

Rogin, Michael (1990). '"Make My Day!": Spectacle as Amnesia in Imperial Politics'. *Representations* 29(Winter):99–123.

Rosenberg, Steve (2014). 'Eurovision's "Bearded Lady" Winner Divides Russia'. BBC News, May. http://www.bbc.co.uk/news/world-europe-27404406, downloaded March 27, 2015.

Rostow, W. W. (1960). *The Stages of Economic Growth: A Non-Communist Manifesto.* Cambridge: Cambridge University Press.

Rothman, Stanley (1971). 'Functionalism and Its Critics: An Analysis of the Writings of Gabriel Almond'. *Political Science Reviewer* 1(1):236–276.

Rousseau, Jean-Jacques (1978). *The Social Contract.* Translated by Judith R. Masters. London: Macmillan.

Ruback, Timothy J. (2011). 'Sovereignties (Once Again) in Question'. *International Studies Review* 13(4):631–636.

Rubin, Gayle (1992). 'Thinking Sex: Notes for a Radical Theory of the Politics of Sexuality'. In Carole S. Vance, ed., *Pleasure and Danger: Exploring Female Sexuality,* 267–293. London: Pandora.

Runyan, Anne S., V. and Spike Peterson (1991). 'The Radical Future of Realism: Feminist Subversions of IR Theory. *Alternatives* 16:67–106.

Rutenberg, Jim (2001). 'Fox Portrays a War of Good and Evil, and Many Applaud'. *New York Times*, December 3.

Sabsay, Leticia (2013). 'Queering the Politics of Global Sexual Rights?' *Studies in Ethnicity and Nationalism* 13:80–90.

Said, Edward (1978). *Orientalism.* London: Penguin.

Salecl, Renata (2004). *On Anxiety.* London: Routledge.

Schotten, Heike, and Haneen Maikey (2012). 'Queers Resisting Zionism: On Authority and Accountability beyond Homonationalism'. *Jadaliyya*, October 10. http://www.jadaliyya.com/pages/index/7738/queers-resisting-zionism_on-authority-and-accounta, downloaded June 12, 2015.

Schulman, Sarah (2012). *Israel/Palestine and the Queer International.* Durham, NC: Duke University Press.

Schulman, Sarah (2013). *The Gentrification of the Mind.* Berkeley: University of California Press.

Scott, A. O. (2002). 'Film Review: Where the Drag Queens Wore Beards'. *New York Times*, June 28. http://www.nytimes.com/2002/06/28/movies/film-review-wh ere-the-drag-queens-wore-beards.html, downloaded March 8, 2015.

Scott, J. (2013). 'The Distance between Death and Marriage'. *International Feminist Journal of Politics* 16(4):534–551.

Seckinelgin, H., and D. Paternotte (forthcoming). '"Lesbian and Gay Rights Are Human Rights": Multiple Globalizations and Lesbian and Gay Activism'. In D. Paternotte and M. Tremblay, eds., *The Ashgate Research Companion to Lesbian and Gay Activism.* Burlington, VT: Ashgate.

Sedgwick, Eve Kosofsky (1990). *Epistemology of the Closet.* London: Penguin.

Sedgwick, Eve Kosofsky (1993). *Tendencies.* Durham, NC: Duke University Press.

Sedgwick, Eve Kosofsky (2003). *Touching Feeling: Affect, Pedagogy, Performativity.* Durham, NC: Duke University Press.

Sedgwick, Eve Kosofsky (2011). 'Melanie Klein and the Difference Affect Makes'. In Janet Halley and Andrew Parker, eds., *After Sex? On Writing since Queer Theory*, 283–301. Durham, NC: Duke University Press.

Shapiro, Michael J. (1991). 'Sovereignty and Exchange in the Orders of Modernity'. *Alternatives* 16(4):447–477.

Shapiro, Michael J. (1994). 'Moral Geographies and the Ethics of Post-Sovereignty'. *Public Culture* 6(3):479–502.

Shapiro, Stephen (2004). 'Marx to the Rescue! Queer Theory and the Crisis of Prestige'. *New Formations* 53(Summer):77–90.

Shaw, Kara (2008). *Indigeneity and Political Theory: Sovereignty and the Limits of the Political*. London: Routledge.

Shepherd, Laura J., and Laura Sjoberg (2012). 'Trans-bodies in/of War(s)'. *Feminist Review* 101:5–23.

Shinko, Rosemary E. (2012). 'Geniuses, Exiles and (Liberal) Postmodern Subjectivities'. *Journal of International Relations and Development* 15(2):177–200.

Simon, Sunka (2000). '*Der vord're Orient:* Colonialist Imagery in Popular Postwar German *Schlager*'. *Journal of Popular Culture* 34:87–108.

Sjoberg, Laura (2012). 'Toward Trans-gendering International Relations?' *International Political Sociology* 6(4):337–354.

Sjoberg, Laura (2014). 'Queering the "Territorial Peace"? The Value of Queer Theory Conversing with Mainstream IR'. *International Studies Review* 16(4):608–612.

Sjoberg, Laura (forthcoming). 'The Counterterrorist in the Bedroom'. *Critical Studies on Terrorism*.

Sjoberg, Laura, and Caron Gentry (2007). *Mothers, Monsters, Whores: Women's Violence in Global Politics*. London: Zed Books.

Sjoberg, Laura, and Cynthia Weber, eds. (2014). 'Forum: Queer International Relations'. *International Studies Review* 16(4):596–622.

Smith, Andrea (2005). *Conquest: Sexual Violence and the American Indian Genocide*. Cambridge, MA: South End Press.

Smith, Andrea (2010). 'Queer Theory and Native Studies: The Heteronormativity of Settler Colonialism'. *GLQ: A Journal of Lesbian and Gay Studies* 16(1–2):41–68.

Smith, Nicola J. (2015). 'Toward a Queer Political Economy of Crisis'. In Jacqui True and Aida Hozic, eds., *Scandalous Economics: The Spectrum of Gender after Global Financial Crisis*. New York: Oxford.

Smith, Nicola J., and Donna Lee (2015). 'What's Queer About Political Science?' *British Journal of Politics and International Relations* 17(1):49–63.

Smith, Rhona K. M. (2003). 'European Convention on Human Rights—Respect for Private Life—Fight to Marry—Legal Status of Transsexuals—Effect of Judicial Precedent—Evolution of Human Rights Standards'. *American Journal of International Law* 97(3):659–664.

Soguk, Nevzat (1997). 'Predicaments of Territorial Democracy and Statecraft in Europe'. *Alternatives* 22:313–352.

Soguk, Nevzat (1999). *States and Strangers*. Minneapolis: University of Minnesota Press.

Somerville, Siobhan B. (2000). *Queering the Color Line: Race and the Invention of Homosexuality in American Culture*. Durham, NC: Duke University Press.

Soto, Sandra K. (2010). *Reading Chican@ Like a Queer: The De-mastery of Desire.* Austin: University of Texas Press.

Spade, Dean (2004). 'Fighting to Win'. In Mattilda/Sycamore and Matt Bernstein, eds., *That's Revolting! Queer Strategies for Resisting Assimilation*, 31–37. Brooklyn: Soft Skull Press.

Spade, Dean (2013). 'Under the Cover of Gay Rights'. *NYU Review of Law and Social Change* 37(79):79–100.

Spillers, Hortense J. (2003). *Black, White and in Color: Essays on American Literature and Culture.* Chicago: University of Chicago Press.

Spivak, Gayatri Chakravorty (1988). 'Can the Subaltern Speak?' In Cary Nelson and Lawrence Grossberg, eds., *Marxism and the Interpretation of Culture*, 271–313. Basingstoke: Macmillan Education.

Spurlin, W. J. (2013). 'Shifting Geopolitical Borders/Shifting Sexual Borders'. *Studies in Ethnicity and Nationalism* 13:69–79.

Stanley, E. A., and N. Smith, eds. (2011). *Captive Genders: Trans Embodiment and the Prison Industrial Complex.* Oakland, CA: AK Press.

Stoler, Ann Laura. (1995). *Race and the Education of Desire.* Durham, NC: Duke University Press.

Stoler, Ann Laura (2002). *Carnal Knowledge and Imperial Power: Race and the Intimate in Colonial Rule.* Berkeley: University of California Press.

Stone, Sandy (1991). 'The Empire Strikes Back'. In J. Epstein and K. Straub, eds., *Body Guards: The Cultural Politics of Gender Ambiguity.* London: Routledge.

Stryker, Susan (2008). *Transgender History.* Berkeley, CA: Seal Press.

Stryker, Susan, and Paisley Currah (2014). Introduction. *Trans*gender Studies Quarterly* 1(1–2):1–18.

Stryker, Susan, Paisley Currah, and Lisa Jean Moore (2008). 'Introduction: Trans-, Trans, or Transgender?' *Women's Studies Quarterly* 36(3–4):11–22.

Stryker, Susan, and Jim Van Buskirk (1996). *Gay by the Bay: A History of Queer Culture in the San Francisco Bay Area.* San Francisco: Chronicle Books.

Stryker, Susan, and Stephen Whittle (2006). *The Transgender Studies Reader.* New York: Routledge.

Sunderland, Patricia L. (1997). ' "You may not know it, but I'm black": White Women's Self-Identification as Black*'. *Ethnos* 62(1–2):32–58.

Sycamore, M. B., ed. (2006). *Nobody Passes: Rejecting the Rules of Gender and Conformity.* Emeryville, CA: Seal Press.

Sycamore, M. B., ed. (2008). *That's Revolting! Queer Strategies for Resisting Assimilation.* New ed. Brooklyn: Soft Skull Press.

Tagma, Halit Mustafa (2009). 'Homo Sacer vs. Homo Soccer Mom'. *Alternatives* 34:407–435.

Tagma, Halit Mustafa (in progress). *Mancraft as Statecraft.*

Tagma, Halit Mustafa, and Dogu Durgun (in progress). 'The Gendering of Geopolitical space: "Mancraft" as Statecraft'.

Telegraph Foreign Staff (2014). 'Conchita Wurst Caused Balkan Floods after Eurovision Win, Say Church Leaders'. *Telegraph*, May 22. http://www.telegraph.co.uk/news/world-news/europe/serbia/10850219/Conchita-Wurst-caused-Balkan-floods-after-Eurovision-win-say-church-leaders.html, downloaded January 26, 2015.

Thoreson, R. R. (2011). 'The Queer Paradox of LGBTI Human Rights'. *Interalia:* 6:1–27.

Tickner, J. Ann (1992). *Gender in International Relations.* New York: Columbia University Press.

Tompkins, Avery (2014). 'Asterisk'. *Transgender Studies Quarterly** 1(1–2):26–27.

Turner, Bryan S. (2005). 'Talcott Parsons's Sociology of Religion and the Expressive Revolution: The Problem of Western Individualism'. *Journal of Classical Sociology* 5(3):303–318.

Walker, R. B. J. (1993). *Inside/Outside: International Relations as Political Theory.* Cambridge: Cambridge University Press.

Walker, R. B. J. (2000). 'Europe Is Not Where It Is Supposed to Be'. In Morten Kelstrup and Michael Williams, eds., *International Relations Theory and the Politics of European Integration: Power, Security and Community,* 14–32. London: Routledge.

Wallace, Lewis (2014). 'Bearded Woman, Female Christ: Gendered Transformations in the Legends and Cult of Saint Wilgefortis'. *Journal of Feminist Studies in Religion* 30(1):43–63.

Wallsten, Peter, and Scott Wilson (2012). 'Obama Endorses Gay Marriage, Says Same-Sex Couples Should Have Right to Wed'. *Washington Post,* May 9. http://www.washington-post.com/politics/2012/05/09/gIQAivsWDU_story.html, downloaded November 9, 2014.

Warner, Michael (1999a). *The Trouble with Normal.* Cambridge: Harvard University Press.

Warner, Michael (1999b). 'Normal and Normaller: Beyond Gay Marriage'. *GLQ: A Journal of Lesbian and Gay Studies* 5:119–171.

Warner, Michael (2012). 'Queer and Then?' *Chronicle of Higher Education,* January 1. http://chronicle.com/article/QueerThen-/130161/, downloaded August 29, 2014.

Weber, Cynthia (1994a). 'Something's Missing: Male Hysteria and the U.S. Invasion of Panama'. *Genders* 19:171–197.

Weber, Cynthia (1994b). 'Shoring Up a Sea of Signs'. *Environment and Planning D: Society and Space* 12(5):547–558.

Weber, Cynthia (1995). *Simulating Sovereignty: Intervention, the State and Symbolic Exchange.* Cambridge: Cambridge University Press.

Weber, Cynthia (1998a). 'What's So Queer about IR? Or Beware of the Sexuality Variable. Paper presented at the Millennium Annual Conference, London School of Economics, September 13–14.

Weber, Cynthia (1998b). 'Performative States'. *Millennium* 21(1):77–95.

Weber, Cynthia (1998c). 'Reading Martin Wight's "Why Is There No International Theory?" as History'. *Alternatives* 23(4):451–469.

Weber, Cynthia (1999). *Faking It.* Minneapolis: University of Minnesota Press.

Weber, Cynthia (2002). 'Flying Planes Can Be Dangerous'. *Millennium* 31(1):129–147.

Weber, Cynthia (2005). 'Not without My Sister(s): Imagining a Moral America in Kandahar'. *International Feminist Journal of Politics* 7(3):358–376.

Weber, Cynthia (2006). *Imagining America at War: Morality, Politics and Film.* London: Routledge.

Weber, Cynthia (2010). 'Interruption Ashley'. *Review of International Studies* 36(4):975–987.

Weber, Cynthia (2011). 'I Am an American': Filming the Fear of Difference.* Chicago: University of Chicago Press.

Weber, Cynthia (2013). *International Relations Theory: A Critical Introduction*. 4th ed. London: Routledge.

Weber, Cynthia (2014a). 'Why Is There No Queer International Theory?' *European Journal of International Relations*, April 3. doi:10.1177/1354066114524236.

Weber, Cynthia (2014b). 'You Make My Work (Im)Possible: Reflections on Professional Conduct in the Discipline of International Relations'. *Duck of Minerva*, April 9. http://www.whiteoliphaunt.com/duckofminerva/2014/04/you-make-my-work-impossible-reflections-on-professional-conduct-in-the-discipline-of-international-relations.html, downloaded August 29, 2014.

Weber, Cynthia (2014c). 'From Queer to Queer IR'. *International Studies Review* 16(4):596–601.

Weber, Cynthia. (2015). 'Queer Intellectual Curiosity as International Relations (IR) Method: Developing Queer IR Theoretical and Methodological Frameworks'. *International Studies Quarterly*. doi: 10.1111/isqu.12212.

Wee, Darren (2014). 'Liberian Gays Attacked over Ebola'. *Gay Star News*, October 24. http://www.gaystarnews.com/article/liberia-gays-attacked-over-ebola241014, downloaded October 31, 2014.

Weiner, Rachel (2013). 'How Hillary Clinton Evolved on Gay Marriage'. *Washington Post*, March 18. http://www.washingtonpost.com/blogs/the-fix/wp/2013/03/18/how-hillary-clinton-evolved-on-gay-marriage/, downloaded November 9, 2014.

Weiss, Meredith L., and Michael J. Bosia (2013a). *Global Homophobia*. Urbana: University of Illinois Press.

Weiss, Meredith L., and Michael J. Bosia (2013b). 'Political Homophobia in Comparative Perspective'. In Meredith L. Weiss and Michael J. Bosia, eds., *Global Homophobia*, 1–29. Urbana: University of Illinois Press.

Wiarda, Howard (1989–1990). 'Rethinking Political Development: A Look Backward over Thirty Years, and a Look Ahead'. *Studies in Comparative International Development* 24(4):65–82.

Wiegman, Robyn, and Elizabeth A. Wilson, eds. (2015). 'Introduction: Antinormativity's Queer Conventions'. *differences* 26(2):1–25.

Wight, Martin (1960). 'Why is There No International Theory?' *International Relations* 2(1):35–48.

Wilcox, Lauren (2014). 'Queer Theory and the "Proper Objects" of IR'. *International Studies Review* 16(4):612–615.

Wilkinson, Cai (2013). 'Putting Traditional Values into Practice: Russia's Anti-gay Laws'. *Russian Analytical Digest* 138(November 3):5–7.

Wilkinson, Cai (2014). 'Putting "Traditional Values" into Practice: The Rise and Contestation of Anti-homopropaganda Laws in Russia'. *Journal of Human Rights* 13(3): 363–379.

Wilkinson, Cai, and Anthony J. Langlois (2014). 'Introduction to Special Issue: Not Such an International Human Rights Norm? Local Resistance to Lesbian, Gay, Bisexual, and Transgender Rights—Preliminary Comments'. *Journal of Human Rights* 12(3):249–255.

Winter, Sam, and Mark King (2013). 'Well and Truly Fucked: Transwomen, Stigma, Sex Work, and Sexual Health in South to East Asia'. In R. L. Dalla, L. M. Baker, J. DeFrain, and C. Williamson, eds., *The Prostitution of Women, Men, and Children: A Global Perspective*, 245–253. Lanham, MD: Lexington Books.

Wogan, Terry (2014). 'Better the Devil You Know: The Life and Loves of a He-Devil by Graham Norton: A Memoir'. November 1, *Irish Times*. http://www.irishtimes.com/culture/books/better-the-devil-you-know-the-life-and-loves-of-a-he-devil-by-graham-norton-a-memoir-1.1983605, downloaded March 28, 2015.

World Bank (2000). Argentina—Family Strengthening and Social Capital Promotion Project—PROFAM (LIL). Project Information Document, Report No. PID9623. Project Id. ARPE70374, July 31.

World Bank (2001). Project appraisal document on a proposed learning and innovation loan in the amount of US $5.0 million to the Argentine Republic for a family strengthening and social capital promotion project—PROFAM, October 30. Report No. 21344-AR. Project ID P070374.

World Bank (2014). 'The Economic Cost of Homophobia: How LGBT Exclusion Impacts Development'. *World Bank Live*, March 12. http://live.worldbank.org/economic-cost-of-homophobia, downloaded July 8, 2015.

Wurst, Conchita, as told to Daniel Oliver Bachmann (2015). *Being Conchita: We Are Unstoppable*. London: John Blake.

Yuval-Davis, Nira, Floya Anthias, and Jo Campling, eds. (1989). *Women-Nation-State*. New York: St. Martin's Press.

Zivi, Karen (2011). *Making Rights Claims*. Oxford: Oxford University Press.

Zivi, Karen (2014). 'Performing the Nation: Contesting Same-Sex Marriage Rights in the United States'. *Journal of Human Rights* 13(3):290–306.

Žižek, Slavoj (1998). 'Love Thy Neighbor? No, Thanks!' In C. Lane, ed., *The Psychoanalysis of Race*, 154–175. New York: Columbia University Press.

CPSIA information can be obtained
at www.ICGtesting.com
Printed in the USA
BVHW032316060122
625104BV00003B/103